Policy Matters

Transforming Education Through Critical Leadership, Policy and Practice

Series editors: Stephanie Chitpin, Sharon Kruse and Howard Stevenson

Transforming Education Through Critical Leadership, Policy and Practice is based on the belief that those in educational leadership and policy-constructing roles have an obligation to educate for a robust critical and democratic polity in which citizens can contribute to an open and socially just society. Advocating for a critical, socially just democracy goes beyond individual and procedural concerns characteristic of liberalism and seeks to raise and address fundamental questions pertaining to power, privilege and oppression. It recognizes that much of what has gone under the name of 'transformational leadership' in education seeks to transform very little, but rather it serves to reproduce systems that generate structural inequalities based on class, gender, race, (dis)ability and sexual orientation.

This series seeks to explore how genuinely transformative approaches to educational leadership, policy and practice can disrupt the neoliberal hegemony that has dominated education systems globally for several decades, but which now looks increasingly vulnerable. The series will publish high-quality books, both of a theoretical and empirical nature, that explicitly address the challenges and critiques of the current neoliberal conditions, while steering leadership and policy discourse and practices away from neoliberal orthodoxy towards a more transformative perspective of education leadership. The series is particularly keen to 'think beyond' traditional notions of educational leadership to include those who lead in educative ways – in social movements and civil society organizations as well as in educational institutions.

Policy Matters: Perspectives, Procedures, and Processes

BY

DAVID C. YOUNG
St. Francis Xavier University, Canada

ROBERT E. WHITE
St. Francis Xavier University, Canada

AND

MONICA A. WILLIAMS
St. Francis Xavier University, Canada (Retired)

emerald
PUBLISHING

United Kingdom – North America – Japan – India – Malaysia – China

Emerald Publishing Limited
Emerald Publishing, Floor 5, Northspring, 21-23 Wellington Street, Leeds LS1 4DL

First edition 2024

Copyright © 2024 David C. Young, Robert E. White and Monica A. Williams.
Published under exclusive licence by Emerald Publishing Limited.

Reprints and permissions service
Contact: www.copyright.com

No part of this book may be reproduced, stored in a retrieval system, transmitted in any form or by any means electronic, mechanical, photocopying, recording or otherwise without either the prior written permission of the publisher or a licence permitting restricted copying issued in the UK by The Copyright Licensing Agency and in the USA by The Copyright Clearance Center. Any opinions expressed in the chapters are those of the authors. Whilst Emerald makes every effort to ensure the quality and accuracy of its content, Emerald makes no representation implied or otherwise, as to the chapters' suitability and application and disclaims any warranties, express or implied, to their use.

British Library Cataloguing in Publication Data
A catalogue record for this book is available from the British Library

ISBN: 978-1-80382-482-6 (Print)
ISBN: 978-1-80382-481-9 (Online)
ISBN: 978-1-80382-483-3 (Epub)

Printed and bound by CPI Group (UK) Ltd, Croydon, CR0 4YY

INVESTOR IN PEOPLE

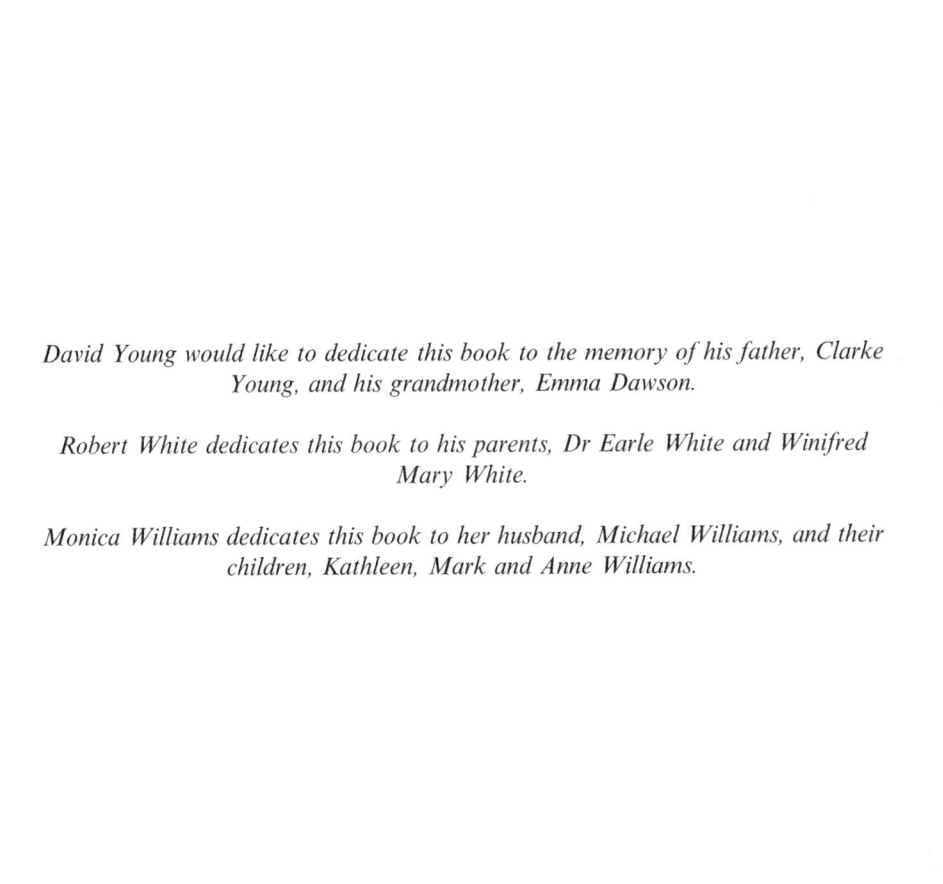

David Young would like to dedicate this book to the memory of his father, Clarke Young, and his grandmother, Emma Dawson.

Robert White dedicates this book to his parents, Dr Earle White and Winifred Mary White.

Monica Williams dedicates this book to her husband, Michael Williams, and their children, Kathleen, Mark and Anne Williams.

Table of Contents

About the Authors — *ix*

Preface — *xi*

Acknowledgements — *xiii*

Chapter 1   So, What Is Policy, Anyway?   *1*

Chapter 2   Policy, Power and Politics in Education   *17*

Chapter 3   Policy Alignment: Connecting School, District and System Policies   *31*

Chapter 4   Contemporary Models of Policy Development   *43*

Chapter 5   The Policy Continuum   *63*

Chapter 6   The Roles of Educational Leaders in the Policy Process   *83*

Chapter 7   Policy Implementation   *103*

Chapter 8   Bridging Policy-Practice Gaps and Building Policy Capacity   *123*

Chapter 9   Leadership of Change   *135*

**Chapter 10 Navigating the Policy Process: Intended and
 Unintended Consequences** *155*

Chapter 11 Conclusion *175*

Index *187*

About the Authors

Dr David Young is a Full Professor in the Faculty of Education at St Francis Xavier University, Director of the Frank McKenna Centre for Leadership, as well as a Resident Fellow of the Brian Mulroney Institute of Government. Dr Young is the past Chair of the Department of Curriculum and Leadership and previously served as Chair of the Inter-University Doctoral Programme in Educational Studies. Dr Young is also an Editor of *International Studies in Educational Administration*, one of the oldest journals in the field of educational leadership. Dr Young's research is focused on the broad topic of educational administration and policy. More particularly, his current writing deals with issues pertaining to law and education.

Dr Robert White began his teaching career in 1972, and, since 2003, has been a member of the Faculty of Education at St Francis Xavier University, where he currently holds the position of Senior Research Professor. Dr White's research interests include educational administration and policy, postmodernity and globalization, qualitative research methodologies and critical pedagogy. Dr White is Associate Editor of the *International Journal of Leadership in Education*.

Dr White has also received numerous Social Sciences and Humanities Research Council of Canada grants to pursue his research. In 2013, he received the President's Research Award, granted by St Francis Xavier University.

Dr Monica Williams is a career educational leader who has held senior leadership positions in the Nova Scotia public education system. During 2017–2018, Dr Williams served as a commissioner on the Nova Scotia Commission on Inclusive Education. She subsequently joined the Faculty of Education at St Francis Xavier University as an Assistant Professor specializing in the leadership of inclusive education. Dr Williams' research interests include educational leadership, inclusive education and education policy, law and standards. Following her retirement from the university in 2022, Dr Williams was awarded the Queen Elizabeth II Platinum Jubilee Medal.

Preface

Policy Matters: Perspectives, Procedures, and Processes has been developed for educational leaders, practitioners and theoreticians. This book provides readers with the means to think critically and in so doing, understand policy initiatives and their ramifications. The goal is for theoreticians and practitioners to be able to understand the purpose of policy, how it may be effectively developed and efficiently implemented. Never have policy initiatives been so important and necessary. Neoliberal manifestations, climate change, civil rights movements and governmental reactions to these and other global forces have made education in policy analysis, development and implementation crucial to educational leadership and the evolution of school systems, at home and abroad.

Policy is often created for purposes of accruing power, expanding privilege and further marginalizing oppressed groups. Educating policy developers and consumers is but one means of harnessing the positive power of policy while restraining baser instincts that tend to pervert policy for the betterment of the more powerful hegemonic elite. Simply put, this book strives to put policy into perspective by demystifying it and making it accessible to a wide audience. This book is premised on the notion that policy development, analysis and implementation, both traditionally and historically, has sought to preserve the status quo rather than to formulate policy that is liberating and transformative. This book also focuses on the future, including the creation of educational policies that are grounded in research-based theories, practices and frameworks, and dedicated to strengthening teaching and learning for the benefit of *all* students.

This volume explores how policy formulation may truly be transformative in combatting hegemonic and neoliberal incursions into the educational arena. This book addresses some of the challenges associated with current neoliberal conditions which have spawned a plethora of social and structural issues. It will appeal broadly to a myriad of formal and informal leaders within social movements and civil society organizations as well as in educational institutions. As such, this publication will strive to eliminate the theory/practice divide by uniting educational policy with educational reality in order to empower educators, education stakeholders and citizens to use policy, policy development and policy initiatives for the betterment of society in general.

Acknowledgements

The authors wish to thank the editors of the book series Transforming Education Through Critical Leadership, Policy and Practice: Stephanie Chitpin, Howard Stevenson and Sharon Kruse. They also extend a sincere debt of gratitude to the entire team at Emerald Publishing who have been unbelievably supportive as this book has unfolded.

David Young would also like to recognize the love and support of his wife Lori and daughter Emma. On more than one occasion they overlooked and tolerated his absence as he engaged in writing and research. He also wishes to acknowledge his mother, Barbara Ann Young, for all that she has done and continues to do.

Robert White would also like to acknowledge the people who have supported him on this journey; you know who you are. Chhunly Tiv, Bopha Ong and their daughter, Cibo, have offered unstinting support throughout this process. A special debt of thanks is also due to Karyn Cooper, who allowed numerous projects to slide so that this volume could be completed in a timely fashion.

Monica Williams would also like to acknowledge the unfailing love and support of her husband Mike and their children, Kathleen, Mark and Anne, who have made it possible for her to contribute to the field of education in many ways, including this publication, which is her first book.

Chapter 1

So, What Is Policy, Anyway?

From our first days in the classroom to the end of our careers, education policy shapes all aspects of our work as educators. Beginning with the hiring policies that regulate the recruitment and appointment of teachers, continuing with the curriculum and assessment policies that guide classroom instruction and concluding with the retirement policies that frame professional departures, policies underpin each stage of our careers. Despite their pervasive impact, policies often remain invisible to educators until a policy disrupts their daily routines, adds to their workloads and/or challenges their core beliefs and values. Sudden policy changes and major policy reforms may provoke considerable consternation and uncertainty, especially given the increasing number of competing policy demands placed on teachers and educational leaders today.

Each of us has vivid memories of our first major encounter with education policy. On her first day on the job as a newly minted Speech-Language Pathologist, one of the authors of this book (Monica Williams) was asked by the Superintendent of Schools of a large rural school board to establish this new service by creating an operating budget, purchasing supplies and equipment, and drafting a school board policy and supporting procedures. This baptism by fire marked the beginning of a long career in educational leadership that centred on the development, implementation and reform of an ever-expanding network of school, school board and provincial policies for special education and inclusive education.

For another author (David Young), policy, at least in the practical sense, became readily apparent during his stint as a student teacher. From policies around accepting late submissions to after-school supervision, it seemed as though everything teachers could or could not do was regulated, at least to a degree, by some type of policy. While this author recognized that policies were vital to ensuring that disparate parties to the educational enterprise remained on the same page and teaching and learning operated smoothly, there was also a gradual realization that some policies can be ineffective, leading to barriers associated with interpretation, understanding and co-operation. Because of this early experience, this author has spent much of his career examining how policies can be used as a legitimate vehicle to improve education.

According to a third author (Robert White), he recounts an experience in high school that centred upon attendance policies. Unfortunately, this author firmly

---

Policy Matters, 1–16
Copyright © 2024 David C. Young, Robert E. White and Monica A. Williams
Published under exclusive licence by Emerald Publishing Limited
doi:10.1108/978-1-80382-481-920231001

believed and continues to believe that schooling should never be fully responsible for one's education. The recognition of policy transgression occurred one Friday afternoon at the Winnipeg Art Gallery when the author was educating himself regarding the nuances of modern art, when he ran directly into his school principal. After a stilted conversation and a hasty exit from the gallery, this author became dimly aware that Friday afternoons were routinely reserved for schooling. Years later, while reminiscing about this misadventure, it suddenly dawned upon this author to question what his principal was doing in the art gallery on a Friday when school was still in session.

For each of us and for educators everywhere, our first forays into education policy often spawn many questions: What is education policy? Why is it developed? Who is responsible for implementing it? How does it impact educators' daily work? As we progress through different stages of our careers and navigate successive policy changes and reforms, more questions arise concerning our evolving roles and responsibilities as policy developers, interpreters, implementers and challengers. The purpose of this book is to address common questions about education policy by examining different policy perspectives, procedures and processes and exploring their impact on educators, at home and abroad.

To offer an illustration, some time ago, an individual purchased a new keyboard for their computer. The old one had keys that tended to stick, an irritating habit that often prevented any reasonable communication. In fact, this is reminiscent of the old joke about the person who put dozens of monkeys in one room, equipped them with typewriters (you see how old this joke is?), and waited to see if one of the monkeys would eventually reproduce a classic work of literature. To this person's wonderment and consternation, after some months, one of the monkeys typed, 'To be or not to be, that is the gzorgnplatz'.

The old, key-stuck keyboard was behaving like this exceptional monkey, so a decision was made to replace it. The consumer asked all the right questions about compatibility, the return policy and the like and brought the new keyboard home. Unfortunately, the new keyboard was ultimately returned to the store. The clerk greeted the consumer warmly and reassured them that, indeed, if necessary, the keyboard could be returned for a full refund. The consumer then produced the keyboard and placed it on the counter. The still smiling clerk asked after the box that it had come in, with the consumer noting that the box had been thrown out. The smile faded. The clerk told the consumer they could not return it without the box. The consumer asked why and the clerk said they could no longer resell it as a new keyboard if the box was missing. Suspecting the consumer was about to run up against 'policy', the consumer announced that the keyboard *was* used, as they had in fact used it several times, already.

Suddenly, the 'return policy' evaporated. The consumer was unable to return the product, even though they had never been told about the box. This gave the consumer pause to consider how porous and flexible the term 'policy' had become. Although the consumer was not disgruntled, they returned home somewhat less than gruntled, and decided to investigate the store's policies around returned items and the re-selling of used goods as new products.

To dive deeper into this illustrative case, we begin with the definition of 'policy'. The online Merriam-Webster dictionary (https://www.merriam-webster.com/dictionary/policy) defines policy as: (1) a definite course or method of action selected from among alternatives and in light of given conditions to guide and determine present and future decisions, and alternately, as (2) management or procedure based primarily on material interest, and finally, (3) a high-level overall plan embracing the general goals and acceptable procedures especially of a governmental body. Clearly, this aforementioned brush with policy was an embodiment of the second definition. A legal definition of policy, also from the Merriam-Webster dictionary, identifies policy as an overall plan, principle or guideline that is formulated outside of the judiciary obligated to consider policy on the matter to be decided upon. This definition stresses the fact that most policies are developed independently of the people who are expected to implement that policy. This topic will be expanded upon in subsequent chapters.

Definitions of Policy

Many different types and kinds of policy abound, not to mention the act of deploying policy. For example, policy may be introduced as a contract, such as an insurance policy that is legally binding for all parties concerned. Policy may also be a system of guidelines or rules determining a specific course of action (Merriam-Webster). This is an interesting definition in that it may be a system of rules, which brings it close to the level of the legally binding policy, but not quite. On the other hand, it may also be seen as a set of guidelines. This means that it may be flexible enough to offer some form of social justice for those would typically be influenced by such a set of guidelines. In addition, policy may be 'in the eye of the beholder', meaning that different implementers of a particular policy may view that policy in different ways. For example, one may see a particular policy as an inviolate rule, whereas a different individual may have a much more relaxed interpretation of how that particular policy is to be implemented. At any rate, the term is suitably malleable enough to give pause for consideration as to how its meaning should be interpreted whenever one hears the word being used.

Given that the English language has the largest word pool of any language, there are numerous words that may act on behalf of 'policy'. Policy may alternately be viewed as a code of conduct, a guideline for action, a prescription for managing affairs, a method of practice or even a programme or protocol. Softer versions of the term may be found in words such as custom or design. Order is another way that policy may be used and has also been referred to as 'red tape' (Merriam-Webster).

The first mention of the word, 'policy', in the English language, seems to have occurred in fifteenth century, either from the Middle English or Middle French '*policie*'. From here, it can be traced back even further to the Italian '*polizza*', and further still to the ancient Roman 'apodeixis' and ancient Greek 'apodeiknynai' (Merriam-Webster). In its more current iterations, 'policy' bears a strong resemblance to the word 'police', seeming to imply that one should take the notion of policy very seriously. It also bears a striking resemblance to the term 'politics', which many of us have come to understand as entertainment, although there was a time when politics was an intensely important activity, particularly during the time of nation-building, several centuries past. Seriously enough, however, the notion of politics and its attendant and seemingly incessant policy construction are clearly and inextricably intertwined.

In conjunction with the many definitions of the term, 'policy', according to Proctor English Dictionary (https://www.ldoceonline.com/dictionary/policy), it may also be used as a way of doing something that has been agreed upon, thus making it a de facto instrument that, once introduced and maintained within the system into which it has been introduced, disappears within the framework of customs, values and beliefs that we tend to refer to as 'culture'. Thus, embedded within any culture are a multiplicity of policies in terms of procedures, protocols, guides and rules, which keep us connected to the society within which we serve as citizens.

Within the field of education, policy takes on a different hue. Cunningham (1963) noted that 'Policy is like an elephant – you recognise one when you see it, but it is somewhat more difficult to define' (p. 229). This may be very true, as illustrated by the following parable - a version of which, taken from a much more ancient parable, originated in China during the Han dynasty (202 BC–220 AD).

Three Blind Men and an Elephant

One day, three blind men happened to meet each other and gossiped a long time about many things. Suddenly one of them recalled, 'I heard that an elephant is a strange animal. Too bad we're blind and can't see it'.

'Ah, yes, truly too bad we don't have the good fortune to see the strange animal', another one sighed.
The third one, quite annoyed, joined in and said, 'See? Forget it! Just to feel it would be great'.
'Well, that's true. If only there were some way of touching the elephant, we'd be able to know', they all agreed.
It so happened that a merchant with a herd of elephants was passing, and overheard their conversation. 'You fellows, do you really want to feel an elephant? Then follow me; I will show you', he said.
The three men were surprized and happy. Taking one another's hand, they quickly formed a line and followed while the merchant led the way. Each one began to contemplate how he would feel the animal, and tried to figure how he would form an image.
After reaching their destination, the merchant asked them to sit on the ground to wait. In a few minutes he led the first blind man to feel the elephant. With outstretched hand, he touched first the left foreleg and then the right. After that he felt the two legs from the top to the bottom, and with a beaming face, turned to say, 'So, the strange animal is just like that'. Then he slowly returned to the group.

Thereupon the second blind man was led to the rear of the elephant. He touched the tail, which wagged a few times, and he exclaimed with satisfaction, 'Ha! Truly a strange animal! Truly odd! I know now. I know'. He hurriedly stepped aside.

The third blind man's turn came, and he touched the elephant's trunk, which moved back and forth turning and twisting and he thought, 'That's it! I've learnt'.

The three blind men thanked the merchant and went their way. Each one was secretly excited over the experience and had a lot to say, yet all walked rapidly without saying a word.

'Let's sit down and have a discussion about this strange animal', the second blind man said, breaking the silence.

'A very good idea. Very good'. the other two agreed for they also had this in mind. Without waiting for anyone to be properly seated, the second one blurted out, 'This strange animal is like our straw fans swinging back and forth to give us a breeze. However, it's not so big or well made. The main portion is rather wispy'.

'No, no!' the first blind man shouted in disagreement. 'This strange animal resembles two big trees without any branches'.

'You're both wrong', the third man replied. 'This strange animal is similar to a snake; it's long and round, and very strong'.

How they argued! Each one insisted that he alone was correct. Of course, there was no conclusion for not one had thoroughly examined the whole elephant. How can anyone describe the whole until he has learned the total of the parts?

This parable, which dates back to Buddhist, Hindu and Jain writings, is useful in reminding us that, while numerous definitions and permutations of policy and its subsequent analysis abound, there will be an appropriate choice for the policy initiative at hand. Otherwise, like the three blind men and the elephant, one might suggest a procedure that is completely at odds with what it is that the project is attempting to resolve. As an interesting aside, if the elephant were to represent policy, it becomes clear that the three blind men each interpret the 'policy' in different ways. This underscores the myriad issues relating to policy as written and policy as implemented, simply because those who write policy are rarely the individuals who are expected to implement that policy.

Public Policy

While these previous definitions of policy are suitable for the general public, there are a number of more academic and politically oriented definitions to be found. These definitions go beyond a generic statement of what policy is and offer a more nuanced view of public policy, policy analysis and typical policy contents. First of all, public policy, according to Howlett et al. (2009), comprises the matching of policy goals with policy means, characterised as 'applied problem-solving' (p. 4). At its core, this is about identifying issues and finding solutions for them, using policy 'tools'.

The process has two distinct dimensions – technical and political. The technical aspect requires the identification and application of appropriate instruments for developing the optimal relationship between goals and the processes used to achieve those goals. The political aspect, on the other hand, recognises the inherent problems involved in the policy makers' agreement on what the issues are with respect to the policy required and also what the most appropriate solution would be. This matter is also compounded by the state of current knowledge relating to socio-economic issues, as well as the policy makers' various ideas, norms and principles regarding the best way forward (Howlett et al., 2009). Thus, given the complexity and 'messiness' of creating public policy, it has been described as 'Anything a government chooses to do or not to do' (Dye, 1972, p. 2). However, this definition does little to differentiate between trivial or significant manifestations of government activities, but does address the notion that policy tends to be made by governing bodies. Dye (1972) also notes that there is choice surrounding the initiation of a policy process and its resolution, even if that choice is to maintain the status quo. As such, choices made around policy initiatives are conscious choices. Happenstance is seldom involved, except possibly in terms of unintended consequences of the implementation of the policy (Howlett et al., 2009).

Consistent with Dye's definition, Pal et al. (2021) describe public policy as a guide to action, a plan or a framework. In their view, public policy is a course of action or inaction embarked upon by public authorities to address a specific problem or interrelated set of problems, or to take advantage of an opportunity. Although policies are problem-solving instruments, they express and impact values, as well. The main, overarching value in public policy is the public interest, which is variously defined and comprised of diverse views, interests, and values. As roadmaps or guides for problem solving, the three main elements of public policy are (1) the definition of a problem; (2) the targeted goals to be achieved; and (3) the instruments or means for addressing the problem and achieving the goals. As shall be discussed in a subsequent chapter, and as can be viewed above, most policy initiatives can be characterized by a pre-policy phase (problem definition), a policy phase (meant to address the issue and achieve the policy goal) and a post-policy phase (the means by which the policy is implemented).

Another definition of public policy comes from Jenkins (1978), who states that public policy is

> A set of interrelated decisions taken by a political actor or group of actors concerning the selection of goals and the means of achieving them within a specified situation where those decisions should, in principle, be within the power of those actors to achieve.
> (Jenkins, 1978, p. 15)

As can be ascertained from this definition, policymaking is a dynamic and goal-oriented process that involves a set of interrelated and conscious decisions on the part of the policy-makers. As can also be divined from this definition, numerous internal and external constraints on any policymaking decisions may influence the final policy (Howlett et al., 2009). Perhaps one of the more concise statements relating to policy matters is Pal's (1997) contention that defines policy analysis as the 'disciplined application of intellect to public problems' (p. 233). As an example of this disciplined application of intellect, let us view, for a moment, the Government of Canada's public policy to facilitate immigration of sponsored foreign nationals excluded under the immigration and refugee protection regulations. While this is not educational policy, it does represent a fair example of a 'disciplined application of intellect to public problems'.

An Example of Public Policy

First of all, the immigration and refugee protection regulations act as a policy within the *Constitution* of Canada. The policy selected for closer scrutiny can, therefore, be seen as a policy amendment. However, in order to avoid a very cumbersome dissection of the master policy network, this amendment will serve current purposes. As with any good policy, this policy sets out the background relating to immigration and refugee protection in Canada. This is necessary in terms of recognizing the purpose of the policy. In this case, the 'regulation' was established to encourage full disclosure by immigration applicants in order to protect the health, safety and security of current Canadian citizens. Following this is a section on 'Public Policy Considerations'.

Apparently, 'stakeholders' and the House of Commons Standing Committee on Citizenship and Immigration have concerns regarding the impact, particularly on immigrant children, who would be prevented from entering Canada should one or more parent be ineligible for consideration. This identifies the significance of the policy and establishes why it was required in the first place. Next, conditions are established in the form of eligibility requirements, followed by a section on exactly which eligibility requirements may be waived, typically in the case of an absentee parent who was initially denied entry to Canada. This section is more explicit regarding fees, definition of dependent children, geographic exceptions where policy may vary, as in the province of Quebec, and the duration of the policy in terms of deadlines by which the applicants must apply. A final note states that the policy may be cancelled at any time, ensuring that the balance of power remains in the hands of the Canadian government (Hussen, 2019).

Educational Policy and Policy Analysis

Leaving governance to its own policymaking devices, literally and figuratively speaking, let us move to the development of educational policy. It seems that, in the field of education, there may easily be as many definitions of policy analysis as there are practitioners of policy analysis. These variable definitions reflect contradictory conceptualizations of policy, from Bell and Stevenson's (2015) assertion that education policy is the realization of contested meanings, to the contention by Pal et al. (2021) that policy comes from those invested with the authority to enact normative guidelines for action. However many definitions may be available, Duke and Canady (1991) contend that a commonly accepted definition of policy remains elusive in research literature and in educational practice. This may also be true of public policy, as well.

Taken together, educational policy may be seen as a statement of purpose that embodies broad guidelines that provide a framework for a school and its programmes (Caldwell & Spinks, 1988), an authoritative communication identifying how individuals in certain positions ought to conduct themselves (Sergiovanni et al., 1999), and an authoritative guideline to institutions, including determination of a society's intents and priorities, as well as resource allocation (Downey, 1998). All told, Delaney (2002) identifies four elements that resonate throughout these definitions. They all suggest, to a greater or lesser degree, that policy is a formalized act, has a pre-agreed upon objective, is sanctioned by an authoritative body and provides standards for measuring performance. Once in place, it is important to determine if the policy is responsible for the desired change or if there were other factors that created the change. If other factors *are* responsible, there would be no need for the policy, as framed. As a result, many policy analysts use statistical models in order to ascertain beforehand, if the policy will have the desired effect (Simon, 2020).

As with most policies, especially policies within educational organizations, the enactment of a policy tends to create reciprocity in terms of an interaction of sorts between the school or school system leader and the policy itself. Policy is communicated through texts and artefacts and variously interpreted by educators in different grade levels, subject areas, school contexts, community settings and levels of administration.

The process of interpretation, by which educators understand and respond to policy, is messy, multi-layered and variable from one educator, school and school system to the next. This variability in policy interpretation is due in part to the heterogeneity of schools as highly complex and internally differentiated organizations (Maguire et al., 2014).

Educational leaders have pivotal roles in making sense of educational policy, translating policy dictates into practical actions and discerning and promoting policy values (Cardno, 2018). School leaders create the dynamic for the introduction and implementation of the policy within the policy environment, as determined by the developers of that policy. The policy environment, thanks to the proliferation of technology that has changed the way that we do just about everything, is subject to changes in market, performativity and management, not to mention leadership (Ball, 2012). A danger inherent in education today relates to the neoliberal agenda that strives to standardize many aspects of the educational process, conflating leadership with management and engineering policy to frame educational leadership to serve policy goals (Kim, 2020).

To summarize, broadly speaking, policy engenders three different conceptualizations – policy as text, policy as discourse and policy as lived experience. In short, policy as text can often become 'the word', which may be rigidly adhered to in spite of humane considerations that would encourage policy to be viewed as discourse or policy as lived. Policy as discourse implies a debate with regard to the purpose or function of the policy, which may reflect upon the policy as written. Policy as lived relates to the implementation of the policy, whether it exists in binary form, inviolate, or is implemented judiciously and humanely. This incarnation of policy tends to allow for greater interpretation of policy implementation, whereas policy as discourse appears to be a more academic and less practicable form of policy conceptualization. These three notions are not mutually exclusive in practice, although the majority of policy implementation studies focus primarily on policy as text and tend to overlook discourse and lived experience. This oversight may result in subordinating the purpose of educational leadership to *policy engineering*, particularly in the field of educational leadership and administration.

Purposes of Policy

As you may have already ascertained, policy is deliberate. It adheres to specific principles. Its usefulness is not only limited to guiding decisions but also to achieving meaningful outcomes. As such, policy may be seen as a statement of intent, such as vision and mission statements, which fall under the umbrella of policy, that can be implemented through procedural directives.

Vision statements tend to describe the goal of the organization, while mission statements tend to establish the process by which that goal may be achieved. Thus, a vision statement tends to be much shorter and more succinct than a mission statement. Both vision and mission statements are indispensable to an organization, although their distinct purposes are often conflated and confused within a single policy document.

Policy is made by an authoritative body, such as a government or a committee of senior administrators within an organization. Additionally, policy is neither a subjective enterprise, nor an objective process, but embodies aspects of both. However, the purpose of policy is to assist in the process of decision-making by offering a framework from which to address issues and to make suitable decisions with a minimum of problematic detritus. Consequently, policies strive to offer an unbiased view that can allow the implementers of any given policy to make decisions that are based on a number of conditions, factors and attitudes. Policies, in this way, may be considered to be subjective, while more procedural policies tend to be somewhat more objective in nature.

This allows for a distinction between policies that can be viewed alternately as guidelines or as rules. Occasionally, the distinction between guidelines and rules may become somewhat murky and it is possible for policy to be used as a blunt force weapon to coerce people into following an arbitrary 'rule'. However, compare this with policies that cover many types of hazardous waste disposal. A subjective view of exactly what waste is constituted as hazardous may not be in the public's best interest. As a result, such policies tend to be interpreted more objectively as rules.

Policies, however, should not be confused or conflated with rules of law. Good driving is not determined by policy, but by law. The rules of the road are not guidelines or suggestions, no matter how much we would like them to be. The difference is simply that laws tend to enforce appropriate behaviour, under penalty, while policy, no matter how hard-edged, is still a recommendation. To illustrate this more clearly, take for example the issue of the policeman in the province of Quebec, Canada, who arrested a woman for refusing to hold the handrail as she was travelling on an escalator (Lau, 2019). After numerous admonishments, and after the woman steadfastly refused to grip the handrail, the frustrated policeman took her into custody. Eventually, she was charged and fined. Perhaps it would come as no surprise that the woman, even though she refused the police directive, had done nothing illegal. This clearly illustrates the difference between a law and a policy, as well as identifying subjective and objective perspectives, at the same time. This story will be further explored in Chapter 10.

Intended and Unintended Effects of Policy Deployment

Intended effects of a policy frequently vary widely, depending upon the organization and context within which they have been made. Broadly stated, policies are typically instituted to avoid potential negative effects of previous policies that may have been noticed within an organization, in order to neutralize or bolster underperforming past policies. An example of such a policy may be seen in a number of large corporations and organizations where computer security is an issue. In order to protect sensitive data, and to minimize the possibilities of servers and personal computers from being 'hacked', it is customary for such companies to require a change in passwords periodically, often every quarter or 90 days. This may have a standardizing effect in that all employees must comply in order to protect data from being stolen. Eventually, this policy becomes so engrained in the workplace that, while it is still obeyed, it seems to disappear within the matrix of policies that result in the creation, development and maintenance of the culture of that organization.

Policy initiatives can also be brought into play to encourage certain behaviours or patterns of behaviour. Take for example, the new Transport Canada incentive programme that encourages Canadian drivers to purchase electric cars. To a driver who wishes to take advantage of that programme, the incentive is a $2,500–$5,000 rebate (Canadian Automobile Association, 2020) applied at the point of sale. This policy initiative clearly intends to create conditions to ameliorate issues relating to carbon emissions and, ultimately, will hopefully have a positive effect on deteriorating climate conditions.

Policies created by large, complex organizations – governments or other bureaucracies, such as school boards – may not be implemented as intended, or they may not be able to be implemented at all. Referring to the example above, a local newspaper asked where all the electric vehicles in Nova Scotia were. It seems that, while purchasing initiatives were attractive, Nova Scotia has one of the smallest inventories of electric vehicles in Canada. Apparently, dealerships are not willing to incur the costs of acquiring a license to sell the vehicles, to hire electrical mechanics to work on them or to train sales representatives to become conversant with this new mode of transportation (Moreton, 2019). Other considerations that prevent this policy from becoming a cultural precedent are the notable absences of charging stations and the lack of mechanics to work on the vehicles. Another consequence of this initiative is the recognition that the federal government will not impose a mandate to implement this policy.

Side effects like this are common with the implementation of policies developed by large and complex organizations that are at a distance from those who will be implementing the policy. A similar unintended consequence was experienced by the Canadian government's legalization of cannabis. The huge revenues that were anticipated were never realized or, at least, have not yet been realized. One of the objectives was to wipe out the black market of illegal drug dealers. However, the government's solution to unrealized profits was to systematically raise the price of legal cannabis to levels that saw consumers rushing back to the dealers on the street, creating a 'grey market' where the black market used to be.

Within the realm of education, policy enactment is not always a linear or rational process (Ball, 2015; Cerna, 2013). Rather, it is a complex process of social, cultural, and emotional construction that is contextually bound in diverse school and community settings (Maguire et al., 2014). As a multidimensional change process aimed at putting policy into practice, implementation impacts education systems on several levels (Viennet & Pont, 2017). Through this process, some policies are promoted and others are discarded, some policies are bundled and others are enacted in isolation, and some policies are highly visible while others remain covert. Due to the wide variance in the beliefs, values and priorities held by educators in different education systems, there is no 'one-size-fits-all' approach to policy implementation (Cerna, 2013).

Returning to the policy process, policymakers attempt to consider as many areas of impact as possible, in order to ensure that the policy operates in terms of its overall intended consequences, rather than foundering as an unsuccessful policy, due to damning unintended consequences.

Policy Development and Form

Policy development is the subject matter for subsequent chapters. However, suffice it to say that policy is rarely made in a vacuum, a theme that is repeatedly referenced throughout this book. One of the most common approaches to policy development, however, is a 'stage' approach. Laswell (1971) developed a seven-step stage theory that comprised seven different stages. While it is a somewhat dated approach and will not be delved into here, it offered a view of policy development in general, although it remains an ideal view rather than an actual view as to how policy is actually created. Other leaders in the creation and development of policy include Anderson (2014), who identified five steps in policy development, and Althaus et al. (2018) who provided us with an eight-step model. As can be seen, policy development, by the 'numbers', is not particularly formulaic and can be developed from many differing perspectives. While Lasswell looks at combining implementation with the original intent of the policy, Anderson tends to view policy development in terms of the success of the policy in terms of its impact. Althaus et al. (2018) offer a more holistic approach to policy development and consider a wide range of actors involved in the policy development process. This model, along with the other policy models introduced here, are examined in greater detail in Chapter 4.

Policy typically arrives in a concrete form. Although it may benefit some makers of policy to not commit their policies to paper, there is usually a repository for policy documents in the form of a binder, policy manual, server contents or other means of storage. Policy, however, is frequently communicated by other means, such as email, staff meetings or other ways by which the message can be made public. The original hard copy document is usually signed by the authority in charge or by members of the policy committee. It is noteworthy, here, that membership in policy committees is frequently rotated, depending on the nature of the policy need and the expertise that is available to address the issue. Depending on the organization, most policy documents have a standard format particular to that organization.

Most policy documents, however, arrive in a certain standard form that tends to include the purpose and the intended recipients. Duties and responsibilities of the new approach are included, and tend to address new orders of regulations, requirements and/or behaviours. A date is included so that the time of commencement is also addressed. Less common, but also an integral part of the policy document is the inclusion of any definitions, which may pertain to the new routine of conduct that were not previously included or that were not well understood. Frequently, too, among policy documents is an introduction that supports the reasons for the development of the policy in the first place. In addition to providing a rationale, policies often describe a vision to be achieved, specific goals to be met, and the means for reaching them (Viennet & Pont, 2017).

Political scientist, T. J. Lowi (1972), identified four types of policy. They included distributive and redistributive policies, and regulatory and constituent policies. Distributive policies extend and distribute goods and services, as well as costs incurred for or by those services, to its constituent members. Redistributive policies have been considered to be more dynamic, as these represent 'policy in action'. Redistributive policies may be implemented in the wake of unintended consequences to a previous policy or to a policy that is unpopular or unsuccessful. Regulatory policies, on the other hand, tend to be 'limiting' policies that identify appropriate actions and behaviours within a specific range of meaning. Regulations concerning the operation and responsibilities associated with driving a motor vehicle, regardless of whether it is electric or not, is an example of a regulatory policy. Constituent policies serve to enshrine certain powers or to confer those powers, or the lack thereof, on particular groups of citizens or employees, depending upon their status within the organization with which they are associated.

It may also be noted that policy as written may vary substantially from policy as lived. This may be the result of compromise or by lack of commitment, implementation supports or enforcement of the policy directives. Such variations may also occur whenever a policy overreaches its intended audience, issuing directives that go beyond the issue that it was designed to address (Lowi, 1972).

Features of a Quality Policy Document

High quality policy making is usually preceded by some form of needs assessment. For example, a common way to begin, depending on the perceived need for a specific policy, may be by administering a 'needs' survey, which may serve to gauge how well a policy will be received by those who will be most affected by it. In addition, a cost/benefit or cost/effectiveness analysis may be useful in identifying the parameters or range of the policy, prior to the formal policymaking process. Opportunity costs associated with choosing a particular policy over an alternative policy may also be estimated (Simon, 2020). Cost/benefit calculations are frequently difficult, as, in most cases, benefits must be assigned a numeric value, most frequently in monetary terms, regardless of how difficult that may be. Consequently, the calculation of a benefit is often measured and aggregated in a manner that fails to capture those nuances. In spite of limitations in estimation, policy makers may estimate benefits through survey research by employing scales such as the popular Likert Scale that commonly measures up to five categories that rate reactions in terms of 'strongly agree' to 'strongly disagree'. A four-point Likert Scale is commonly used to 'force' opinions by striking out the middle category, which typically elucidates a neutral stance. Policymakers also view benefit through the output of a policy in terms of the number of people served by the policy (Simon, 2020).

Because policymaking does not occur independently of the society or organization of which it is a part, there may also be a number of other strategies or technologies available that may help to speed the process to a successful conclusion. As with any policy initiative, there is always the risk of policy failure, which may induce 'policy paralysis', where policymakers avoid difficult decisions by ignoring high risk but potentially rewarding policy issues (Simon, 2020).

Educational policies also often fall victim to partisan politics, lack of information, rejection of information and any number of unhelpful influences. For example, the presence of data-driven decision-making, data-informed decision-making and other permutations may fall prey to a reversal of sorts that are commonly referred to as 'decision-driven data-making', where the policy has already been decided upon in the notable absence of any useful information. The decision, once made, then suffers from incursions into research literature that supports that decision. Any information to the contrary is roundly ignored. This does not only occur in educative circles, however. Even powerful national governments have been known to use this time honoured pseudo-method, often with chequered results. Such ad hoc approaches to policy creation tend to result in policies that are generally implemented without discerning how effective the policy will be or even monitoring the policy's effect, once it is in place. Furthermore, outdated, insufficient or otherwise rogue policies tend to become ignored, gathering like dust or autumn leaves at the feet of the erstwhile policymakers. As new policy documents are added to the pile, conflicts or discrepancies between new and existing policies are massaged out, explained away or simply ignored. Here, policymaking really does appear to occur in a vacuum.

Policymaking, educational or otherwise, will benefit from the inclusion of two distinct and separate components. The first component refers to the use of a simple, yet effective policy model that can be easily followed in order to create high quality, future-oriented policies that require a minimum of maintenance. The second component is the awareness of the availability of certain tools, technologies or materials that may be utilized in order to facilitate the policy process. Personal interviews may also offer an important way to improve policy, as the experiences of staff members, administrators and the students themselves can help to inform the policy process and its results. Personal interviews allow for a high degree of flexibility in information collection. These and other issues pertaining to the development of high quality policy will be dealt with in subsequent chapters.

In particular, prevalent themes in policymaking will be explored, including different policy models and frameworks, various iterations of the policy process, the pivotal role of leadership in education policy, and the importance of alignment and coherence in policy reforms and educational change.

References

Althaus, C., Bridgman, P., & Davis, G. (2018). *The Australian policy handbook*. Allen & Unwin.

Anderson, J. E. (2014). *Public policymaking* (8th ed.). Cengage Learning.

Ball, S. J. (2012). *Global education inc: New policy networks and the neoliberal imaginary*. Routledge.

Ball, S. J. (2015). What is policy? 21 years later: Reflections on the possibilities of policy research. *Discourse: Studies in the Cultural Politics of Education, 36*(3), 306–313. https://doi.org/10.1080/01596306.2015.1015279

Bell, L., & Stevenson, H. (2015). Towards an analysis of the policies that shape public education: Setting the context for school leadership. *Management in Education, 29*(4), 146–150. https://doi.org/10.1177/0892020614555593

Caldwell, B. J., & Spinks, J. M. (1988). *The self-managing school*. Falmer.

Canadian Automobile Association. (2020). *Government incentives*. https://www.caa.ca/electric-vehicles/government-incentives/

Cardno, C. (2018). Policy document analysis: A practical educational leadership tool and a qualitative research method. *Educational Administration: Theory and Practice, 24*(4), 623–640. https://doi.org/10.14527/kuey.2018.016

Cerna, L. (2013). *The nature of policy change and implementation: A review of different theoretical approaches*. Organisation for Economic Co-Operation and Development.

Cunningham, C. (1963). Policy and practice. *Public Administration, 43*(3), 229–238.

Delaney, J. G. (2002). *Educational policy studies: A practical approach*. Detselig Enterprises Ltd.

Downey, L. W. (1998). *Policy analysis in education*. Detselig Enterprises Ltd.

Duke, D. L., & Canady, R. L. (1991). *School policy*. McGraw-Hill.

Dye, T. R. (1972). *Understanding public policy*. Prentice-Hall.

Howlett, M., Ramesh, M., & Perl, A. (2009). *Studying public policy*. Oxford University Press.

Hussen, A. (2019). *Public policy to facilitate the immigration of certain sponsored foreign nationals excluded under paragraph 117(9) or 125(1)(d) of the immigration and refugee protection regulations*. Government of Canada. https://www.canada.ca/en/immigration-refugees-citizenship/corporate/mandate/policies-operational-instructions-agreements/excluded.html

Jenkins, W. I. (1978). *Policy analysis: A political and organizational perspective*. St: Martin's Press.

Kim, T. (2020). What is the meaning of educational leadership in a time of policy engineering? *International Journal of Leadership in Education, 26*, 37–53.

Laswell, H. (1971). *A pre-view of policy sciences*. Elsevier.

Lau, R. (2019, November 29). Supreme Court rules in favour of Montreal woman fined for not holding escalator handrail. *CTV News*. https://montreal.ctvnews.ca/supreme-court-rules-in-favour-of-montreal-woman-fined-for-not-holding-escalator-handrail-1.4708211

Lowi, T. J. (1972). Four systems of policy, politics, and choice. *Public Administration Review, 32*(4), 298–310.

Maguire, M., Braun, A., & Ball, S. (2014). 'Where you stand depends on where you sit': The social construction of policy enactments in the (English) secondary school.

Discourse: Studies in the Cultural Politics of Education, 36(4), 485–499. https://doi.org/10.1080/01596306.2014.977022

Moreton, B. (2019, May 19). Where are all the electric cars in Nova Scotia? *The Chronicle Herald.* https://www.thechronicleherald.ca/news/local/where-are-all-the-electric-cars-in-nova-scotia-308004/

Pal, L. A. (1997). *Beyond policy analysis: Public issue management in turbulent times* (5th ed.). Nelson Education Ltd.

Pal, L. A., Auld, G., & Mallett, A. (2021). *Beyond policy analysis* (6th ed.). Nelson Education Ltd.

Policy. (n.d.). *Merriam Webster dictionary.* https://www.merriam-webster.com/dictionary/policy

Proctor, P. (2015). Policy. *Longman dictionary of contemporary English.* Pearson.

Sergiovanni, T. J., Burlingame, M., Coombs, F. S., & Thurston, P. W. (1999). *Educational governance and administration.* Allyn & Bacon.

Simon, C. A. (2020). Policy analysis. *Encyclopædia Britannica.* https://www.britannica.com/topic/policy-analysis#accordion-article-history

Viennet, R., & Pont, B. (2017). *Education policy implementation: A literature review and proposed framework* (OECD Working Paper No. 162). Organisation for Economic Co-Operation and Development.

Chapter 2

Policy, Power and Politics in Education

In his 1968 work *Pedagogy of the Oppressed*, Freire noted that 'all education is political; teaching is never a neutral act' (p. 19). In 2023, it seems little has changed in this regard, as seldom are matters of education divorced entirely from the political. Neutrality is oftentimes void from educational debates, and what we are left with is a situation where the political can take precedence, sometimes at the expense of what is best for teaching and learning, which is the fundamental enterprise of education. Decisions around curriculum often become 'political hot potatoes' as what is in favour at what one time can be discarded and replaced as often as governments change power. These macro-level decisions have reverberations throughout the entire workings of an educational system and can cause real and tangible impacts on those most directly impacted: teachers and students. But the political reach is not limited to matters as grandiose as curriculum. Rather, matters such as where to build a school, or who should receive the contract for the provision of catering services are wrapped up in the political. Indeed, if one were to scrutinize how education works, it would or at least should not be startling to realize that many forces and actors are involved in the development of policy. Each school year children of appropriate age attend schools where teachers strive to deliver for each student in their class an appropriate education. If one considers the buses that deliver kids from their homes to school, the teachers and support staff, as well as the policymakers formulating directives that drive the system, it becomes clear that education is characterized by many competing forces (Young, 2017). While many of these forces and actors are easily discernible, others tend to be less visible — some by design and others by choice — yet their influence cannot be ignored. These overt and covert dimensions of policy development can and ideally do exist in a harmonious fashion, but there are times when the interchange is disharmonious, and this battle can be both public and private. As Taylor et al. (1997, pp. 26–27) observe, policy is value-laden, and involves competing interests, with the end goal hopefully being some sort of compromise. Ultimately, the crux of the matter should be what is best for education, but simple observation leads one to the unfortunate conclusion that such debates are often framed around issues well beyond the purview of what will result in optimal learning conditions.

This chapter describes the multiple forces that are at play in the development of policy and related processes. And here the reference to forces implies the various layers of government and governmental agencies that are intimately involved in the process. But the reference also further implies non-governmental agencies whose reach and scope are worth examining. And this also includes economic forces that often exist and operate outside the political realm. This chapter also discusses the interplay among the sometimes-competing interests of the policy as written/lived, power dynamics and political agendas that drive the policy process. Specific attention is devoted to unpacking the social context and forces in which policy is developed and implemented. To the lay person, most of these forces often appear hidden, and in fact, many involved in education are also oblivious (Young, 2017). Yet, it is important to recognize that policy does not exist in a vacuum, and in fact, is very much a contextual response to real initiatives and espoused personal proclivities.

The Multiple Layers of Policy

For even the most casual observer, it is important to recognize that in thinking about educational policy, there are multiple levels or layers of government that must be considered as part of the overall equation. If one were to try to visualize what this might look like, it could become a confusing endeavour, with the realization that attempting to capture these policy layers is like trying to make sense of a web, with overlap and inconsistency being the norm.

Ultimately, and in a basic sense, most countries have a central or national government, yet the role played by this level of government varies greatly. In centralized countries such as Singapore, France, China, Spain and Norway, education is also highly centralized and falls under the purview of the national government. In other countries such as the United States, Australia, Canada and Germany, the role of the federal government tends to be minimized, with a large degree of power over education delegated to local states or provinces. This decentralized arrangement tends to stem largely from the fact that in countries with a federal system of government, education, which is often seen as a local matter, is vested outside the federal arena. Other countries such as the United Kingdom and Japan have a somewhat more balanced approach where power is shared between the national and local levels of government.

Irrespective of the country, it seems clear that most educational arrangements can be characterized by some diffusion of power, the degree to which varies. Singapore has often been described as an 'educational powerhouse' with students from this country consistently performing very well on standardized international assessments. Chiefly, education in Singapore is very centralized within the Ministry of Education, who oversees the entire education system, from elementary to post-secondary. The Ministry also determines funding for education, establishes course syllabi and examinations, credentials teachers and manages human resources in schools (La Londe & Verger, 2020). Although the Ministry is clearly the main driver of education in Singapore, the system is coherent and aligned, and roles and responsibilities of the various stakeholders are clearly articulated. It is also worth noting that although education is centralized in Singapore, there is a large degree of autonomy and discretion afforded to teachers and administrators. In addition, Singapore has been openly receptive to change and innovation, which has helped it climb to the upper echelons of the world's education systems. In looking at the Canadian situation as another example, it is possible to conclude that it occupies the other end of the spectrum in that it is a highly decentralized education system. The genesis for this decentralization can be traced back through history to the founding of the country in 1867. At this time, schooling was essentially seen as a local matter, because education was so closely tied to transmitting to society's youth a respect and appreciation for such matters as religion, language, customs, and values. Also, there was a general fear among the populace at this time that centralization in the hands of a central government would erode local autonomy. The solution to this dilemma, although difficult to arrive at, was rather simple (Giles & Proudfoot, 1994, p. 19). In effect, control over public education would be under the purview of the provincial governments. The legitimacy for this arrangement was enshrined in Section 93 of the 1867 *British North America Act* (now known as the *Constitution Act*, 1982) (Axelrod, 2001; Young, 2017). This has resulted in education becoming an unequivocal and exclusive constitutional provincial responsibility. However, this is not to suggest the national government is entirely removed from the equation, as federal involvement arises '... incidentally from explicit federal powers or may be a consequence of financial transfers' (Bezeau, 1995, p. 18).

Although Singapore and Canada, as but two examples, have each adopted differing approaches to the management and delivery of education, most jurisdictions have as a constituent feature a ministry or department of education, whose primary responsibility or mission is to give structure to the education system via the enactment of policies. The chief vehicle by which this is accomplished is through a statute that in some jurisdictions is termed an education or school act. These statutes are normally similar in that they specify such things as organization of school boards and schools, teacher duties, student duties and a host of other factors relevant to education. Most ministries/departments of education are headed by a minister or secretary, who is normally an elected official appointed to the position. These ministries/departments are in turn supported by a bureaucracy of civil servants.

As was mentioned above, education or school acts outline specifics in terms of the creation and administration of local school boards. School boards, which depending on the jurisdiction, are also sometimes known as school districts or school divisions, are normally composed of elected or appointed members known as trustees. In a general sense, there are few qualifications required to serve as a trustee. In terms of powers, 'the only authority that an individual board member...has is the right to speak, make and second motions, and vote at school board meetings' (Bezeau, 1995, p. 122). It is important to keep in mind that a school board is a corporate unit, and operates and exists independently, regardless of changes in the composition of the elected members. Besides the trustees, school boards employ a professional unelected staff led by a superintendent or director of education, who in effect manages the schools within the board or district. In a very real sense, the division of responsibility between trustees and the professional staff can at times lead to a dilemma surrounding professional versus lay authority. Or put another way, who exercises power: teachers and administrators or parents and community members (Young et al., 2007, p. 71). 'Superintendents may feel that trustees are uninformed about education, and have agendas that are short term and much too heavily influenced by re-election considerations. Trustees may feel that their professional staff is insufficiently concerned with what the public thinks, and too unwilling to accept any criticism.... This tension can be positive or negative, depending on how well the parties are able to work together to take best advantage of their different viewpoints' (Young et al., 2007, p. 46). This tension surrounding professional versus lay authority is an interesting feature of school boards and does impact the nature and organization of schools, so in a very real sense, reverberations can be felt within individual classrooms.

A recent trend has been the amalgamation of school boards to reduce costs and provide greater efficiency. This has borne witness to the total number of school boards in Canada decreasing (Parkay et al., 2009, p. 119). And interestingly enough, in the Canadian province of New Brunswick, the government actually abolished school boards in 1996. However, the boards did re-emerge in 2001 (Lessard & Brassard, 2009, p. 262). More recently, in Nova Scotia, Canada, the government, acting on recommendations put forward in a 2018 review of the education system, abolished the province's seven elected English language school boards (Williams & Young, 2022). These policy developments are important in that they illustrate that boards to a large degree operate within the parameters dictated by the government. In the current context, English and French Language public school boards are a constituent feature of Canadian education. These boards provide an open education to all students. We also have in Ontario, Saskatchewan and Alberta Roman Catholic separate school boards. These boards are public in the sense that they receive funding from the provincial government but are generally established to provide an education to those students of the Roman Catholic faith. It's also worth noting that in the 1990s, a reorganization of school boards occurred in Québec and Newfoundland and Labrador. In regard to Québec, religion, especially since the Quiet Revolution of the 1960s, had declined in importance. In an almost concurrent fashion, language had become a central identifying theme in the province. As such, Roman Catholic and Protestant school boards were often considered anachronistic, and not attuned with the modern realities of Québec society. As a result, in 1997, via an amendment to the *Constitution*, denominational school boards were eliminated and replaced by English and French language boards. It is interesting to note that the transition from denominational to linguistic education was relatively smooth, and in fact, not even the Catholic or Protestant Churches voiced great opposition to the change (see Young & Bezeau, 2003). In Newfoundland and Labrador, four different denominations enjoyed legal rights and privileges, thus resulting in a Roman Catholic system, a Pentecostal system, a Seventh Day Adventist system, and an Integrated system that drew from the Anglican, United and Presbyterian Churches, as well as the Salvation Army. Despite strong resistance from the Catholic and Protestant churches, declining enrolments, not to mention a weak economy, facilitated the 1998 reorganization of the Newfoundland and Labrador education system along non-sectarian lines. Thus, a complex multi-denominational arrangement that pre-dated 1949, when Newfoundland joined Confederation, disappeared from the landscape.

Despite the seemingly important role school boards assume, remember that these boards can be likened to creatures of the state, and thus their power is a direct result of that which is delegated to them through statutes enacted by government. Currently, two of the most central tasks delegated to school boards are the provision and maintenance of educational facilities, and the staffing of these facilities. Much of the remaining policy issues involved in schooling, such as the nature of curriculum, approved textbooks and a myriad of other factors, is regulated largely by ministries/departments of education. As such, what we are left with is that even in countries that have a decentralized system such as Canada, centralization is part of the landscape in that power is being usurped and absorbed by ministries/departments of education. This results in local school boards merely enacting policies and procedures developed elsewhere. One is thus left with a situation where local authority is somewhat diffused.

In building on this notion of central policy control exercised by ministries/departments of education, even a cursory examination of the funding of the public education system appears to point to a theme of centralization at the ministerial/department level. This stands in stark contrast to the historical record in which revenue to support education was generated largely through fees, local property taxes, and in some instances support from various religious denominations. However, in the current context, few jurisdictions continue to have significant local property taxes. More typical is the arrangement whereby governments account for nearly all of the monies allocated to school boards (Young et al., 2007, pp. 148–149). Under this type of centralized funding regime, the government allocates to boards financial support as drawn from the general revenue. In a very simplistic sense, most of this funding is provided via (1) a block grant; (2) categorical funding; and (3) equalization funding. A block grant accounts for the largest financial transfer and is based normally on the number of students enrolled in a school board. Categorical funding involves money earmarked for programs, such as special education. And last, equalization funding is a mechanism to align a board's fiscal capacity to deliver programs and services. In essence, it is a means to ensure a level playing field (Young et al., 2007, pp. 156–159). Despite this, because of pressures such as declining enrolments, not to mention the increasing effort by governments across the country to get their fiscal houses in order, school boards will continue to face uncertainty from an economic standpoint.

An additional level or layer that has yet to be discussed but is arguably the most important feature of an education system, is the school itself. Schools generally fall under the auspices of local government-sponsored school boards, but it is important to also recognize that other arrangements such as private schools, some of which are affiliated with religious denominations, also exist. Schools are the primary venue where teachers teach, and students learn. As such, their position of importance is undeniable.

Contextualizing the Layers

With so many layers operating in a largely simultaneous fashion, it is worth noting that disharmony and disjuncture is inevitable. In systems where power is dispersed between national and local governments, power struggles are not uncommon. Because of the nature of the arrangement itself, each level tries to safeguard the integrity of those elements under its purview. Put another way, governments often view their respective jurisdictions as sacrosanct, and resist any encroachment from outside forces or actors. Nonetheless, there is a general principle whereby federal laws can and oftentimes do encroach on other jurisdictions. As an example, the 2001 federal *No Child Left Behind Policy* in the United States instituted a requirement that in order to receive federal school funding, states would have to develop and administer assessments in basic skills at select grade levels. Clearly, this is a prime example whereby a federal law had implications for individual states. Another example comes from Canada, where the 1982 *Charter of Rights and Freedoms* guaranteed all Canadian fundamental rights, which extends to schools. As a result, any provincial education policy needs to accommodate for this federal statute (Young, 2017).

At the local (state or provincial) level we also find numerous policies related to education. These policies only apply within the geopolitical boundaries of the state or province. As an example, Louisiana has a Supplemental Course Academy to provide educational opportunities for students that would otherwise not be available at their local schools, but again, the programme itself is only available within the state of Louisiana.

School boards also actively pursue policy development, although such policies are only relevant within their respective jurisdictions. It is not uncommon within the same province or state to have school boards with dissimilar policies in effect. The School Board of Broward County in Florida has, as an example, a policy which stipulates that principals must maintain a physical screening form for high school athletes. As was the case with the Supplemental Course Academy policy in Louisiana, this particular policy would only apply to schools under the jurisdiction of the school board itself.

In addition to school boards, schools also develop policies that apply solely to students enrolled within that particular educational institution. Moree Public School in Australia has, like many schools across the globe, a policy around bullying. This is hardly atypical, but what is interesting is that in comparing school policies, difference is often the norm, and this even occurs among schools within the same school board. This is problematic in that it would be logical to assume that policy symmetry would be a feature found within and among schools.

In examining the interplay between governmental actors and agencies, it is clear that what we find can be likened to somewhat of a hierarchy (see Fig. 2.1). That is, federal or national policies can be positioned at the top of the hierarchy, and as such, all other polices must conform with federal statutes. If they do not, they are deemed *ultra vires* (beyond their scope of jurisdiction or competence). In a related manner, school board policies need to adhere to state/provincial polices, and school polices should not contravene board policies.

```
┌──────────────┐
│  Federal /   │
│   National   │
│   Policies   │
└──────┬───────┘
       │    ┌──────────────┐
       └────│   State /    │
            │  Provincial  │
            │   Policies   │
            └──────┬───────┘
                   │   ┌──────────────┐
                   └───│ School Board │
                       │   Policies   │
                       └──────┬───────┘
                              │   ┌──────────────┐
                              └───│   School     │
                                  │   Policies   │
                                  └──────────────┘
```

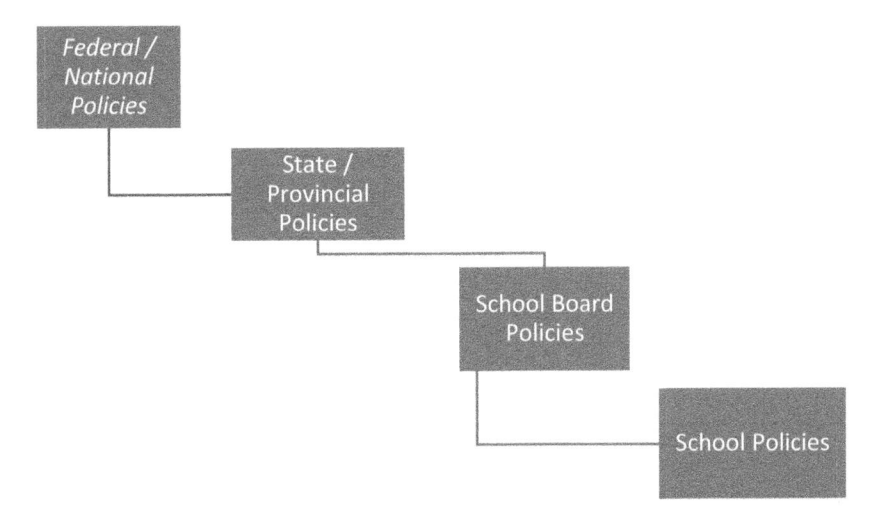

Fig. 2.1.   Hierarchy of Policies.

This hierarchy is an important dimension of debates around educational policy. Basically, policy makers need to ensure they are operating *intra vires* (within their sphere of jurisdiction). Otherwise, they risk the potential of having their policies struck down by relevant authorities such as courts of law, thereby rendering the statute of no force or effect.

Besides this hierarchy, another layer of the policy web that is important to consider is the nature of educational policy itself. To borrow a nautical term, educational policies are not watertight compartments. That is, they simply don't exist as separate and distinct entities. To continue with this somewhat perhaps laboured theme, spillage between various levels of policy is inevitable. Policies within the educational realm have real-world implications beyond the mere educational. Thus, it is impossible to look at educational policy as existing within a vacuum, when in actuality it is a social by-product. Any attempt to treat educational policy in isolation is a futile endeavour. In thinking about the recent and perhaps ongoing pandemic, the move to online learning for schools was indeed an educational policy initiative. But to divorce this from the larger picture is to misconstrue reality. The emergence of COVID-19, once deemed a public health emergency, prompted governments around the globe to introduce restrictive measures to reduce the spread of the disease. As terms like 'social distancing' became part of our vernacular, educational polices around remote learning emerged which were in large measure a response to policies first enacted by public health. At the same time, policies within education also had a ripple effect on other fields including higher education, who also found themselves pivoting to online instruction. The bottom line is no one policy exists within a bubble. Outside forces are at play constantly, and ministries/departments of education can sometimes collide with other departments or organizations. Often, these collisions are unintentional, but reverberations are still part of the equation. In trying to offer an analogy, the best example is that of bumper cars often found at amusement parks. As one navigates around the obstacles, which in many cases are other drivers, a collision between cars can result in a vehicle coming into contact with your car, thus resulting in a thud. This thud is like the policy reverberations mentioned above. While not intentional, they still produce a real and lasting effect for all the parties involved.

An additional feature within the government realm that deserves consideration is the notion of political agendas, and the role they play. And here, the reference to political agendas entails '... what is relevant in public life, how issues are defined, whose views are taken seriously, and what sorts of "solutions" are tenable' (Brooks, 1993, p. 14). Even someone completely unfamiliar with the political process would not be surprised to learn that once elected, governments strive to be re-elected. As such, election platforms are designed to capture voters before they head to the polls. Also, a further feature is governments investing heavily in various programs in anticipation of an election. The prevailing logic is that spending capital will resonate with voters, thus ensuring electoral success. Another related aspect is the policies pursued by governments once elected. While promises are often broken by governments, various parts of their electoral platform are pursued as policy initiatives. Relatedly, some policies are never pursued because of systemic bias, 'a term intended to capture the selectiveness of the policy system' (Miljan, 2008, p. 9). As a consequence, some policy considerations are never 'articulated and some policy outcomes are virtually precluded by the biases inherent in the cultural and institutional fabric of society' (Brooks, 1993, p. 17).

In some cases, policies stem from the leaders themselves. For example, in the Canadian province of Ontario, former Premier Bill Davis, who had long opposed extending full funding to Grade 13 in Ontario Catholic schools, ultimately saw political advantage in extending this funding and as a result reversed his position in 1985. Another Ontario Premier, Mike Harris, was a politician that was driven by a plan, coined the 'common sense revolution'. Harris, who served as Premier from 1995 to 2002, believed that the entire education system was inefficient and ineffective, and that reform was needed. As such, standardized testing became a constituent feature of provincial education policy, with additional efforts to institute teacher testing and re-certification (Gidney, 2002). Although not always the case, politicians, and especially those with strong political agendas, might occupy various positions on the political agenda. It seems indisputable that Premier Harris was pursuing a right-wing agenda, while others who occupy positions of power may be more closely aligned with centre or left of centre policies.

An additional related feature that is worth mentioning is that there can also be scenarios where politicians do not have a strong agenda or lack a vision of what to pursue once in office. This creates a fertile situation for policymakers within the bureaucracy to influence elected officials to pursue various courses of action. And this concern over the influence that bureaucrats could have on policy is not new, and in fact can be found in the earliest writings about bureaucracy. The concern was 'bureaucrats, it was believed, had a tendency to act in their own interests, which meant behaving in ways that might not be in the public's interest' (Miljan, 2008, p. 91). Ideally, public servants should endorse and espouse a position of political neutrality, which is a 'constitutional doctrine or convention according to which public servants should avoid activities that are likely to impair — or seem to impair — their political impartiality or the impartiality of the public service' (Kernaghan & Siegel, 1995, p. 326). Yet, there are well-documented cases in Canada and elsewhere where the ideological preference of members of the bureaucracy has had a direct impact on policy development.

> It is difficult for bureaucrats to separate completely their role as citizens or voter from that of government employee and it is, therefore, reasonable to assume that sympathy for a political party will carry over into decisions or recommendations on the job. Equally problematic is assessing the effect of the ideological commitments of bureaucrats. These commitments need not be manifested by a formal or emotional attachment to a particular political party; the bureaucrat who is politically neutral in the partisan sense still has ample opportunity to inject personal ideological preferences into the policy-making process. These preferences will obviously affect the bureaucrat's views on major policy issues involving such social values as the redistribution of income and the protection of human rights.
> (Kernaghan & Siegel, 1995, p. 490)

While much of the discussion thus far has centred around government actors and agencies, we do need to acknowledge the role played by non-governmental actors, chief among them lobbyists. Lobbyists undertake 'activities aimed at persuading, encouraging, and sometimes even coercing authoritative office-holders to adopt preferred options and avoid undesirable ones' (Howlett et al., 2009, p. 140). So, while there may be an impulsive temptation to automatically think of lobbyists in a negative light given their portrayal in the media, and to accrue undue importance to these actors, in the end, lobbyists have only a voice in the process and not a vote (Sarpkaya, 1988). Yet, their role should not be discounted as it is a force that can play a role in the shaping of policy.

Related to lobbyists is the role played by pressure groups, whose goal is to attempt to influence government policy. Pressure groups take different forms, such as the Canadian Labour Congress, which is concerned with a wide range of policy issues. Conversely, pressure groups can also coalesce around a single issue, and thus their membership would be typically smaller. Regardless of their form, pressure groups occupy a position of importance, and their growth has caused some commentators to observe that in some ways, pressure groups have 'diminished to some extent the role of political parties as intermediaries between the citizen and the state' (Kernaghan & Siegel, 1995, p. 490).

Like lobbyists and pressure groups, the media is another external force that needs to be considered in issues of policy. However, unlike lobbyists and pressure groups, the media has a very wide reach, and can influence a large audience. As

Kernaghan and Siegel put it, 'the media play a critical role as two-way channels of communication between the governors and the governed' (1995, p. 503). One need look no further than the situation in the United States, where Fox News has been labelled as a megaphone for the Republican Party, which was especially evident during the presidency of Donald Trump. In the end, the media 'influence the attitudes and behaviours of both government officials and members of the public. Thus, the media both reflect and influence public opinion' (Kernaghan & Siegel, 1995, p. 503).

As a final point of consideration around the role of lobbyists, pressure groups and the media, it is worth noting that one barometer by which to measure the overall impact of these actors is the extent to which policy initiatives for which they advocate are endorsed by government. Admittedly, this is a simplistic means of analysis, but does offer some window into 'whose arguments, interpretations, and proposals are taken seriously in the policy-making process' (Brooks, 1993, p. 16).

Another external dimension that comes into play is social forces. While these social forces can be domestic in nature, they can also originate on the international stage. Regardless of point of origin, they exert real pressure on how and which policies are pursued by the government. As an example, international test scores have become somewhat of a fascination or preoccupation for policy makers. The question that is often posed is why students in certain countries are performing well, while students in other countries lag behind. As a response mechanism, many countries developed policies designed to focus emphasis on reading, writing and arithmetic. In an almost concomitant manner, governments introduced standardized tests as a means to measure and gauge how students were performing in schools. While the merits of such policy initiatives are well beyond the scope of this chapter, it still serves as a prime example of how policy is designed to meet outside pressures and forces.

Conclusion

Writing in 1995, Silver discussed the concept of 'policy rage'. While our initial inclination might be to think about the many ways that policies infuriate us, Silver was actually referring to society's general preoccupation with policy. And if we fast-forward to the current context, Silver's writing still rings true. Policies truly abound, and what we are left with is a world inundated with policies. While some policies work well and are advantageous, critics also lament the fact that other policies wreak havoc and are broken beyond repair. But even the critics don't advocate for abandoning policies completely; rather, they argue that what is broken should be replaced with a new and improved policy.

In thinking about what a good policy should entail, a glaring truth is that no policy is perfect, and anyone seeking such will be left utterly disappointed (Ripley, 2013). Rather, policies must be examined within their own contexts to tease out what works, and conversely, what might need reform. And as a caveat, education reform is very complex, and takes time (Martin et al., 2017, p. 62). 'Policy makers' hunger for immediate answers is always frustrated by the snail's pace at which the development of data, evidence and research advances' (Schleicher, 2018, p. 61). In the end, arriving at a policy takes time. The decision-making stage involves

> ... the choice among policy alternatives that have been generated and their likely effects on the problem estimated.... It is the most overtly political stage in so far as the many potential solutions to a given problem must somehow be winnowed down and but one or a select few picked and readied for use. Obviously most possible choices will not be realized and deciding not to take particular courses of action is as much part of selection as finally settling on the best course.
> (Brewer & DeLeon, 1983, p. 1790)

In the end, education is a most valuable enterprise, and 'high-performing systems tend to align policies and practices across the entire system. They ensure that the policies are coherent over sustained periods of time, and they see that they are consistently implemented' (Schleicher, 2018, p. 64).

The power dynamics at play in the development of policy are real and have the potential to overtake or control the entire process, and this is a danger if left unchecked. In thinking about policy, one comes to the realization that the idea of a 'fair' policy is something of a myth. Policy makers, regardless of political stripe, bring to the table certain values, beliefs and principles they embrace. As such, partisan influence is a feature of policy development. This is not to say that all policies are corrupt, but it is appropriate to posit that policies inevitably tilt in one direction, much like the Leaning Tower of Pisa itself. And all the braces in the world will not erase or eradicate this tilt.

This chapter has focused on the notion of multiple layers or levels that play a role in the policy process. Some of these layers can best be described as governmental, while others exist outside the realm of government. Often, what we have is a dynamic interplay among these layers that causes friction among competing interests within the policy process. Thus, the policy as written may not be implemented as written, due to various, unpredictable, and insurmountable issues relating to the process of developing and implementing a new policy. It is within these parameters that policy becomes 'policy as lived', rather than policy as written. Thus, no unbiased policy exists that is completely free of power dynamics, political agendas, and other possible forms of influence. This is the nature of policymaking, then. It does not exist in a vacuum but is representative of a function of the society within which it was created. At the end of the day, policy remains a contextual response to concrete initiatives, which must be responsive to personal and societal proclivities. And although 'we might like to think that all decisions and policies in education are developed and undertaken with the best interests of students as the ultimate objective. However, the reality is that this is not always so' (Delaney, 2017, pp. 77–78). In the end, as Marshall and Gerstl-Pepin note, 'policy is what governments choose to do' (2005, p. 5).

References

Axelrod, P. D. (2001). *The promise of schooling: Education in Canada, 1800–1914*. University of Toronto Press.

Bezeau, L. M. (1995). *Educational administration for Canadian teachers* (2nd ed.). Copp Clark.

Brewer, G. D., & DeLeon, P. (1983). *The foundations of policy analysis*. Dorsey.

Brooks, S. (1993). *Public policy in Canada: An introduction* (2nd ed.). McClelland & Stewart.

Delaney, J. G. (2017). *Education policy: Bridging the divide between theory and practice* (2nd ed.). Brush.

Freire, P. (1968). *Pedagogy of the oppressed*. Herder and Herder.

Gidney, R. D. (2002). *From Hope to Harris: The reshaping of Ontario's schools*. University of Toronto Press.

Giles, T. E., & Proudfoot, A. J. (1994). *Educational administration in Canada* (5th ed.). Detselig.

Howlett, M., Ramesh, M., & Perl, A. (2009). *Studying public policy: Policy cycles & policy subsystems* (3rd ed.). Oxford University Press.

Kernaghan, K., & Siegel, D. (1995). *Public administration in Canada: A text* (3rd ed.). Nelson Canada.

La Londe, P. G., & Verger, A. (2020). Comparing high-performing education systems: Understanding Singapore, Shanghai, and Hong Kong. *Discourse: Studies in the Cultural Politics of Education, 43*(1), 158–171.

Lessard, C., & Brassard, A. (2009). Education governance in Canada, 1990–2003: Trends and significance. In C. Levine-Rasky (Ed.), *Canadian perspectives on the sociology of education* (pp. 255–274). Oxford University Press.

Marshall, C., & Gerstl-Pepin, C. (2005). *Reframing educational politics for social justice*. Pearson.

Martin, L. E., Kragler, S., & Frazier, D. (2017). Professional development and education policy: Comparison of two important fields in education. *Journal of Educational Research and Practice, 7*(1), 60–73.

Miljan, L. (2008). *Public policy in Canada: An introduction* (5th ed.). Oxford University Press.

Parkay, F. W., Hardcastle Stanford, B., Vaillancourt, J. P., & Stephens, H. C. (2009). *Becoming a teacher* (3rd Can. ed.). Pearson.

Ripley, A. (2013). *The smartest kids in the world and how they got that way*. Simon & Schuster.

Sarpkaya, S. (1988). *Lobbying in Canada: Ways and means*. CCH Canadian.

Schleicher, A. (2018). *World class: How to build a 21st-century school system*. OECD.

Silver, H. (1995). Policy problems in time. In E. W. Ricker & B. A. Wood (Eds.), *Historical perspectives on educational policy in Canada: Issues, debates and case studies* (pp. 30–40). Canadian Scholars' Press.

Taylor, S., Rizvi, F., Lingard, B., & Henry, M. (1997). *Educational policy and the politics of change*. Macmillan.

Williams, M. A., & Young, D. C. (2022). The encouragement and constraint of distributed leadership via education policy reform in Nova Scotia, Canada: A delicate balancing act. *International Journal of Education Policy and Leadership, 18*(2), 1–18.

Young, D. C. (2017). Educator rights and duties. In D. C. Young (Ed.), *Education law in Canada: A guide for teachers and administrators* (pp. 83–111). Irwin Law.

Young, D. C., & Bezeau, L. M. (2003). Moving from denominational to linguistic education in Quebec. *Canadian Journal of Educational Administration and Policy, 24*.

Young, J., Levin, B., & Wallin, D. (2007). *Understanding Canadian schools: An introduction to educational administration* (4th ed.). Nelson.

Chapter 3

Policy Alignment: Connecting School, District and System Policies

As the preceding chapter has illustrated, there are various layers or levels involved in the policy process. Some of these layers fall under the umbrella of what might be termed government/governmental actors, while others fall outside this construct as external forces. Within the former, three particular entities occupy positions of particular importance in that they are directly and intimately involved in the arena of educational policy. The first entity is the school, which is where teaching and learning occurs. In any given day during the academic year, students can be found in classrooms across the globe receiving instruction from educators on a wide variety of topics. While schools develop internal policies, in many ways they are receptors and implementors of policy created at higher levels within the educational hierarchy. A second entity that warrants consideration is the school district or school board. Boards or districts are local entities that serve and operate schools within a particular geographic locale. In many countries, these boards/districts are organized along linguistic lines, but there are situations where they can be constituted around other factors such as religion. Like schools, boards develop and institute policies that apply to those schools they operate and administer. Board/district policies need to correspond with higher-level state policies; otherwise, they may be deemed *ultra vires*. A final entity in this equation is the system or government, with the reference here largely being to individual states and provinces. System policy is developed and uniformly applies to all districts/boards and schools within a defined geopolitical boundary (e.g., a state or province).

In thinking about the interaction of these various entities, it would be ideal if everyone worked together, policy alignment was the norm and harmony abounded (Rice & Prince, 2000). In fact, if there was mutual and widespread agreement, we might not even have a need for policy. However, this utopian ideal is not the nature of the situation and policies are needed to provide structure and coherence. Oftentimes, what we encounter is a situation where policies are not created uniformly and, in some cases, may be characterized by a conflict of interests at the school, district, and system levels.

In this chapter, specific attention will be devoted to identifying the necessary features that may help to ensure consistent, coherent policies that are functional at each level of governance. Reference will be given to theoretical constructs and how they may be practically applied to ensure policy alignment.

Policy Alignment: Connecting Theory and Practice

Policy alignment is an ideal, and something to strive towards. It is a situation where all of the entities operate in concert, working towards a common goal. To use an agricultural analogy, if one were ploughing a field using a team of horses, all the equines need to work together pulling in the same direction; otherwise, what results is a futile endeavour where each horse operates as an independent contractor, and the field never gets ploughed so that the crops might be planted. In the end, there is no winner.

A first consideration and one that might seem obvious, but is nonetheless missing from many a conversation, is the need to study public policy.

> As the scope of state intervention ... has increased and the forms of state action have grown more complex, it has become more difficult for laypersons to understand public policy. Yet the importance of such understanding has never been greater. Today the state really does accompany its citizens from the cradle (if not the womb) to the grave. But it is not always easy to make sense of what governments do and why. Confusion is a natural response to the enormous range of government programs, the Byzantine complications introduced by bureaucracy and multiple layers of government, and the information overload that seems to await anyone intent on sorting out what it all means. Retreat into apathy or uninformed cynicism (not the same as informed cynicism) is a common reaction, though not a helpful one.
> (Miljan, 2008, p. 19)

Policy is by its very nature dense and difficult to understand. Perhaps part of this stems from the fact that there exist multiple and sometimes competing definitions of what the term policy actually means. If we start from a position of ambiguity and uncertainty, it should hardly be startling to be able to foresee potential pitfalls. While it would be facile to expect that increased education would result in uniformity of thought, not to mention that this too is highly undesirable, possessing some degree of shared and/or common literacy in the area of policy would be highly advantageous. If we all depart from the same starting line, there is greater likelihood we will all cross the same finish line. Ultimately, all those involved with policy need not be policymakers, but it is not hyperbolic to suggest that those who understand and are familiar with the system in which they work will be able to do their job with increased effectiveness and efficiency. As Delaney notes, 'the educator — whether a teacher in the classroom, a principal, or a district-level administrator — regularly confronts some aspects of policy in the multitude of decisions he or she makes every day' (2017, p. 2). As such, education is an important foundation upon which to build policy alignment.

Besides the educational component, there also needs to be a breaking down of barriers. Too often in government, departments become so siloed that mere cooperation becomes a bit of a foreign concept. In the case of schools, districts and systems, it seems obvious that their sheer inter-connectedness would dictate that cooperation would be the norm. However, fracture and disjointedness, not to mention in some cases mutual distrust of the other, lead to competition and disharmony. Inter-departmental boundaries are a real impediment to working together for the common good, which ultimately should be the betterment of the educational enterprise. To borrow from the nautical metaphor employed in the previous chapter, watertight compartments might be well-suited for marine vessels, but they are fundamentally ill-suited when discussing educational policy. Policies developed at the system, district and/or school level spread across all three entities, so it only makes rational and logical sense that the parties would work in tandem. Ideally, policy development, implementation and review should involve all constituents and not occur behind closed doors, but rather, should evolve as a process of mutual sharing. Certainly, no one entity owns this process or possesses a monopoly over it, as a plurality of actors are needed. As the old saying goes, two heads are better than one, and in this case, multiple heads can only serve to improve the process. One might think of the educational policy dynamic as like a wheel one would find on a bicycle, where the system, district and school serve as spokes. As long as the spokes remain sturdy and the tire is fully inflated, the wheel will rotate in a somewhat smooth and unencumbered manner. While it is inevitable that divergences can and will occur, working through these spats as a cohesive unit is the key. For Pal, democratic governance is about working together to arrive at a common goal. As he writes: '...democratic politics is...-about working through...differences, or reaching beyond them to some common ground' (1997, p. 274). Politics is often regarded as the art of compromise, and in this regard, compromise is a key feature of democratic governance, as without this, quarrels will remain.

In addition to education and the breaking down of barriers, there also needs to be some sort of agreement or symmetry between the entities to arrive at a common goal. Many scholars have noted that in order to facilitate the development of policy, what is often required is an agenda-setting protocol involving all players (Howlett et al., 2009, p. 101).

Cobb and Elder (1972) speak about the informal and institutional agendas, and each holds merit when discussing the need to ensure policy coherence. In terms of the former, the reference is to any matters that deserve public attention and that fall within the purview of the organization or institution. As an example, a case of bullying at an educational institution could very well be an issue that would merit the attention of the school, the district and the system, and as such, could be included as an item for consideration in an informal agenda. Certainly, the number of issues that could be addressed in any policy sphere is numerous, and as such, choices need to be made about what is formally addressed by government. Those items that make the cut comprise the institutional agenda and are but a small fraction of all existing issues. Falling test scores across all schools within a district is a concern that would capture attention, and as a result, could very well be an issue that gets catapulted onto the institutional agenda.

According to Cobb et al. (1976), there are four phases to consider as policies move from the informal to the institutional agenda: (1) issues are initiated; (2) solutions are specified; (3) support for the issue is expanded; and (4) the issue enters the institutional agenda. What is useful about this construct is that it provides a framework to allow policymakers to arrive at a decision as to whether an issue should be elevated to the status of a formal agenda item. Too often, knee jerk reactions or personal proclivities confuse and muddy the waters, leading to an absolute lack of coherence. When this occurs, policy development is doomed from the outset. Further complicating the issue is that too often, policy is pursued at breakneck speed, with no consideration given to the potential consequences. By adopting an agenda setting model, it causes one to pause, consider the issue fully, and then proceed with hopefully all parties on the same page. We might liken this to the role played by the Senate in Canada's parliamentary democracy. Essentially, while the House of Commons is charged with developing policy, it is the Senate that reviews such policies prior to endorsement. As a result, the Senate has often been seen as the place of sober second thought. Sometimes, it is wise to pump the brakes rather than the accelerator, and in terms of policy, this rings true. Setting an agenda as a first step is advantageous, and would serve schools, districts and systems well.

Another factor that schools, districts and systems would be wise to attend to in aligning policy is the notion of 'decision criteria' as posited by Gallagher (1992). According to this model, there are four criteria that policy makers should consider: (1) technical feasibility; (2) economic and financial possibility; (3) political viability; and (4) administrative operability.

Technical feasibility refers to if the policy will actually work and deliver what is intended. Gallagher does note that 'no one program will always bring about its intended effect' (p. 46). If we think about the problem of bullying and school violence, schools have adopted a number of proactive and reactive strategies to address this problem. One such strategy that gained widespread traction were the zero-tolerance policies. While the theory behind this approach perhaps had some merit, their impact on schools was less than stellar. In fact, these policies did little to address bullying and school violence, and in fact, had a negative impact on minority students in that they were disproportionately singled out as a result of the zero-tolerance approach. In retrospect, schools, districts and systems were looking for a quick-fix to tackle a real problem, and although zero-tolerance policies promised an immediate impact with its get-tough approach, it simply did not deliver. Consequently, they have largely been abandoned as a tool used within education. Had policymakers at all levels done a complete and thorough analysis of zero tolerance prior to implementation, it may have become apparent from a technical feasibility standpoint that the potential results were not promising. In deciding on which policy course to pursue, technical feasibility needs to be part of the conversation.

The second criterion under Gallagher's model is economic and financial possibility. At the heart of this matter is how much will a policy cost, and what are the intended benefits. In purely economic terms, it is a prime example of a cost-benefit analysis. In the current context, the problem of the purse is widely acknowledged and trumpeted by governments as a rationale to support decreased spending. While it might be argued that cost should not be a consideration when discussing public education, this simply ignores the reality of the situation. Schools, districts and systems are trying to make do with less in an effort to curb spending. To illustrate this cost-benefit analysis, a Canadian example will be provided. As the number of children diagnosed with Autism continues to climb, education systems have been striving to provide learning environments that allow for these students to reach their full potential. For many parents of children with Autism, specialized therapies such as intensive behaviour intervention or applied behaviour analysis show the greatest promise, and as such, there have been concerted efforts to have governments pay for these therapies. In the 2004 case of *Auton v. British Columbia*, the Supreme Court of Canada found that the decision by the British Columbia government to not provide these specialized therapies was not discriminatory. The Court's rationale was that these therapies were not deemed to be a core service under the *Health Act*. Others have speculated that the Court was aware of the hefty price tag that accompanied such therapies and as a result, decided that the extension of full funding would be problematic from an economic standpoint. As a sort of compromise, the Court found that governments could choose to provide funding for these therapies but were not obliged to do. In so doing, they did not close the door entirely but instead allowed governments to exercise discretion in the matter. These types of decisions are not easy as parents want what they perceive to in the best interests of their child, but this needs to be balanced against other factors, including economics.

Gallagher also addresses the notion of political viability. Essentially, as Delaney (2017, p. 11) points out, this refers to whether a policy will 'fly'. As we have seen from the previous chapter, the nature of educational policy is highly political. As a result, schools, districts and systems need to read the tea leaves to gauge if a policy is palatable. While achieving unanimous support for any policy is a steep hill to climb, majority support is highly desirable when undertaking any course of action. In borrowing from another Canadian example, in 2021, the provincial government of Manitoba announced plans to eliminate school boards. Public consultations held after this announcement revealed deep civic dissatisfaction with the plan, and in 2022 the government signalled its intention to scrap the plan, leaving school boards intact. In the end, even though the politicians who occupied the government benches had developed a plan to reform the governance structure in the province, it simply did not 'fly' with the general public and thus was abandoned. Political viability is yet another factor that needs to be part of any policy discussion between and among schools, districts, and systems. Proactively examining the pros and cons of any proposed policy at the outset can reduce or minimize the potential for political egg on one's face at a later juncture.

A last point advanced by Gallagher is administrative operability. The reference here is to how practical a policy actually is in terms of implementation. A myriad of issues potentially fall under this criterion, and in fact, most every aspect of schools and schooling would intersect or fall under this heading. As an example, the recent experience with the pandemic and the move to remote learning served as an excellent example of how administrative operability can be tested. COVID-19, as we all recall, brought with it a host of macro-level challenges, and education was not spared from being impacted. As governments across the globe issued stay-at-home orders, policymakers were left with the challenge of how to provide an education for school aged children. Congregating in a school classroom was no longer a possibility, so moving classes online became the solution. From a practicality standpoint, schools were not ready for this, and in many ways, few could have foreseen the impact this virus would have on our way of life. Teachers had to scramble and learn how to use platforms like Zoom, migrate their lessons to learning management systems, and envision new and novel ways to deliver curriculum. Administrators had to secure laptops for student use, and for those households who lacked internet service, curriculum was delivered by regular mail. While the pandemic did test the system, in the end, schools, districts and systems came together in an effort to provide kids with a basic education. There were growing pains, and not everything unfolded smoothly, but in the face of adversity, the system and its actors rose up and met the challenge head-on.

Ultimately, the criteria put forth by Gallagher is valuable in that it provides policy makers with a set of useful and operational factors to consider. Having schools, districts and systems adhere to these provides an opportunity for policy coherence and alignment to be realized.

An additional and related factor that schools, districts and systems must keep in mind is the very nature of what a good policy entails. If there is agreement among these constituencies, policy alignment and coherence is more likely to be realized. For Clemmer (1991), the following criteria constitute good policy: (1) only policies directed at relevant issues should be pursued; (2) policies should respond to real needs; (3) policy should be functional; and (4) policies must be feasible in terms of implementation. Clemmer commented further, noting the following:

> Although good policies allow for a reasonable measure of interpretation, they are stated in language specific enough that they provide real guidance. Good policies treat broad, general issues that have long-term implications; poor policies often respond to specific incidents and prescribe narrow judgements, and they often prove unenforceable. Unlike those fostered in business, where profit is an abiding incentive, a school district's policies should enhance the achievement of its own goals, which are educational or service-oriented. (p. 105)

Another issue to consider when trying to connect theory with practice is the notion of policy analysis. There are many definitions of policy analysis, such as the following offered by Gallagher (1992, p. 4):

In its most basic sense, *policy analysis* is the process of locating information relevant to the identified purpose. In this broad sense, *policy analysis* is synonymous with *problem solving*. Policy analysis has two characteristic features: the information collected has a practical orientation and the information will help guide action rather than be an end in itself. So the aim of policy analysis is to provide decision makers with information that can be used to make reasoned judgements in finding solutions to practical problems.

For Pal (1997, p. 15), policy analysis is 'a way of thinking, an ability to sift the extraneous from the essential, to get to the bottom, to see patterns and connections such as historical or international comparisons. It's the ability to think ahead a few more moves, about the consequences downstream. It's the ability to organize information'.

Regardless of the definition adopted, policy analysis is a vital cog in determining what is working and what is not. If schools, districts, and systems adopt a similar blueprint to undertaking policy analysis, this could go a long way to ensuring coherence and alignment. Pal (1992) offers some very valuable tips that stakeholders should keep in mind.

- *Dive deep.* Sound analysis is characterized by exploring the issue in full. There are no shortcuts in policy analysis, and one must complete a thorough analysis of all facets surrounding the issue. Doing your homework is always advantageous.
- *Know the law.* When in doubt, familiarize yourself with any relevant laws that might have an impact on the policy. Again, there are absolutely no shortcuts as breaching a law can have serious ramifications.
- *Count the stakes.* In any policy, some will benefit while others will not. It is always important to consider the impact of policy on others, but in the end, decisions must be taken and not all parties will be satisfied. Tough choices are part of the terrain.
- *Look at the big picture.* The analogy of not being able to see the forest for the trees is appropriate in this regard. While it might be useful to focus analysis on the micro, it is equally important to consider the macro when thinking about policy.
- *Be cautiously sceptical of experts.* As a policy analyst, it is always important to remain objective and be aware of your blind spots. At the same time, always exercise caution when something seems too good to be true. A snake oil salesman is just that, a snake oil salesman.
- *Be cautiously respectful of common sense.* While there is a saying that common sense is not so common anymore, there really is no substitute for relying on what one believes. As such, trust your gut as it won't steer you wrong.

- *If possible, have a bias towards small solutions.* While the temptation might be to search for a complex answer, most times the straightforward answer is what is being sought. Keep things simple!
- *Choose policy targets you have a reasonable chance of controlling.* Some things may simply be out of reach or unattainable, so always be driven by reason, and not by passion.
- *Try to structure choice into policy.* It is crucial that choice is a constituent feature of policymaking.
- *Be balanced in considering interests, but err on the side of diffuse interests over concentrated, organized interests.* Remember that policy should always be driven by a focus on the greater good.

These tips are useful to consider for those from school, district and system levels. But as Pal (1992, p. 277) notes, 'tips will not necessarily guarantee good work but ignoring them is almost certain to lead to shoddy analysis'. In the end, 'whether they realize it or not, actors engaged in policy evaluation are often participating in a larger process of policy learning, in which improvements or enhancements to policy-making and policy outcomes can be brought about through careful and deliberate assessment of how past stages of the policy cycle affected both the original goals adopted by governments and the means implemented to address them' (Howlett et al., 2009, p. 180).

A final point that requires addressing is the notion of policy dissemination, which involves 'the initial diffusion of information about the program [policy] among potential users' (Scheirer & Griffith, 1990, p. 164). Clemmer offers sage advice when he discusses dissemination:

> Because relatively few persons may have assisted in the development of a particular policy, unless it is controversial and has attracted public attention the vast majority of...students, employees, and patrons will most likely be unaware of its existence or its implications. All major district players should be informed about the new policy and how it will be administered, but the audience of first magnitude is always the one comprised of the persons most *affected* by the policy (1991, p. 186).

And because policy dissemination is a complex process with the real potential to cause upset and confusion, the advice offered by Rich (1974, p. 31) is prescient.

> [T]he policy-maker must anticipate and evaluate a host of factors prior to deciding on the proper course of action; such factors as the complexity of policy change, the degree to which the policy breaks with past practices, the ability of personnel to execute the policy successfully, and the possible conflict of the policy with vested interests are all matters that merit careful assessment in determining dissemination procedures.

In thinking about the process of dissemination, a few points are worth noting for those from the school, district, and system levels. First, 'the onus is on those in leadership positions both at the building and district levels to ensure that dissemination is given the attention it warrants' (Delaney, 2002, p. 79). Second, transparency is always preferable to obfuscation. Issues shrouded in secrecy are bound to provoke distrust, which can be a real impediment to the success of any policy. Third, and this ties into the notion of transparency, making available a policy manual is simply good practice. In days gone by, it was not uncommon to have large binders crammed full of papers in the principal's office. This binder contained all of the rules and regulations that pertained to the school. It is probably safe to say that very few principals would have fully digested this manual, but it was nonetheless a valuable resource as a reference. For some administrators, the policy manual was likened to a safety blanket. In the current context, not much has really changed. As Delaney (2017) notes, 'one challenge of school administrators is to keep their heads above the continuous flow of communication that enters their worlds daily; keeping everything in order and easily accessible is not an easy task' (p. 64). Given the proliferation of technology, developing online virtual policy manuals seems logical, given their ease of access and ability to be maintained and updated in an almost real-time manner.

> The policy manual...should be a living document that serves as the chief guide for...management and, therefore, is a signpost for administrators, board members, teachers, and other staff who are responsible for carrying out their duties. Unfortunately, in today's legalistic world, policy manuals have become far thicker and wordier than they should be, but still they are very necessary and important enough that a district [or school] should make time and resources available to do a good job on the initial and subsequent updates.
> (First, 1992, p. 237)

A last word of advice to those from the school, district, and system levels is that in addition to being transparent, communication must be consistent and uniform. By this, what we are referring to is policymakers speaking with one voice. There is nothing more disruptive to policy than having multiple talking heads, each espousing something different. In the military, there is a protocol whereby certain individuals are given the task of providing briefings, and there always appears to be an internal and logical consistency among the speakers. Nowhere was this more readily apparent than during the first Gulf War, where all the military commanders spoke from the same script. Now, the recommendation here is not to adopt a military-style approach, but simple adherence to a common message. Remember that communication is a powerful medium, and when used effectively, can yield positive results. But at the same time, miscommunication can prove disastrous.

Conclusion

This chapter has focused on aligning policy at the school, district, and system levels. While it might be hoped that policy develops in a logical, coherent and seamless fashion, this is simply not the case. In fact, it is no exaggeration to state that '…most policy is developed in a more disjointed, less rational and more political fashion' (Taylor et al., 1997, p. 25).

> The path leading from an idea to its embodiment in public policy is sometimes short and direct. More often, however, it is long and sinuous, marked by detours, roadblocks, and even dead ends. Sometimes the path is barely visible, obscured by the struggle of contending interests and ideas, by the inconsistencies or contradictions of government action (and inaction), or by the fuzziness in how an issue is defined.
> (Miljan, 2008, p. 50)

Policymakers would be well-advised to do their homework and become students of policy. By knowing the field, they can arguably do their jobs more effectively. As well, and this might arguably be the most important consideration in aligning policy, but at the end of the day, barriers need to be eradicated. Schools, districts and systems are not distinct entities, but rather, subsets of a larger whole. Cooperation needs to be the *terra firma* upon which the entire process of educational policy rests. Certainly, the use of agenda-setting protocols could help in this regard. Decision criteria is another factor that has a place in this debate, and this ties in nicely with the notion of good policy. Policy analysis and policy dissemination are additional features that should be included in any conversations around alignment. Schools, districts and systems are entities that are uniquely intertwined, and operating in a transparent manner and communicating with one voice can only be seen as advantageous. In the end, alignment and coherence of policy is an ideal, and even though ideals are difficult to realize, it is something to strive towards.

References

Clemmer, E. F. (1991). *The school policy handbook*. Allyn and Bacon.
Cobb R. W., & Elder, C. D. (1972). *Participation in American politics: The dynamics of agenda-building*. Allyn and Bacon.
Cobb, R. W., Ross, J. K., & Ross, M. H. (1976). Agenda building as a comparative political process. *American Political Science Review, 70*, 126–138.
Delaney, J. G. (2002). *Educational policy studies: A practical approach*. Detselig.
Delaney, J. G. (2017). *Education policy: Bridging the divide between theory and practice* (2nd ed.). Brush.
First, P. F. (1992). *Educational policy for school administrators*. Allyn and Bacon.
Gallagher, K. S. (1992). *Shaping school policy: Guide to choices, politics, and community relations*. Corwin.

Howlett, M., Ramesh, M., & Perl, A. (2009). *Studying public policy: Policy cycles and policy subsystems* (3rd ed.). Oxford University Press.

Miljan, L. (2008). *Public policy in Canada: An introduction* (5th ed.). Oxford University Press.

Pal, L. A. (1992). *Public policy analysis; An introduction* (2nd ed.). Nelson Thomson Learning.

Pal, L. A. (1997). *Beyond policy analysis: Public issue management in turbulent times.* Nelson.

Rice, J. R., & Prince, M. J. (2000). *Changing politics of Canadian social policy.* University of Toronto Press.

Rich, J. M. (1974). *New directions in educational policy.* Professional Educators.

Scheirer, M. A., & Griffith, J. (1990). Studying micro-implementation empirically: Lessons and dilemmas. In D. J. Palumbo & D. J. Calista (Eds.), *Implementation and the policy process: Opening up the black box* (pp. 163–179). Greenwood.

Taylor, S., Rizvi, E., Lingard, B., & Henry, M. (1997). *Educational policy and the politics of change.* Macmillan.

Chapter 4

Contemporary Models of Policy Development

It may become very difficult to create policy without the benefit of a policy model. However, because there are many different forms of policy models in abundant supply, it may also be very difficult to choose one particular model over another. Suitability is the key here, and, depending upon the purpose or need for a particular type of policy, it behoves policy architects to choose wisely.

This chapter describes a variety of contemporary policy models. At one end of the policy model spectrum is an 'all inclusive' model, such as the one favoured by Leslie Pal (2014) that addresses multiple external influences that impact internal policy development. At the other end of the spectrum is Yehezkel Dror's (1983) more structured approach to creating policy, which identifies three distinct phases of policy creation and implementation. Typically, however, most policy models appear to be a combination of these extremes.

It must be stated that there is no ideal model for developing policy. One must choose the 'best fit' and hope that this model will be suitable for the task at hand. It may not follow, if the eventual policy is less than successful, that the policy itself is flawed, although that may often be the case. It may be that the policy model that has been chosen for the task is not up to the rigours required of it. The easy solution, however, may be to examine the policy initiative through the lens of a different policy model. Nonetheless, it may also be that a thorough re-envisionment of the need for the policy or its intended purpose may become necessary, rather than merely inscribing a new policy reformulation.

Creating the Policy

For an eventual policy to meet with any degree of success, there needs to be some form of policy model in place for the policy makers to follow. Most policy models tend to have three distinctive phases – pre-policy, policy and post-policy phases. These may take on different names, depending on the model and the policy-makers, but all models tend to have some form of these three phases.

Pre-Policy Phase

The pre-policy phase occurs prior to the initiation of the other two phases. However, it is common for this phase to be revisited many times during the policy process. This phase may run concurrently with other phases; it may become recursive and may need to be considered anew as new revelations occur during the process. In some cases, the policy process-in-the-making may be scrapped in favour of returning to the pre-policy phase in order to proceed with greater clarity.

The pre-policy phase must take into consideration many factors, including the reason for the policy. Every policy must have a motivation; otherwise, there is little need for the policy. Another consideration relates to timeframe. Any policy requires some investment in terms of time. Policies do not spring into being without some commitment on the part of policymakers. One of the greatest commitments is the recognition that there may be 'interminable' policy meetings. Depending on the perception of the policy need, the managerial organization and characteristics, and the possible need to 'plead one's case' for a policy initiative, time considerations may vary enormously.

In addition to the 'soft concerns', of time constraints and investment, the pre-policy phase must also consider the power structures operating within the organization. The simple question is, 'Who gets to play?' Participants in the policy process may vary enormously, depending on the structure of the organization. Key questions involve whether management alone will craft the policy, whether it will be middle management or lower, or whether it will be a combination of all of the above. Japanese management (Crocker et al., 1986), popular during the 1960s and 1970s, included policy making at all levels of the organization, allowing even the most lowly of employees to engage in the policy process, thus creating greater and renewed company loyalty, among other things.

Other elements of the pre-policy phase include resources above and beyond those of time and participation. A budget, itemizing resources available and resources needed in order to facilitate the process are frequent necessities. There may be other concrete issues such as meeting places, as well as schedules and replacements or substitutes for those who will be participating in the policy process. Meetings to schedule meetings are commonplace, as well. As a final consideration, even the position that participants will hold during the policy-making process will be important to define, ahead of the actual policymaking process. Such internal considerations are invaluable in promoting the health of the policymaking body.

The Policy Phase

Once the requirements of the pre-policy phase have met with satisfaction, it is time to concentrate on the actual policymaking process. As noted before, this process may not be a linear process and may involve revisiting the pre-policy phase or jumping ahead to the final phase in order to maintain or gain a perspective that will lead to the eventual crafting of a successful policy. There are multiple approaches to this phase. However, they may be roughly divided into two camps, the 'unstructured' approach, which takes into consideration myriad elements that may impact and influence the process, and the more 'structured' approach, that tends to view less crucial considerations as being 'optional'.

However the task is approached, there are a number of necessary steps required to produce a policy that may be successful. The first step may be the 'information gathering' step. Participants explore the perceived need for policy. What do they know about the issue(s) surrounding the policy call? About the organization and the employees? Familiarizing oneself with the background of the yet-to-be-framed policy is an essential step in developing a successful policy. Historical considerations, political nuances and understanding the nature of the workforce and those impacted by the policy are all important concerns. As well, not only does implementation of policies change over time, the culture within which the policy is made may transform itself over time. This means that the policy created today may not be as effective tomorrow, depending on how it will be interpreted and implemented, and depending on how the culture of the organization and, perhaps, the society in general, shifts over the years.

Once the 'homework' is deemed complete (and there may be many 'trips to the well' throughout this process), identifying similar policies that are in place in the organization or in similar organizations will serve to educate policy maker participants. Of interest, here, is to recognize the organization's tolerance for risk. This may mean that radical policies may present a threat to the organization in some way, shape or form. Conversely, too 'meek' a policy may not be sufficient in fostering the change that the organization requires.

Along the road to policy, there will be a constant need to update information and to share intelligence, material or wisdom. These activities may constitute 'external activities', as there may be a requirement to disseminate information to the rest of the organization on a more or less regular basis. In addition to this, information, experiential knowledge and other key data may find its way from outside the formal policy process into the purview of the participants in the formal policymaking process. Professional development activities may rate highly throughout this phase of the process.

Thus, the entire policymaking process may not represent a black box, but may essentially be a very porous process, where prevailing issues, existing policies and current practices can and, perhaps, should be discussed with those who will be affected by the eventual policy. Such analysis and discussion are always an iterative practice, as new information or data may impact the current status and state of the policy under development. As ever, the mission for the policy and the analysis of findings is both interminable and finite.

Like any work of art, the artist (in this case, read 'policymaker') must choose a point at which the work of art (the policy) is deemed to be finished. This may occur with saturation, where no new information or knowledge is uncovered. Other steps may include brainstorming possible alternatives, testing potential policy alternatives, trial policy implementation in a limited arena, and adopting the 'best fit'. At this point, it is time to adopt and write the policy; or, if already crafted, the nascent policy may require a level of fine-tuning.

Post-Policy Phase

The post-policy phase is distinct from the policy phase, if only for the simple reason that the policy, by now, will have become a concrete artefact. What remains is the implementation of the policy. Interestingly enough, the policy, as written, is almost never implemented by those who have crafted the policy. Consequently, policy is almost exclusively written for implementation by other members within or outside of the organization. In a perfect world, imagine if those who declare war had to fight the war themselves. Perhaps a small change – one that would have the policymakers write policy that they would then have to implement – would be an unequivocal call for peace throughout every nation on earth. However, we are not there, yet. The policy, as written, is now ready to be put into practice.

In educational circles, policy may be crafted by educators at any level. Increasingly, however, policy is being made, not at local levels, but at international levels, by 'standardizing' organizations, such as the OECD, which seek to commodify education by determining what passes as knowledge and at what grade level. To editorialize for a moment, it seems to this author that any policy that is not for the benefit of the student may not be a good policy. After all, is it not the student for whom we ultimately work? While there may be arguments that seem to support policies of standardization as being a boon to the society by creating and maintaining a vibrant economy, these policies may appear to be flawed if they were primarily expected to benefit students rather than the society at large. Policies that may benefit students somewhat but which benefit corporations more, in terms of developing an obedient, consumer-driven workforce, may not truly be in the best interests of the student.

In light of such examples, and there are many such examples in the halls of education, policy evaluation is necessary. While it is not specifically a part of the policy process, such elements get tucked into the post-policy phase. In some cases, the policy may do exactly what it is intended to do. In other cases, the policy may create obstacles that make it difficult to support. However, any policy has a 'disappearance' clause. As policies become enacted, no matter how the policy is implemented, it may at first be 'novel'. Then, through common practice, the policy becomes routinized and, eventually, becomes a part of the organizational culture. At this point, the policy tends to 'disappear' and becomes 'just the way we do things around here'. From the implementation to the routinization and 'disappearance' of the policy into the substrate of the culture may take as long as seven years.

Old policies never really die. They simply become ignored if they have not served their purpose. The reason for this appears to be that the policy tends never to be reversed or terminated, as that would require untold numbers of meetings and this would typically be a cost item. Any policy, however, would benefit from evaluation and revision. This constitutes a review element that is not always present in policy models. Good models tend to offer an initial review phase, instituted at some point after the inception of the policy, in order to assess its effectiveness. This may be followed by a periodic review that will assess the continued efficacy of the original policy. Minor tweaks may become necessary over the effective life span of the policy. These may take the form of amendments or minor changes to the original policy. Such changes may or may not require the input of the original policy makers.

Standard and Optional Policy Elements

All policies feature 'standard' elements that are intended to address specific issues. However, different policy models may exhibit different standard elements simply because tradition and practice tend to determine the purpose for the policy. As a result, although the purpose for the policy may be consistent across a variety of models, the practice of that policy may differ, depending on the model used to author the policy. Standard elements are found in all policies regardless of the field or subject matter of the policy initiative.

For example, a typical standard element of a policy may be a general principle statement. This statement may include a vision and/or mission statement as well as a brief synopsis of the organization's core activities. Philosophy statements and values identification may find their way into this section of the eventual policy, along with a list of definitions that may serve to clarify the content. Other standard elements may include administrative statements, such as the reason for or purpose behind developing this policy. Also important in the development of a policy document is the identification of those who will be affected by the eventual policy. Additionally, a policy administrator may be appointed. This individual may, among other responsibilities, be tasked with oversight duties.

Within the policy or post-policy phase, any exceptions to the eventual policy will be spelled out. For example, in certain areas of educational policy, copyright is an important issue. Any exceptions or usage concerns will be addressed within the policy document.

The post-policy phase, identified above, may also include a policy review function. This is always beneficial, as older, successful policies may be reviewed with an eye to modernization, while those policies that have met with little success may be excoriated from the policy manual. Thus, the policy 'certification' or even its approval ratings and history may become more transparent. Additionally, the policy initiative may include a mechanism for resolving potential disputes. Within the policy manual, the new policy may be grouped with related policies or policies upon the same or similar topics.

In addition to standard elements that grace the policy initiative, there are also a multitude of 'optional' elements to be considered. These optional elements tend to be of a more topical nature and tend to embrace current views relating to the society in general and the perceived needs of that society. The applicability of these optional elements to the policy differs from policy initiative to policy initiative, depending on the subject and on the perceived needs of the institution that requires a policy mandate. Consequently, each institution tends to select those optional elements that apply to the specific association, establishment or foundation that has sponsored the policy development. Whether the optional element is a reflection of human rights or a more objective corporate consideration, each optional element must be justified by the policy makers.

Designing for Policy Success

Attempting to create a policy model that is successful in all applications is an impossible task. At best, one may be able to develop a policy initiative that is successful – meaning applicable and transparent (Howlett, 2014). It is also likely that this will be specific to the policy initiative under construction. Finding, discovering or developing a model that fits all occasions, considerations and situations is akin to the Holy Grail of policy analysis. Thus, based on a very limited notion of 'successful policy', the way forward appears to be a consideration of research tools (Howlett, 2014) that may assist in the creation of 'successful' policy.

Charles Lindblom's seminal article, 'The Science of Muddling Through' (1959), underscores the complexity and the limitations of policy development. Lindblom's main argument was the observation that, while policy development may benefit from a rational and comprehensive methodology, most policy developers are not experts in the field. As a result, claims Lindblom, many policymakers, analysts included, lack the intellectual capacity and disposition to develop successful policies. His solution was incrementalism; this is the notion that multiple successive policies, each building on the previous one, may be better suited to eventually achieving a successful policy, albeit one that would be constantly in the making.

While this may seem suspiciously like building the plane while it is flying, utilizing an incremental approach may allow the policy to 'become' more successful, rather than banking on one iteration of a policy to be either successful or to represent yet another failed policy. Essentially, this approach almost guarantees full-time employment for policymakers and this may run counter to the organization's purposes if the policymakers are more or less permanently pulled from their responsibilities within the institution.

Perhaps it was, is and always will be that policy making will be problematic. In fact, Compton et al. (2019) claim that there is a general mood of scepticism with regard to the problem-solving capacity of large organizations, such as governments. However, it must be noted that, governing bodies do, from time to time, develop and implement successful policy initiatives. Compton et al. (2019) note that policy analysis has languished as a result of an emphasis on development of general descriptive and explanatory models of policy process and implementation. Additionally, emerging trends, such as globalization and the move by governments to manage rather than to lead (Howlett, 2014), have led to a dearth of 'tangible, practical and actionable strategies' relating to policy formulation and development (Compton et al., 2019, p. 120). Even so, a return to design-oriented policy offers no panacea, either, as such conceptually elegant 'formulations are difficult to operationalize and do not allow analysts to address the well-documented conceptual and methodological challenges inherent in making goal achievement the main criterion for policy success' (Compton et al., 2019, p. 120).

What follows, below, is a categorization of policy models, ranging from less structured models to more structured models. Also, included in this battery of models is an example of a 'quasi-model' that emanates from other lines of endeavour but which is still, at its heart, a model that assists in decision-making; and decision-making lies at the heart of any policy model.

Unstructured Approaches

In his book, *Beyond Policy Analysis* (2014), Leslie Pal describes three key elements of policy content: (1) goals, (2) problem definition and (3) instruments. How these elements interconnect is illustrated in Fig. 4.1. Of interest to the reader

Problem Definition
- Recognition
- Definition
- Appearance of problems in clusters
Causality

Elements of Policy Content

Goals
- Intermediate vs. Ultimate
- Specific vs. general or vague
- Policy goal vs. real goal

Instruments
- Theoretically a wide menu
- Distinct from implementation
- Constrained by legitimatcy, legality, and practicality

\+ Actors   \+ Related policy frameworks

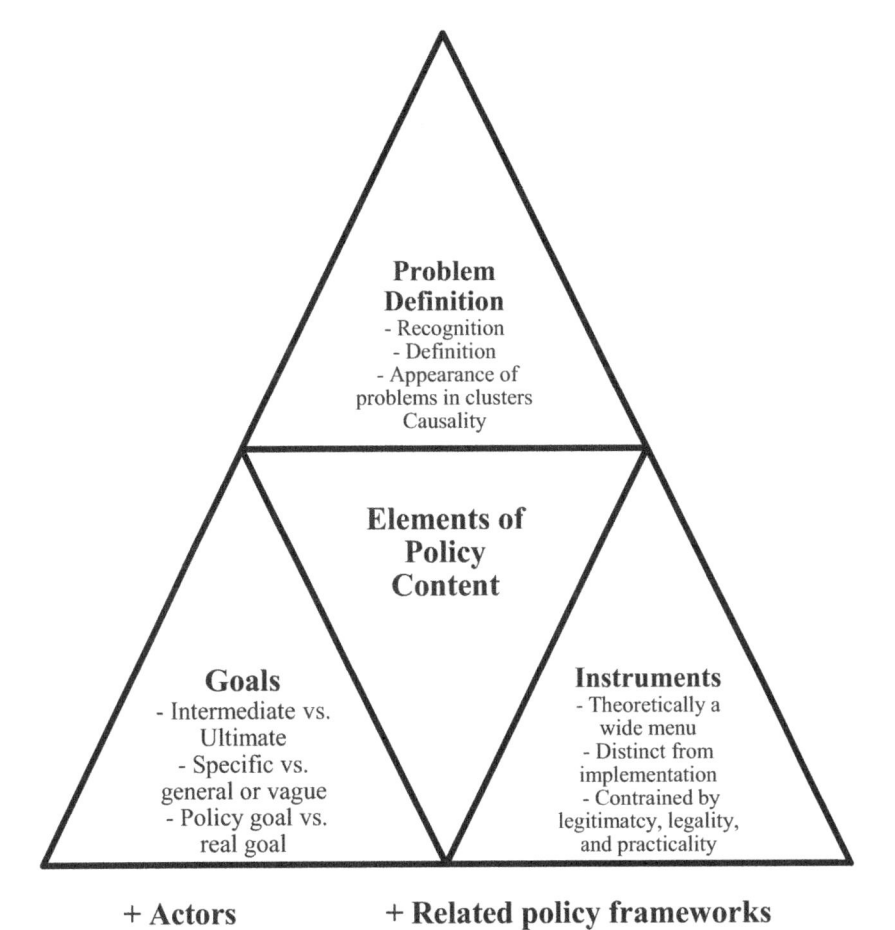

Fig. 4.1. Elements of Policy Analysis.
Adapted from: Pal, L. (2014). *Beyond policy analysis: Public issue management in turbulent times* (5th ed.). Nelson Education.

may be the fact that these three elements are influenced by a plethora of actors and related policy frameworks.

These three elements – goals, problem definition and instruments – circulate within a loop. Accordingly, Pal notes that, 'Although problem definition is central to an understanding of policy in a logical sense, in reality, the three elements are inextricably entwined' (Pal, 2014, p. 11). As a result, the goal of policymaking is oriented towards specific issues that policy architects believe require resolution. As previously noted, a particular set of policy tools with which these architects are familiar encourages them to seek out problems and goals consistent with what is achievable with the tools. This might appear to be a case of the tail wagging the dog; however, it is a realistic endeavour because not every policy model will yield the same or even similar results. As Pal (2014) notes, it is almost impossible to isolate any one of these elements from the others, making this policy model iterative. As with many of the less structured policy models, Pal's policy model cycles through the loop multiple times, each time (hopefully) creating or refining understanding of each element, illuminated by the other two elements.

> The loop also suggests that there will be consistency between the different elements. A definition of a problem should 'fit' somehow with the instruments and goals. Policy consistency is an important concept to appreciate, since it underpins both what we do as policy analysts and how we perceive public policies as citizens.
> (Pal, 2014, p. 12)

The attending diamonds at the bottom of the loop represent actors and other related policy frameworks. Although these are not true elements of policy content, they operate as 'contextual factors' (p. 12) that may serve to extend, enrich and/or mediate understanding of any particular policy initiative.

Structured Approaches

In his book, *Public Policymaking: Reexamined* (1983), Yehezkel Dror, a senior consultant on policymaking and planning for the Israeli government, and who founded the Jewish People Policy Planning Institute, offered a controversial systematic approach for policy study. This volume is generally acknowledged as a modern classic for teaching and researching public policy, planning and policy analysis, and public administration. Dror (1983) combines policy analysis, behavioural science and systems analysis in examining the reality of public policymaking and offering suggestions for reform. Here, policymaking is evaluated with explicit criteria and standards, based on an optimal model approach.

Yehezkel Dror's Normative Optimum Model

Once again, the confounding issue with contemporary policymaking remains the continually widening gap between what is known about policymaking and how policy is actually made. According to Dror (1983), contemporary societies rely on outmoded policymaking machinery. Contemporary policymaking is very complex and dynamic, wherein various components offer significant but different contributions. Somewhat like striving to predict the weather accurately, contemporary policy models endeavour to identify major guidelines for action aimed at the future. This necessarily involves a series of difficult issues that have yet to be resolved.

The task, according to Dror (1983), requires explicit criteria and standards that replace implicit assumptions and one-sided views that tend to accompany policy development. Another part of the problem is that it is more convenient to regard net output as the primary criterion for ascertaining the quality of policymaking. This may be useful when output cannot be quantified in terms of units for measuring desirability and satisfaction, and when the opportunity costs or other possible but unrealized uses of input cannot be calculated. Thus, a secondary set of criteria for determining the actual quality of policymaking is required. Both of these measures – output and quality – are necessary and sufficient for evaluating policymaking (Dror, 1983).

Also, according to Dror (1983), policymaking is a cumulative process, where the quality of the decision-making and sub-policymaking done by individuals, small groups and organizations may suffer from two hyperbolic presumptions; regarding human history as an unbroken series of mistakes and inadequacies or regarding human history as a rather successful 'muddling through' (Lindblom, 1959). At this point, Dror (1983) offers a rather grim prediction that, given the date of publication of *Public Policymaking: Reexamined*, appears to have come to pass. Dror's dire warning can be summarized in three points. The first is that policymaking is not as good as it could be. The second observation, predicated upon the first, is that policymaking fails to achieve satisfactory quality for many specific issues. Thirdly, given its current state of unreadyness and dishabillement, policymaking may be unlikely to achieve survival quality for such issues in the foreseeable future.

Dror (1983) does, however, offer a sliver of hope. He suggests that a subjective impression of policymaking may be improved, without identifying new alternatives, by way of incremental changes, as per Lindblom's (1959) analysis. A second way to offer improvement is to analyse, identify and innovate alternatives that may correct the weaknesses in current models. Dror (1983) then proceeds to identify three stages of the policy making process – meta-policymaking (or the pre-policy phase, as noted above), policymaking and post-policymaking, all of which are interconnected by communication and feedback channels.

Dror's Metapolicy Phase

This phase of the policymaking process, similar to the pre-policy phase, described above, is comprised of seven steps – the first three of which are processing values, reality and problems. Societal and organizational values are important and cannot be disregarded if the eventual policy is intended to flourish. It is likewise important to be realistic as to the constraints, limitations and eventual benefits of the intended policy. This has implications for the problem or problems, which the eventual policy is intended to address. Policymakers ignore these points at their peril.

A fourth step of the process is to identify and accumulate resources that will be required for the process of making policy. The fifth step is to redesign the policymaking system so that it reflects the needs of all of the stakeholders – those who make the policy as well as those who will be affected by the policy. Allocating problems, values and resources is represented by Step Six of Dror's model. The final step in the meta-policy phase is to determine the exact strategy or strategies by which the policy will be developed.

Dror's Policy Phase

Dror (1983) outlines three contingencies for the development of successful policy. Relating to his previous notion that reality must be attended to, Dror suggests that the knowledge that can develop the policy must already be in existence. To generate new knowledge would only serve to prolong and/or derail the policymaking process. Secondly, he notes that there must be a mechanism by which the policy process can be integrated into the actual making of the policy. His third point is a lesson in governance. Here, he states that policymakers must want the changes that will be incurred by the ensuing policy enough to overcome ideologies that act contrary to the forces of change and other forms of inertia (Dror, 1983).

Dror's Post-Policy Phase

Because this phase of the policy process is dependent on implementation of the policy, if the first two stages are attended to conscientiously, the eventual policy may exhibit symptoms of success. As ever, the 'British System of Architecture' may be a useful strategy at this point. This tongue-in-cheek approach claims that, if the details have been attended to and everything has been reinforced, then, if it looks all right, it probably is.

However, Dror is not yet finished with us. He contends, in his seminal work, the quality of personnel is the most important variable determining the quality of the eventual policy. As he previously opines, without improving the qualifications and performance of policymakers, institutional improvements are doomed to be less than successful. In addition, he claims that changes in structure and process are a major way to improve policymaking processes. Such changes may include, but are not limited to, minor changes in subcomponents to a radical redesign of the entire system, which may be easily identified by comparing the actual process of policymaking with the optimal model (Dror, 1983). As a *caveat*, Dror notes that almost none of these changes can be operationalized unless the input into policymaking and its stipulated output are increased or improved. This *caveat* occurs because policymaking remains a subset of society, which constantly interacts with the local and societal culture, opinion, social and stakeholder groups, as well as economic, religious and other components of the society at large. In essence, then, policymaking is both bounded and shaped by social ecology, particularly in modern western democratic states (Dror, 1983).

Dror (1983) also notes that distinctions between different policy models and their methods are not necessarily obvious and that alternative choices abound. He likens society to being lost in the wilderness and it must choose some direction in which to travel, adjusting method and direction as the topography and available resources permit or require. By way of summary, Yehezkel Dror condemns Lindblom's incremental approach as unsatisfactory and conservative because, he claims, it creates a division between powerful and less powerful groups. However, Dror's (1983) model offers a combination of economic rationalism within an extra-rational model that combines 'muddling through' with a rational comprehensive model to create his 'normative optimum model'.

Additional Policy Models

Building upon the introduction to multi-step policy models presented in Chapter 1, we now turn our attention to the policy models developed by Anderson (2014), Lasswell (1971), Grindle and Thomas (1991), and Althaus et al. (2018). James Anderson, in his book, *Public Policymaking* (2014), identified five steps in policy development. First and foremost, according to Anderson, is the need to identify a problem. That is to say, there must be a justification for the eventual policy. Step Two is to set the agenda. These first two steps may fit neatly into the pre-policy phase, as noted above. At Step Three, one moves into the policymaking phase through the evaluation of policy in order to arrive at the best policy alternative available. This may sound like a 'black box' of policy analysis, but it is, in reality, very similar to the policy phase, discussed at the beginning of this chapter. Moving into the post-policy phase, Anderson identifies the final two steps of his policy model. Step Four relates to the revision of an extant policy – implementation is a taken-for-granted condition – and Step Five illuminates the possible need to terminate an existing policy.

This is an important consideration, as not all policies do what they set out to do and the success of an existing policy may not only be chequered, it may, through unintended consequences, do more harm than good. Not all policy models feature review or termination strategies, which may become necessary should the policy's performance become less than stellar or even problematic. It is clear that Anderson views policy development in terms of the success of the policy. That success is measured in terms of its impact.

In the 1950s, Harold Lasswell, a significant figure with respect to the development of 'policy sciences' at the University of Chicago and at Yale University, established a policymaking model still used today. This model of policymaking, Lasswell's (1971) 'stage' approach, transformed the social sciences through his notion of 'policy sciences'. This movement, offering an unprecedented approach to the development of public policy, was originally based on the work of John Dewey and other pragmatists. What was original in this approach was the view that not only was the generating of knowledge essential to the process of policymaking, the knowledge generated by this process was essential to improve the process of policymaking itself (Dunn, 2018). According to Leslie Pal, 'In Lasswell's view, the policy sciences would integrate the other social sciences in a multidisciplinary enterprise devoted to dealing with public problems and the policy processes of democracy' (Pal, 2014, p. 15).

Lasswell combined implementation with the original intent of the policy. While this remains a somewhat dated approach and will not be delved into here, this model offered a view of policy development in general, although it remains more of an idealized view rather than an actual view regarding how policy is actually created. Lasswell's (1971) model comprised six different stages, commonly relied upon to provide for adequate and accurate policy initiatives at a time when formal policymaking was in its infancy.

Agenda Setting remains the first step in this model. At this point, as with other models, a problem or challenge is recognized and identified. Solutions may be proposed by interested parties or stakeholders from inside and from outside of the organization. Agenda setting is similar to the pre-policy phase, described earlier in this chapter. There are typically four stages in the agenda-setting step – A 'policy initiation' phase identifies all issues that 'officials' believe to be worth pursuing. This is followed by an 'institutional agenda' which has been developed from the systematic agenda. These items are the ones the policymakers will focus on. A 'discretionary agenda' follows, which comes from lawmakers. This informs the institutional agenda in terms of what is possible. A final 'decision agenda' is generated that policymakers will consider actionable.

The second step is *Policy Formulation*, which involves the development of policy options. By now, the participants in the policy process, or 'officials', have narrowed the range of possible policy alternatives through disqualifying those alternatives that do not pass a feasibility test. This step is often marked by intense debate. This step is followed by the *Policy Selection* phase, where a decision is made to accept a particular policy, usually predicated on a 'best fit' philosophy that will, hopefully, best address the problem for most members of the organization. The nascent policy may or may not be tested or measured against other possibilities. Steps Two and Three, policy formulation and policy selection, would typically be found in the policy phase of the process described earlier in this chapter.

Policy Implementation is the fourth step identified by Lasswell, and is similar to the post-policy phase, described earlier, if only for the simple reason that policymakers rarely implement their own policies, particularly in educational policymaking. At this stage of the policy process, the governing body is ready to put the chosen policy into effect. In educational settings, the policy may be implemented by administrators and put into effect by teachers and other education workers. The changes should reflect the sentiments and values of the affected parties. If the policy has originated beyond the school board level, it may be that the school district will put the policy into effect. The policy initiative will then descend the various levels of implementation until it reaches those for whom it was intended.

Policy Evaluation and *Policy Termination* are the final two steps in Lasswell's policy model. At this juncture, interested parties both inside and outside of the organization assess the policy to determine whether it has achieved its intended objective. At this point, it may still be possible to tweak the policy in order to fine-tune its impact. This may also lead to further changes in light of the impact of the original policy. Should the policy turn out to be unsuccessful, it may be terminated by the policymakers who brought it into existence in the first place. However, in many cases, unsuccessful policies may exist within a 'conspiracy of silence', where they are simply ignored. Unlike successful policies, which eventually become routinized in education practice and so disappear within the matrix of the school or organizational culture in order to become 'We have always done it this way', unsuccessful policies may disappear to never be invoked (or revoked) again.

The linear model of policy described above, developed by Lasswell (1951), was modified by Meier (1991) to include four steps taken in policymaking. In the first phase of Meier's model, policymakers predict or prescribe solutions to issues that may be addressed through policy. In the second phase of this model, policymakers arrive at a policy choice. In Phase Three, the policy is implemented and, by Phase Four, an outcome is noted and experienced.

This is a simple framework which does not make use of feedback loops. Thus, there is no ability for this model to be recursive, as there are no opportunities for the process to move backward or forward. This is an example of a very structured and simple policy model that will clearly, to even the most novice reviewer, exhibit a tendency to 'develop' as it is practiced, leading the policymakers into new territory as they progress through the model. While this may be said of any policy model, it is the streamlined, linear policy models, such as this, that tend to become more complex as the process progresses.

In reality, the policymaking process is not so linear as this and other models would suggest. However, Lasswell's policy model and others that have been presented here offer a framework for a better understanding of policy formulation. As can be seen, there have been numerous policy models developed to describe the policy formulation process. Some may be quite linear and therefore idealistic, while others try to capture the complexity and messiness of the reality of policy development.

Grindle and Thomas (1991), however, suggest a more elegant framework, one that is at once more complex but which exhibits fewer phases of the policy development process. In their three-step model, Grindle and Thomas made use of an agenda phase, a decision phase and an implementation phase. In order to truly capture the dynamic nature of policy making, the model allows for decisions to be made for or against the policy-in-process at each step along the way. As such, in the first step, any issue may be added to the agenda, or not. This, in essence, changes any iteration of the process. By the time the decision step is reached, the decision can be supportive or unsupportive of the current policy choice. If and when the chosen policy is at the implementation stage, the newly minted policy will either be put into practice or it will simply be derailed (Grindle & Thomas, 1991).

Althaus et al. (2018) provide us with an eight-step model. As can be seen, policy development, by the 'numbers', is not particularly formulaic and can be developed from many differing perspectives. Althaus et al. (2018) offer a much more holistic approach to policy development and consider a wide range of actors involved in the policy process. As can be seen, there are many, many models from which to choose.

There is also absolutely no reason why an individual cannot mix and match models in order to customize an approach that is tailor-made for the policy initiative at hand. In fact, that same individual is also free to create his or her own policy model. The test, of course, will be the successful development of a policy that actually does what it is intended to do.

Additional 'Quasi-Policy' Models

As illuminated above, all policy models appear to have three major components – the pre-policy phase, the policy phase and the post-policy phase. Given this, it may be true to suggest that any policy model is also a decision-making model. However, not all decision-making models are policy models.

Of interest to educators may be a much less complex 'quasi-policy' model, found in the form of qualitative research methodologies such as Action Research (White & Cooper, 2022). What is useful about this quasi-policy model is that it is much less complex than full policy models required at advanced administrative levels. This model is suitable for decision-making at the school or classroom levels. It is not surprising that teachers and administrators make daily policies – be they rules or guidelines – about any number of things relating to the complex nature of the educational project. While a full-on policy model might be quite overwhelming in terms of both complexity and time allocations, the quasi-policy model that follows may prove useful for those policy makers who require a fast, efficient means of creating guidelines and rules that may help them to lead more effectively.

Action Research

Action research, also known as 'practitioner research', 'teacher research' or 'participatory action research', allows action researchers to occupy multiple positions, even simultaneously, as insiders and/or outsiders, depending on social or ideological constructs (Herr & Anderson, 2005). Action research's strength lies in generating solutions to practical problems and its ability to empower practitioners by having them engage with research and with its ensuing policy development or implementation activities (Meyer, 2000). Like most policy initiatives, the impetus for action research is a perceived issue between reality and a desire for change. Consequently, action researchers can be viewed as 'interested in resolving, reformulating or refining dilemmas, predicaments or puzzles in their daily lives through systematic planning, data-gathering, reflection and further informed action' (O'Brien, 2001, p. 100) in much the same way that policymakers are. Thus, like any policy model, action research represents both an exploratory procedure and a decision-generating process (Burns, 2015) and can be undertaken by individuals or institutions to improve knowledge, strategies and practices. As designers and stakeholders, action researchers, like any policymakers, propose new courses of action to help their communities improve work practices (O'Brien, 2001).

Action research originated with the work of innumerable different scholars from so many different backgrounds that 'there is no single generally accepted narrative of its origins' (Charles & Ward, 2007, p. 2), although John Dewey (1859–1952) and Kurt Lewin (1890–1947) have been credited with its inception. An early model of change, often ascribed to Lewin, is characterized as a three-stage process, involving 'unfreezing', 'changing' and '(re)freezing'.

When faced with a new policy initiative, the individual or group needs to 'unfreeze' (pre-policy) in order to overcome inertia, dismantle existing mindsets and accumulate talent and resources. 'Changing' (policy) occurs as the situation is diagnosed and new alternatives are explored and tested. The third and final stage, called 'freezing' (post-policy) (Lewin, 1947) or 'refreezing' (Owens & Valesky, 2015), occurs when the new mindset or new behaviour is evaluated and, if approved, is adopted. Fig. 4.2 illustrates Lewin's original model of action research.

Depending upon the policymakers involved in action research, there is a multiplicity of ways to describe the permutations of action research. According to Burns (2015), there are approximately 30 typical representations of action research that utilize a three or four stage spiral approach, such as planning, action, observation and reflection. These spirals are interwoven, fluid and

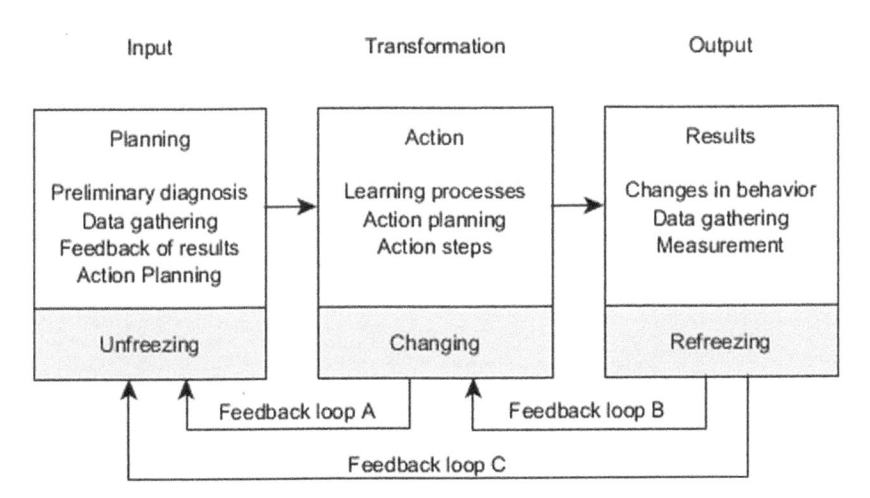

Fig. 4.2. Kurt Lewin's Action Research Model (Lewin, 1958).

repeated throughout the policy process, encouraging the policymaker(s) to prepare themselves for unexpected and unanticipated variations and reiterations in the research process. As such, action research has the capacity to move beyond reflective knowledge, created by 'experts', to active and immediate policymaking occurring in the midst of emergent structures or methods.

As Kemmis and McTaggart (2000) maintain, in reality, the process of planning, acting, reflecting and revising may not be as neat as the spiral stages suggest. The process is likely to be more fluid, open and responsive, as Charles Lindblom (1959) has noted in his incrementalist policy model. The plan, act, observe, reflect spiral is, by necessity, iterative and appealing, as it allows for the re-envisionment of policy-in-the-making at progressively higher levels of understanding. In fact, as Koshy (2010) explains, excessive reliance on a particular model, or following the stages or cycles of a model too rigidly, may adversely affect the emerging nature and flexibility of the ensuing policy. Action research lends itself to systematic inquiry that is eventually made public policy. However, it will not look like an action research project at the time, nor will it will incorporate a set number of steps, as the process is recursive and re-iterative. Fig. 4.3 summarizes the steps and processes involved in planned change through action research, depicted as a cyclical process of policy analysis and policymaking.

As major adjustments or re-evaluations in any of the stages of these models occur, the cycle tends to revert to the planning or 'pre-policy' stage. Thus, the organizational development (or individual development) project would exhibit the basic change that initiated the revision. Then, the action or 'policy stage' of any of

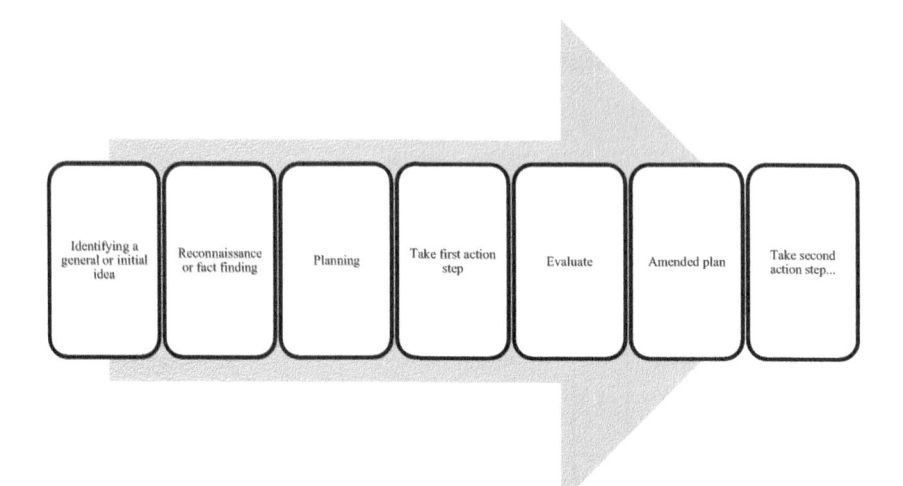

Fig. 4.3. A Systems Model of the Action Research Process.
Source: Adapted from French and Bell (1973).

these models signals a period of change, often resulting in new behaviours in the 'post-policy' stage that can result in improved understanding. Action research is not only participant- or problem-centred, it is also oriented towards action in an attempt to provide identification of problems, a diagnosis of issues and an active direction-taking which tends to recycle and transform incrementally until an appropriate solution materializes, much as with any policy model.

Conclusion

As can be observed, policymaking is not a straightforward enterprise. Although all policy models have a pre-policy, policy and post-policy phase, conditions may vary within and amongst them, depending on internal and external circumstances. However, according to Walker et al. (2013), there are several key principles that influence the long-term sustainability of policy planning. Firstly, it behooves the policy maker to explore a wide variety of relevant uncertainties, such as natural viability, external changes and pertinent past policy responses. This should be accomplished in a dynamic manner, rather than merely assuming that uncertainties exist. Secondly, it is important to connect short-term targets and long-term goals. In this way, 'big picture' thinking does not obliterate immediate and shorter-term 'small picture' thinking. And, finally, drawing from the previous point, it remains vital to deal with short-term actions while keeping options open for the future. In this way, current successful policies may be 'tweaked' as necessary in order to continue to be successful into the future.

Policy analysts and policymakers may be acutely aware that their policies may be planned on specific, concrete situations. However, there is a deep uncertainty (Walker et al., 2013) that may elude even the best of policy planners. Consequently, most policymakers continue to create policy based on what they know or on the assumption that the future, while it may be uncertain, continues to remain predictable. However, the hoped for, planned for, hypothesized future may not materialize in ways that support the policy that has, in essence, been created in a semi-vacuum. In such cases, the policy is likely to fail, simply because, as conditions change, the policy planners need to constantly adjust to new information that informs their policies and to the subsequent policies, themselves. As a consequence, such adjustments are uncommon, as it is rare that such adaptation has been planned for in advance (Walker et al., 2013).

This chapter has discussed policy models from a variety of perspectives and has hopefully identified the ongoing complexity of developing successful policies. In addition to this, there may be numerous unintended consequences related to even the most carefully crafted policy, to be discussed in a future chapter in this volume. However, in the next chapter, our attention is turned to policy contexts, frameworks, actors, and networks, as well as the different types of education policy that impact all aspects of educators' daily work.

References

Althaus, C., Bridgman, P., & Davis, G. (2018). *The Australian policy handbook*. Allen & Unwin.

Anderson, J. E. (2014). *Public policymaking* (8th ed.). Cengage Learning.

Burns, A. R. (2015). Action research. In J. D. Brown & C. Coombe (Eds.), *The Cambridge guide to research in language teaching and learning* (1st ed., pp. 99–104). Cambridge University Press.

Charles, L., & Ward, N. (2007). *Generating change through research: Action research and its implications*. Discussion Paper Series No. 10. Centre for Rural Economy Newcastle University.

Clark, I. (2017). *Atlas of policy analysis*. https://www.atlas101.ca/pm/concepts/pals-elements-of-policy-content/

Compton, M., Luetjens, J., & Hart, P. (2019). Designing for policy success. *International Review of Public Policy, 1*(2), 119–146.

Crocker, O., Charney, C., & Leung, J. S. (1986). *Quality circles*. Berkley.

Dror, Y. (1983). *Public policymaking: Reexamined*. Taylor & Francis.

Dunn, W. N. (2018). *Harold Lasswell and the study of public policy*. https://doi.org/10.1093/acrefore/9780190228637.013.600

French, W. L., & Bell, C. (1973). *Organization development: Behavioral science interventions for organization improvement*. Prentice-Hall.

Grindle, M. S., & Thomas, J. (1991). *Public choices and policy change: The political economy of reform in developing countries*. Johns Hopkins University Press.

Herr, K., & Anderson, G. L. (2005). *The action research dissertation: A guide for students and faculty*. SAGE Publications, Inc.

Howlett, M. (2014). From the 'old' to the 'new' policy design: Design thinking beyond markets and collaborative governance. *Policy Sciences, 47*(2), 187–207.

Kemmis, S., & McTaggart, R. (2000). Participatory action research. In N. K. Denzin & Y. S. Lincoln (Eds.), *Handbook of qualitative research* (pp. 567–595). SAGE.

Koshy, V. (2010). *Action research for improving educational practice: A step-by-step guide* (2nd ed.). SAGE.

Laswell, H. (1971). *A view of policy sciences*. Elsevier.

Lewin, K. (1947). Frontiers in group dynamics: Concept, method and reality in social science; Social equilibria and social change. *Human Relations, 1*, 5–41. https://doi.org/10.1177/001872674700100103

Lewin, K. (1958). *Group decision and social change*. Holt, Rinehart & Winston.

Lindblom, C. E. (1959). The science of muddling through. *Public Administration Review, 19*, 79–88.

Meier, G. M. (1991). Policy lessons and policy formulation. In G. M. Meier (Ed.), *Politics and policy making in developing countries: Perspectives on the new political economy* (pp. 3–12). ICS Press.

Meyer, J. (2000). Using qualitative methods in health related action research. *British Medical Journal, 320*(178). https://doi.org/10.1136/bmj.320.7228.178

O'Brien, R. (2001). Um exame da abordagem metodológica da pesquisa ação [An Overview of the Methodological Approach of Action Research]. In R. Richardson (Ed.), *Teoria e Prática da Pesquisa Ação [Theory and Practice of Action Research]*. Universidade Federal da Paraíba. (English version). http://www.web.ca/~robrien/papers/arfinal.html

Owens, R. G., & Valesky, T. C. (2015). *Organizational behavior in education: Leadership and school reform*. Pearson.

Pal, L. A. (2014). *Beyond policy analysis: Public issue management in turbulent times* (5th ed.). Nelson.

Walker, W. E., Haasnoot M., & Kwakkel, J. H. (2013). Adapt or perish: A review of planning approaches for adaptation under deep uncertainty. *Sustainability*, 5, 955–979. https://doi.org/10.3390/su5030955

White, R. E., & Cooper, K. (2022). *Qualitative research in the postmodern era: Interpretive and critical approaches*. Volume II. Springer.

Chapter 5

The Policy Continuum

Introduction

As we have seen in the first four chapters of this book, policy is conceptualized and defined in a multitude of ways, policy models take many different forms, and policy processes are constantly evolving. This chapter continues the examination of these and other facets of educational policymaking in a rapidly changing world. In education, as in other government sectors, the rise of complex social problems has exacerbated the technical, operational and political challenges faced by all levels of government (Wu et al., 2018). To tackle these challenges and strengthen education systems, robust policymaking is required that is grounded in a deep understanding of how policies create transformational change, how policies are interpreted and implemented in practice, and how policy implementation is helped and hindered by external variables (Cobb et al., 2013; Viennet & Pont, 2017; Wu et al., 2018). Accordingly, this chapter examines key aspects of education policy and policymaking, including policy processes, actors, networks, contexts, and frameworks. The chapter concludes with an Education Policy Continuum that illustrates different types of education policies, their distinctive features, and the various functions that they serve.

Education Policy

Education policy, like many aspects of education, is variously defined, sharply contested and fiercely debated in theory, research and practice because 'education policy is broad, and there is no clear agreement as to what it encompasses' (Pont, 2018, p. 180). One of the reasons for this lack of agreement is the complex, multifaceted nature of education policy. It is theoretically grounded, contextually bound, values-based, embedded in power and politics, and closely intertwined with the practice of teachers and educational leaders (Bell & Stevenson, 2006). Moreover, education policy is an amalgam of diverse ideologies, philosophies, agendas, activities and discourses that are permeated by the demands, expectations and political viewpoints of diverse education stakeholders (Starr, 2019).

Adding to this complexity, education policy serves a variety of functions including problem resolution, the promotion of beliefs and values, and the translation of principles into practice (Bell & Stevenson, 2006; Ward et al., 2016).

Policies also provide teachers with frames of reference and vocabulary for reflecting on, discussing and evaluating their teaching practice (Ball et al., 2011). Given its myriad functions, the comprehension and definition of education policy require a broad understanding of multiple, interconnected processes (Bell & Stevenson, 2006). Many scholars frame their definitions within the constructs of education governance, educational leadership and management, and the politics of education.

Definitions of Education Policy

Governance

Educational institutions, including schools and colleges, operate within the governance frameworks enacted by national, provincial and state legislatures (Bush, 2020; UNESCO, 2021). Governance refers to the legislation, policies, standards and leadership structures that underpin and regulate the operation of schools and education systems (Campbell & Fullan, 2019). Thus, education policy is a key part of the governance processes and structures that frame all aspects of the work of teachers and educational leaders (Bell & Stevenson, 2006; Campbell & Fullan, 2019; Viennet & Pont, 2017).

Good governance occurs when education systems operate in a unified, cohesive manner that is dedicated to student learning, supported by well-developed organizational infrastructures, and focused on clearly defined goals. Supportive legal and policy frameworks, progressive accountability standards, and active stakeholder engagement and participation support the translation of theories of good governance into practice (Hutton, 2015). As a key component of governance frameworks, education policy is a mechanism for changing practice through formal government mandates, initiatives, legislation and regulations (Pollock et al., 2017).

The most important governance decision is setting the strategic direction that an education system will follow in ensuring that students excel to the best of their abilities and are well prepared for success in school, life and the workplace (Campbell & Fullan, 2019). Thus, good governance involves translating concepts of student learning into actions, including the development and implementation of readily understandable and easily measurable policies, strategic goals and implementation indicators. As integral components of setting, pursuing and achieving strategic directions, governance and policy are closely intertwined. 'Governance is the connection between communities and professionals, between policy and application, between strategy and tactics' (Campbell & Fullan, 2019, p. 15).

Education policies are developed by political and educational leaders at the national, regional and local levels, and implemented by educators and other stakeholders (Campbell & Fullan, 2019; Hutton, 2015; Viennet & Pont, 2017). Viewed from a governance perspective, education policies encompass laws or regulations developed by policymakers, as well as the guiding principles, overarching objectives, and specific actions that are undertaken to achieve targeted objectives (Nilsen et al., 2013). Thus, education policy may be defined as the actions undertaken by governments in relation to educational practices, as well as the approaches they employ to support the production and delivery of education (Viennet & Pont, 2017).

Educational Leadership and Management

Definitions of education policy are often embedded in discussions of educational leadership and management. While the two terms are sometimes used interchangeably and are closely interwoven in practice (Bush, 2019, 2020; Leithwood, 2017; Spillane, 2017), leadership and management have distinctive meanings. Whereas educational leadership is focused on building and maintaining shared visions, collaborative cultures and positive interpersonal relationships in education, educational management is concerned with the coordination, oversight and monitoring of the daily operation of schools and education systems (Day et al., 2001). Although leadership has surpassed management in importance in recent years, efforts to shift the balance from management duties to leadership activities in leaders' daily work have proven very difficult because both processes remain essential to the operation of contemporary schools and education systems (Bush, 2019, 2020; Leithwood, 2017; Spillane, 2017).

Policies frame the leadership and management of education by shaping the structure, resources, staffing and administration of schools, and dictating how, for what purpose, and by whom education funds are spent (Young et al., 2007). Policies also underpin key aspects of educational leaders' work in areas such as student assessment and evaluation; school safety and security; staff hiring and supervision; student discipline; and the day-to-day running of schools and school systems (Viennet & Pont, 2017). Therefore, from a leadership and management perspective, education policy may be defined as guidelines that are developed and enacted by ministries of education and school boards to govern their own activities (McKay & Sutherland, 2020).

Politics

Some definitions of education policy reflect the dynamic political contexts of education. Simply put, 'education and politics are intertwined' (Pont, 2018, p. 180) because policymaking is an inherently political process (Starr, 2019). The policy decisions taken by governments carry significant weight and impact many people (Starr, 2019). In many instances, governments use policies to amass greater control over multiple facets of education. As new regulations are rolled out, teachers and educational leaders are expected to comply with constantly changing policy agendas and mandated policy reforms. In many instances, policy agendas are controlled by political parties who announce new policies to rectify 'failing' education systems, a strategy which often attracts negative media attention and paints a bleak picture of teachers and schools (Starr, 2019).

Bell and Stevenson (2006) provide an in-depth exploration of power and politics in education policy. They contend that policy is hierarchical, subject to pressure from competing advocacy groups, and governed by rapidly changing political agendas. Consequently, policy development in education is a complex process characterized by negotiation and compromise.

> Policy is political: it is about the power to determine what is done. It shapes who benefits, for what purpose, and who pays. It goes to the very heart of educational philosophy- what is education for? For whom? Who decides?
>
> (Bell & Stevenson, 2006, p. 9)

In the authors' view, education policies are political and centred on the power to reach desired objectives (Bell & Stevenson, 2006). Therefore, understanding who has political power and how it is wielded is crucial to understanding how education policy is developed and enacted to promote diverse organizational values, principles and practices. In addition, an appreciation of the impact of the contrasting priorities and views of education stakeholders on policy development in political forums is vital. This is because policy revolves around the power to determine what does and does not get done in education, which are deeply political and frequently contested issues (Bell & Stevenson, 2006). Consequently, from a political perspective, education policy is the realization of contested meanings (Bell & Stevenson, 2015). As a dual construct, education policy is a product and a process that enables the expression and operationalization of values, which are shaped by diverse contexts, policy actors and sociopolitical environments (Bell & Stevenson, 2006).

Informed by governance, leadership and political perspectives, education policy is defined in this chapter as guidelines, rules and regulations that are developed and enacted by school, district, provincial and state, and national leaders to (a) promote core values, principles and priorities in education; (b) support teaching, learning and the success of all students; and (c) advance the efficient, effective and equitable leadership and management of schools and education systems.

The translation of policies into practices in the daily work of educators is a complicated and iterative process (Ball et al., 2011; Bell & Stevenson, 2006; Berkovich, 2018; Braun et al., 2011; Viennet & Pont, 2017). Teachers, school leaders and others who put policies into practice interpret policies in different ways through the lenses of their varied experiences, contexts and backgrounds (Maguire et al., 2015). In addition, the ways in which educators read, interpret and respond to education policies are influenced by the diverse settings and education hierarchies in which they work. Therefore, accomplishing the difficult transition from 'policy on paper' to 'policy in practice' requires custom-made approaches that are tailored to the diverse contexts of education.

Policy Contexts

Within the realm of education policy, context refers to the precursors and pressures that lead to the development of a specific policy, including the social, economic and political factors that propel issues to the top of policy agendas (Bell & Stevenson, 2006; Braun et al., 2011). Contexts encompass the different levels of education at which policies are formulated and enacted, the diverse ethnic, linguistic, cultural, economic and political environments in which schools and education systems operate, and the different kinds of educational institutions in which educators work (Bell & Stevenson, 2006). Given their considerable influence, the diverse contexts of schools and education systems merit careful consideration because the policy process cannot be separated from the interconnected contexts in which it unfolds (Pont, 2018, p. 182). Within these multilayered contexts, various factors, conditions and people impact the policy process, including community groups and societal movements that exert pressure on policymakers to address specific policy issues. Therefore, it is important to understand the contexts in which policies emerge, take shape and are enacted as part of the policy process (Bell & Stevenson, 2006).

Careful consideration of policy contexts and their many interactive components and members is central to education policy because every country faces unique circumstances and contexts in education (Darling-Hammond et al., 2017). By tailoring policy implementation strategies to their distinctive national contexts, policymakers are able to address the specific challenges that they encounter in their respective environments. Educational policymaking is also shaped by the ideologies, priorities and purposes of education espoused by teachers, educational leaders, education systems and other policy actors who are key members of education contexts (Bell & Stevenson, 2006, 2015; Berkovich, 2018). Therefore, successful policymaking requires strong institutional infrastructures and resources that facilitate dialogue, deliberation, shared expertise and knowledge utilization by policy actors (Viennet & Pont, 2017; Wu et al., 2018). In addition, a rigorous policy process is required that enables the recognition of emerging policy problems and their sources, the development and selection of appropriate solutions, the creation of conducive conditions for policy implementation, and the evaluation, revision and replacement of policy solutions, as needed (Wu et al., 2018).

The Policy Process

Theoretical and practical descriptions of the policy process abound (Cobb et al., 2013), including varied definitions and representations of the policy process by various scholars (e.g. Bell & Stevenson, 2006, 2015; Berkovich, 2018; Teodorović et al., 2016; Wisman & Ingle, 2021; Wu et al., 2018). For example, Berkovich (2018) defines the policy process as the chronological sequence of events that transpires when a political system confronts a public problem, considers different solutions, and adopts, implements and evaluates their chosen solution. Wu et al. (2018) define the policy process as the performance of five vital activities that unfold in stages. Bell and Stevenson (2006) describe the policy process as a continuous and contested process in which individuals with different values and levels of power shape policy to suit their own interests. While the definitions of the policy process differ, descriptions of the stages of the policy process often overlap.

Wu et al. (2018) describe a comprehensive public policy process comprising five interconnected activities: agenda-setting, policy formulation, decision-making, policy implementation and policy evaluation. Wisman and Ingle (2021) also describe a five-stage policy process consisting of problem identification and agenda setting, formulation, adoption, implementation and evaluation. Teodorović et al. (2016) similarly describe a policy cycle comprising four phases: policy formation, policy adoption and budgeting, policy implementation, and policy evaluation. Therefore, common, core components of the policy process include agenda setting, policy formulation, decision-making, policy adoption and budgeting, policy implementation, and policy evaluation, as described below.

Agenda setting is the procedure whereby a small number of policy problems are prioritized for government attention and action from the multitude of competing issues that governments face (Berkovich, 2018; Teodorović et al., 2016; Wisman & Ingle, 2021; Wu et al., 2018). *Policy formulation* is the phase in which different alternatives and courses of action for addressing policy problems are developed, vetted and appraised. *Decision-making*, which is embedded throughout all stages of the policy process, is the process through which policymakers select specific courses of action for addressing policy problems. Decision-making is integral to the adoption phase, in which specific policy alternatives and actions are chosen from available options.

As the *adoption* and *budgeting* phases unfold, education policies are formally adopted by governments and supporting budgets are allocated to facilitate *implementation*, the process whereby policies are put into practice (Berkovich, 2018; Teodorović et al., 2016; Wisman & Ingle, 2021; Wu et al., 2018). Once policy implementation is underway, *evaluation* is conducted to determine whether policies have been implemented as intended by policymakers and achieved their stated objectives and desired outcomes. Policy *evaluation* informs ongoing adjustments to policy implementation and provides vital information for future policymaking initiatives to start the cycle all over again (Berkovich, 2018; Teodorović et al., 2016; Wisman & Ingle, 2021; Wu et al., 2018).

While the policy process is often depicted as unfolding in discreet, sequential stages, it is important to bear in mind that the process does not proceed in a straightforward, linear manner (Ball et al., 2011; Maguire et al., 2015). In reality, because policymakers deal with multiple stakeholders and interest groups, policymaking is a convoluted, complex and inherently political process (Ball, 2015; Starr, 2019). It is also a fuzzy, messy, complicated and value-laden undertaking that entails compromise, negotiation and the mediation of disputes and struggles as participants with competing priorities and conflicting values try to advance their policy agendas (Bell & Stevenson, 2006). Consequently, the policy process often veers off in scattered directions in response to shifting power dynamics and competing agendas (Bell & Stevenson, 2006; Pont, 2018; Starr, 2019).

In addition, each phase in the policy process is continuously shaped and reshaped by a plethora of interactive variables. For example, agenda-setting and policy formulation may be influenced by researchers, politicians, advocacy groups, philanthropic organizations and interest groups (Reckhow et al., 2021). As governments grapple with burgeoning information, complex issues and competing societal demands, multiple policy ideas must be narrowed to a few priorities. Throughout this selection process, the policy beliefs and preferences of funding partners, think tanks, advocacy groups and other politically influential actors impact government choices. Thus, agenda setting is significantly impacted by the growing pressure on governments to (a) winnow mushrooming policy initiatives down to a few priorities; and (b) address the competing goals and objectives of various individuals and groups who have a vested interest in the winnowing process (Reckhow et al., 2021).

During policy implementation, multiple variables are also at play (Berkovich, 2018; Coburn et al., 2016; Viennet & Pont, 2017). The full implementation of ambitious instructional policies often takes many years as districts, schools, publishers and professional developers orient themselves to new policy directions and build their capacity to support new teaching practices. Additionally, policy implementation is highly dependent upon the alignment of national, provincial, state, district and school policies and the educational infrastructures that support teachers in learning about and enacting these policies in the classroom (Coburn et al., 2016). As key policy actors, teachers play pivotal roles in policy implementation as they interpret, enact and adapt education policies to their unique school and classroom contexts (Ball et al., 2011; Braun et al., 2011; Darling-Hammond et al., 2017; Farhadi & Winton, 2022). Teachers and educational leaders require multiple supports and resources for successful policy implementation, including policy frameworks that explain and describe how the policy process unfolds in practice.

Policy Frameworks

Policy frameworks are visual representations of the policy process that reflect different theories and models of educational leadership, policy and change. Policy frameworks provide important reference points for policymakers and educators as they introduce, monitor, revise and replace education policies over time (Gouëdard, 2021; Viennet & Pont, 2017). The policy frameworks developed by Cobb et al. (2013) and Bell and Stevenson (2006, 2015) illustrate divergent approaches to the policy process.

The High Leverage Policy (HLP) Framework developed by Cobb et al. (2013) is grounded in the belief that interconnected policy factors impact the degree to which policies produce systemic improvements at the district, school and classroom levels, and whether these improvements produce positive student outcomes. In the authors' view, high leverage policies

(1) expand learning and increase student achievement or attainment for all students;
(2) increase equity in learning, achievement, or attainment among students; and
(3) initiate multiplicative effects in the educational system.
(Cobb et al., 2013, p. 271)

High leverage policies do not simply advance the learning and achievement of some students, but improve the learning, achievement and attainment of all students, including students from historically underrepresented groups. In this way, high leverage policies increase the equity of student outcomes among diverse students (Cobb et al., 2013).

The HLP framework is comprised of three core components or success factors that spawn systems change which, in turn, produces positive student outcomes: (1) leverage points, (2) design features and (3) implementation contingencies (Cobb et al., 2013). These three dynamic and interconnected success factors are underpinned by a policy theory of action centred on the beliefs and expectations of policy actors.

Leverage points refer to the targets and entry points of education policies (Cobb et al., 2013). Policymakers utilize a variety of policy levers to advance system change, including curriculum and assessment standards aimed at enhanced classroom instruction. Design features encompass the operational characteristics of policies, including guidance on how policy initiatives are to be carried out. Key design features include the function, scope, intensity, reach and coherence of education policies, as well as the policy instruments and mechanisms that support them. Implementation contingencies are variables that impact how policies are interpreted and put into practice, such as organizational capacity, educational leadership, stakeholder involvement, and the beliefs, attitudes and motivations of policy actors (Cobb et al., 2013).

Bell and Stevenson's policy framework (2006, 2015) consists of four levels of key variables that influence policy development and enactment. This hierarchical framework emphasizes the pivotal role of government in shaping policy agendas, and reflects the main ways in which education policy is perceived and experienced. Moreover, the framework also represents ongoing tensions between dominant, global discourses and resistant local contexts, as well as the contested nature of policymaking (Bell & Stevenson, 2006, 2015).

The first two levels in the framework influence policy development, and the last two levels implement policy enactment. The first level, the socio-political environment, 'is the context in which policies begin to be framed' (Bell & Stevenson, 2015, p. 148). This top level provides a forum for ideological discussions, philosophical debates and contested discourses. As dominant discourses emerge, policy problems are presented in specific ways and overarching, guiding principles are formulated. At the second level, governance and strategic direction, the policy trends that emerge from the sociopolitical environment are clarified and policy parameters, priorities and conditions are established. As policies crystalize, they form governance structures which frame the organization and strategic direction of educational institutions.

At the third level, the targets, organizational principles and success criteria of specific policies are articulated (Bell & Stevenson, 2015). Additionally, patterns of control are established, national responsibilities are defined, and local flexibility in policy implementation is determined. As policies continue to evolve, different kinds of educational institutions are established. The fourth and final level of the framework consists of operational practices and procedures, whereby governance frameworks and strategic directions are manifested in the daily practice of educators. Multiple changes happen on the ground, as curricula are revised, assessment methods are updated, institutional policies are enacted, and monitoring mechanisms are put in place. At this stage, education policies that originate 'up there' are put into practice 'down here'.

Throughout the framework, policies are contested and reshaped as teachers and educational leaders interpret them and enact them in different ways in varied contexts (Bell & Stevenson, 2015). Thus, policy implementation is highly reliant upon the beliefs, values, priorities, capabilities and contexts of policy actors at all levels of education systems. In summary, the four sequential phases in Bell and Stevenson's (2006, 2015) policy framework unfold as follows:

(1) sociopolitical environments shape the discourse within which education policy is debated;
(2) a strategic direction develops from this discourse in which education policies are defined and success criteria are created;
(3) as education policies are developed and clarified in accordance with the strategic direction, organizational principles and practices are shaped; and
(4) the operational practices shape how education policy is experienced at the school and system levels.

In this framework and other conceptualizations of the policy process, policy actors figure prominently as the individuals who convert education policies into concrete actions on the ground.

Policy Actors

Policy actors are the individuals who execute the activities that comprise the policy process, including government leaders and bureaucrats, frontline workers, and stakeholders (Teodorović et al., 2016; Wu et al., 2018). Policy actors raise and address key questions at the heart of the policy process, including 'Does this policy have to be done? Who will enact it? What does it really mean in practical terms?' (Maguire et al., 2015, p. 486). In contemporary education systems, policy actors include students, parents, educators and community representatives, to name a few.

Policy actors operate at the local, regional, national and international levels (Wu et al., 2018). For example, elected government officials and appointed government ministry bureaucrats at the national, provincial and state levels play pivotal roles in policy development, adoption and enactment in education. In addition, many different stakeholders in the public and private sectors are frequently involved, including members of community agencies, political parties and advocacy groups. Thus, policy actors include countless individuals and groups who attempt to influence policymaking in informal and formal ways (Wisman & Ingle, 2021). International policy actors also play a vital role. At this level, advisors and consultants to national governments and donor organizations, as well as members of international organizations like the World Bank, World Health Organization (WHO), and Organisation for Economic Co-operation and

Development (OECD) influence the policy process (Bøyum, 2014; Hargreaves & Shirley, 2012; Wu et al., 2018).

The number of policy actors involved in specific policy initiatives depends heavily upon the public sector in question, with education typically involving a wide range of government and nongovernment policy actors at different levels of policymaking and service delivery (Wu et al., 2018). Consequently, labour unions, parent associations, religious organizations, advocacy groups, think tanks, political parties, media outlets, university researchers and many other policy actors participate in and shape the policy process (Wu et al., 2018; Yoo, 2019). As the number of policy actors has grown, policy networks have been established in which groups of policy actors communicate and collaborate with each other in pursuit of common goals.

Policy Networks

The ever-expanding number of policy actors involved in policymaking has led to the establishment of policy networks (Ball & Exley, 2010; Wu et al., 2018). Policy networks are comprised of integrated social structures, relational processes, ideas and people that span multiple positions and sites (Ball & Exley, 2010). Policy networks take many different forms, including national and international think tanks and advocacy coalitions (Koch, 2013). Network members continually move within and between various nations, organizations, public and private sectors, locations, and professional positions (Ball & Exley, 2010). They serve on each other's' advisory councils and boards of trustees and appear at each other's forums and functions. Network members frequently straddle different sectors, fields, and boundaries as they produce and share information and innovations. Through members' constant movements and interactions, ideas are exchanged and momentum is gained within the policy networks and beyond. New ideas are promulgated through joint publications, media releases, websites, blogs, special events, advocacy positions, consultancies and joint projects (Ball & Exley, 2010). These new ideas and innovations spur the development of various types of education policies, which serve distinctive functions and enable policy implementation to varying degrees.

Types of Policies

Different types of education policies are variously described and labelled in the literature (e.g. Ball et al., 2011; Delaney, 2017; Koch, 2013; Maguire et al., 2013, 2015; Tuytens & Devos, 2009). For example, Ball et al. (2011) differentiate between imperative/disciplinary policies and exhortative/developmental policies, Koch (2013) describes progressive policies, Maguire et al. (2013) examine substantive policies, and Cobb et al. (2013) describe high leverage policies, as noted earlier. Each type of policy serves distinctive purposes, reflects varied levels and contexts of education, and addresses different facets of education, from curriculum and assessment, to student attendance and discipline, and teacher hiring and evaluation. The various types of education policy are distinguished by policy features or characteristics that often vary along a continuum. For example, Tuytens and Devos (2009) developed a Policy Characteristics Scale that gauges the clarity, complexity, practicality and need for education policies. This scale may be used by government policymakers to evaluate teacher perceptions of the usefulness, practicality and function of new education policies. By using the Scale to collect and address teacher input, policymakers can adjust new policies as necessary. Very importantly, the Scale can support the identification and provision of essential resources to teachers and educational leaders for policy implementation, including adequate time, materials and professional development. In addition, problems associated with policy design and implementation may be readily identified so that timely solutions can be found. Thus, categorizing the core features of different types of education policies, and collecting and addressing teacher input on them, can contribute to policy design, development and implementation (Tuytens & Devos, 2009).

The identification and consideration of the distinguishing policy features is important because different types of education policies may engender different responses by their very nature (Ball et al., 2011; Maguire et al., 2013, 2015). For example, rigid, non-negotiable, high-stakes polices that command attention and require compliance often assume greater prominence than more fluid, informal policies that have lower visibility (Maguire et al., 2015). To this end, school discipline policies often assume high priority and demand strict observance because governments cannot afford to look weak on student discipline. Similarly, high-stakes policies aimed at raising academic standards and increasing student achievement place significant pressure on educators for policy compliance. These non-negotiable, high-stakes policies require regimented responses from teachers and educational leaders (Maguire et al., 2015).

Some policy implementation researchers have concluded that the characteristics of policies affect their implementation (Nilsen et al., 2013). For instance, Hudson et al. (2019) found that policies that are relatively straightforward and supported by a high level of consensus may be more readily implemented than those that are complex and contentious. In addition, the type of policy, the meanings that underpin the policy and the practices and procedures associated with the policy all play important roles in teacher enactment of policies in their diverse work environments, and at different levels of the education system.

Not all policies are created equal, nor do they afford equal opportunities for teachers to exercise their professional judgement (Ball et al., 2011; Hardy & Melville, 2019; Maguire et al., 2013, 2015). Whereas disciplinary policies demand teacher compliance and confine them to the role of policy consumers and implementers, developmental policies provide teachers with opportunities to engage in professional learning, exercise their professional judgement and function as producers of knowledge. This is a significant distinction because, when teachers have the opportunity to be producers of knowledge, they may engage more proactively with policy (Ball et al., 2011; Maguire et al., 2015).

Just as researchers and policymakers classify education policies in different ways, practitioners cluster and categorize education policies as they interact with them, interpret them, and implement them in their daily practice. Over time, teachers and educational leaders may identify key features of education policies that impede or support implementation within their unique work contexts. Based on four decades of experience with education policy as a teacher, educational leader and academic, and the analysis of school, district and system policies, the Education Policy Continuum was developed to identify different types of education policy and assist policymakers and educators with the policy process. Accordingly, the Education Policy Continuum depicted in Fig. 5.1 describes prescriptive, supportive and progressive policies that are located at various points along a continuum based on their function, clarity, consistency and flexibility (Williams, 2018). While these three types of education policies differ in many respects, it is important to bear in mind that all three serve vital functions in education.

CLARITY AND CONSISTENCY

PRESCRIPTIVE POLICIES	SUPPORTIVE POLICIES	PROGRESSIVE POLICIES
• Regulatory	• Practical	• Inspirational
• Focused on the *What* and *How* of policy implementation	• Focused on the *Why*, *What* and *How* of policy implementation	• Focused on the *Why* of policy implementation
• Long, detailed policy statements	• Clear, concise policy statements	• Broad, idealistic policy statements
• Requires compulsory compliance	• Provides helpful guidance and examples	• Promotes ideals and values
• Describes roles and responsibilities in formal, legalistic language	• Describes roles and responsibilities in plain language	• Does not describe specific roles and responsibilities
• Enforces policy implementation with templates, deadlines, and legal consequences	• Supports policy implementation with glossaries, procedures, examples, guides, and checklists	• Recommends policy implementation to advance social justice
• Demands uniformity in policy interpretation and implementation	• Supports clarity, common understandings, and consistency in policy interpretation and implementation	• Promotes variability and flexibility in policy interpretation and implementation

FUNCTION AND FLEXIBILITY

Fig. 5.1. Education Policy Continuum.

Prescriptive Policies

Located at the left of the Education Policy Continuum, prescriptive policies are formal, comprehensive, regulatory policies that require uniform, consistent and constant responses from all policy actors, in all policy contexts (Williams, 2018). These policies fulfil a variety of purposes, most notably the protection of the health and safety of students and staff. Accordingly, prescriptive policies address a wide range of topics such as student travel on school trips, the administration of medication to students during the school day, reporting requirements for communicable diseases, fire safety protocols, student discipline, school bus safety and school lockdown procedures. Because prescriptive policies address complex issues with serious ramifications for students and staff, they require strict adherence to timelines and deadlines, the completion of procedural checklists and other kinds of formal documentation, and periodic practice of required procedures.

Using prescriptive policies for school fire safety as an example, school leaders conduct a mandatory number of fire drills within specific times during the school year to practice school evacuations. During the fire drills, school personnel follow checklists for ensuring that schools are fully and safely evacuated. They also calculate and record the time spent completing the school evacuation during each fire drill, take and record student attendance following each school evacuation, and await clearance from the local fire department before re-entering the school. In addition to conducting fire drills and fire safety education programs, school leaders work with local fire officials to ensure that schools comply with all fire safety rules and regulations.

Given their impact on the health and safety of students and school staff, prescriptive policies must be interpreted and implemented in a uniform, consistent, and constant manner by everyone involved. Students and staff must comply with prescriptive policies at all times and the failure to do so may result in disciplinary actions, penalties, fines and/or legal consequences. The main advantage of prescriptive policies is that they reinforce clarity and consistency in policy actors' responses, across diverse school and education system contexts to protect students and staff. The main disadvantage of prescriptive policies is that they do not afford teachers and educational leaders the flexibility to exercise their professional judgement in tailoring policy responses to their unique contexts.

Supportive Policies

Located in the middle of the Education Policy Continuum, supportive policies are practical, clear and concise policies that promote common understandings and consistent interpretation and implementation by diverse policy actors in varied policy contexts (Williams, 2018). These policies are practice-oriented and advance teaching and learning by supporting the translation of policy statements into action in schools, classrooms and education systems. Accordingly, supportive policies address a variety of topics related to the operation of schools and education systems and the delivery of educational programs and services, such as staff recruitment and hiring, facilities maintenance, budgetary processes, curriculum and programs of study, student records and special education services. Supportive policies assist policy actors with policy implementation by describing what implementation looks like in practice in schools and classrooms. These policies are often augmented by glossaries, procedural guides, templates, exemplars and electronic data systems that promote common understandings among policy actors and facilitate consistent interpretation and implementation across policy contexts.

Using student records policies as an example, school leaders, teachers and support staff are provided with step-by-step procedures to follow when handling sensitive information about student enrolment, attendance, grades, medical conditions, individualized programs and behavioural infractions. Student records policies promote clarity and consistency by defining key terms and stipulating when student information is to be collected, how it is to be recorded, where it is to be entered in paper and electronic formats, how it is to be secured on school premises and in electronic records systems, and who has access to student information. Like other supportive policies, student records policies provide policy actors with guidelines and templates to follow in completing their work, as well as rationales for the recommended procedures.

Supportive policies strike a delicate balance between supporting clarity and consistency in policy interpretation and implementation on the one hand, and accommodating educator professional judgement in how policies are enacted in individual schools and classrooms, on the other. The main advantage of supportive policies is that they assist policy actors with policy implementation by (a) using clear and concise language; (b) fostering common understandings and consistent policy interpretation and implementation with glossaries, templates and practice guides; and (c) affording educators some flexibility in how policy implementation may be adapted to diverse policy contexts once minimum policy requirements have been met. The main disadvantage of supportive policies is that their uniform terminology and procedures do not always exactly match the vocabulary and practices used in individual schools and classrooms.

Progressive Policies

Located at the right of the Education Policy Continuum, progressive policies are broad, idealistic statements that promote values, visions, principles and priorities in education (Williams, 2018). By design, progressive policies spur progress towards greater diversity, equality, equity, fairness and excellence in all aspects of education. To this end, progressive policies address topics such as equity, inclusive education and personalized learning (e.g. Maguire et al., 2013). Progressive policies support policy interpretation and implementation by reinforcing the underlying values and principles of schools and education systems, providing policy actors with goals to strive towards, and promoting the continuous evolution of schools and education systems. These policies are inspirational rather than regulatory or practical in nature. Whereas prescriptive policies focus on *what* must be done and *how* it is done, and supportive policies focus on *what* must be done, *how* it is done, and *why*, progressive policies focus on *why* education programs and services should evolve in specific directions. Because they uphold diversity in all its' forms, progressive policies are not focused on uniform, unvarying interpretation and implementation by all policy actors, in all contexts. Instead, these policies encourage variable interpretation, implementation, and adaptation by policy actors, including the development of procedures and practices that are custom-made for school and community contexts. Consequently, progressive policies are often stand-alone documents that are not augmented by detailed procedural guides, glossaries or templates.

Using policies for equity and inclusion as an example, these policies often explicitly endorse the core values of equity, diversity and fairness, acknowledge the existence of systemic racism, and describe the negative impacts of discrimination and bias, especially for historically disadvantaged groups. In addition, equity and inclusion policies often describe prohibited grounds for discrimination, such as gender, ability, language and sexual orientation. Included in these policies, as well, are guiding principles, such as honouring cultural and linguistic diversity, and ensuring the full membership and participation of all students in welcoming and inclusive school communities.

Equity and inclusion policies promote creativity and variability in policy interpretation and implementation, and the tailoring of policy responses to diverse students, schools, and communities. The main advantage of progressive policies is that they advance social justice ideals in education and accommodate variability in how these ideals are conceptualized and put into practice in diverse contexts. The main disadvantage of progressive policies is that they are often difficult to implement because they do not describe how core values and guiding principles look in practice. Unfortunately, the vagueness of these policies can undermine the implementation of the very ideals that they uphold because policy actors are unsure of the meaning of key terms, and their specific roles and responsibilities in putting these values and principles into practice in their daily work (Williams, 2018).

In summary, while all three types of policies serve vital functions, supportive policies are the most conducive to implementation by teachers and educational leaders because they feature clearly-defined terminology, supporting procedures and templates, and differentiated roles and responsibilities while still affording educators the opportunity to pursue core values and exercise their professional judgement. Thus, supportive policies support the policy process and enable teachers and educational leaders to put theory and research into practice in their daily work.

Conclusion

Education policy is a complex, multifaceted enterprise that is framed within governance structures, manifested in the policy process, enacted by policy actors and embedded in diverse contexts. Education policy encompasses integrated processes, products and procedures aimed at the advancement of core values, the management of schools and education systems, the leadership of teaching and learning, and the achievement of desired student outcomes. Education policy also ranges along a continuum, with different types of policy distinguished by defining features that both constrain and facilitate policy implementation. Amid all of these interconnected facets, the overarching purpose and biggest challenge of education policy is strengthening teaching and learning for the benefit of all students. Educational leaders, in tandem with teachers and other policy actors, play pivotal roles in advancing education policy towards this overarching goal, as discussed in Chapter 6.

References

Ball, S. J. (2015). What is policy? 21 years later: Reflections on the possibilities of policy research. *Discourse: Studies in the Cultural Politics of Education, 36*(3), 306–313. https://doi.org/10.1080/01596306.2015.1015279

Ball, S. J., & Exley, S. (2010). Making policy with 'good ideas': Policy networks and the 'intellectuals' of new labour. *Journal of Education Policy, 25*(2), 151–169. https://doi.org/10.1080/02680930903486125

Ball, S. J., Maguire, M., Braun, A., & Hoskins, K. (2011). Policy subjects and policy actors in schools: Some necessary but insufficient analyses. *Discourse: Studies in the Cultural Politics of Education, 32*(4), 611–624. https://doi.org/10.1080/01596306.2011.601564

Bell, L., & Stevenson, H. (2006). *Education policy: Process, themes and impact.* Routledge.

Bell, L., & Stevenson, H. (2015). Towards an analysis of the policies that shape public education: Setting the context for school leadership. *Management in Education, 29*(4), 146–150. https://doi.org/10.1177/0892020614555593

Berkovich, I. (2018). *Education policy, theories, and trends in the 21st century: International and Israeli perspectives.* Springer. https://doi.org/10.1007/978-3-030-63103-1

Bøyum, S. (2014). Fairness in education – A normative analysis of OECD policy documents. *Journal of Education Policy, 29*(6), 856–870. https://doi.org/10.1080/02680939.2014.899396

Braun, A., Ball, S. J., Maguire, M., & Hoskins, K. (2011). Taking context seriously: Towards explaining policy enactment in the secondary school. *Discourse: Studies in the Cultural Politics of Education, 32*(4), 585–596. https://doi.org/10.1080/01596306.2011.601555

Bush, T. (2019). Models of educational leadership. In T. Bush, L. Bell, & D. Middlewood (Eds.), *Principles of educational leadership and management* (3rd ed., pp. 4–17). SAGE Publications Ltd.

Bush, T. (2020). *Theories of educational leadership and management* (5th ed.). SAGE.

Campbell, D., & Fullan, M. (2019). *The governance core: School boards, superintendents, and schools working together.* Corwin.

Cobb, C. D., Donaldson, M. L., & Mayer, A. P. (2013). Creating high leverage policies: A new framework to support policy development. *Berkeley Review of Education, 4*(2), 265–284. https://doi.org/10.5070/B84110010

Coburn, C. E., Hill, H. C., & Spillane, J. P. (2016). Alignment and accountability in policy design and implementation: The common core state standards and implementation research. *Educational Researcher, 45*(4), 243–251. https://doi.org/10.3102/0013189X16651080

Darling-Hammond, L., Burns, D., Campbell, C., Goodwin, A. L., Hammerness, K., Low, E. L., McIntyre, A., Sato, M., & Zeichner, K. (2017). *Empowered educators: How high performing systems shape teaching quality around the world.* Jossey-Bass.

Day, C., Harris, A., & Hadfield, M. (2001). Grounding knowledge of schools in stakeholder realities: A multi-perspective study of effective school leaders. *School Leadership & Management, 21*(1), 19–42. https://doi.org/10.1080/13632430120033027

Delaney, J. G. (2017). *Education policy: Bridging the divide between theory and practice* (2nd ed.). Brush Education Inc.

Farhadi, B., & Winton, S. (2022). Ontario teachers' policy leadership during the COVID-19 pandemic. *Canadian Journal of Educational Administration and Policy, 200*, 49–62. http://doi.org/10.7202/1092707ar

Gouëdard, P. (2021). *Developing indicators to support the implementation of education policies.* OECD Education Working Papers No. 255. OECD Publishing. http://doi.org/10.1787/b9f04dd0-en

Hardy, I. J., & Melville, W. (2019). Professional learning as policy enactment: The primacy of professionalism. *Education Policy Analysis Archives, 27*(90), 1–23.

Hargreaves, A., & Shirley, D. (2012). *The global fourth way: The quest for educational excellence.* Corwin.

Hudson, B., Hunter, D., & Peckham, S. (2019). Policy failure and the policy-implementation gap: Can policy support programs help? *Policy Design and Practice, 2*(1), 1–14. https://doi.org/10.1080/25741292.2018.1540378

Hutton, D. M. (2015). Governance, management and accountability: The experience of the school system in English-speaking Caribbean countries. *Policy Futures in Education, 13*(4), 500–517. https://doi.org/10.1177/1478210315572652

Koch, P. (2013). Progressive and sustained school reforms: Framing and coalition building in Swiss cities. *Journal of Urban Affairs, 35*(1), 43–57. https://doi.org/10.1111/juaf.12000

Leithwood, K. (2017). The Ontario leadership framework: Successful school leadership practices and personal leadership resources. In K. Leithwood, J. Sun, & K. Pollock (Eds.), *How school leaders contribute to student success: The four paths framework* (pp. 31–43). Springer International. https://doi.org/10.1007/978-3-319-50980-8_3

Maguire, M., Ball, S. J., & Braun, A. (2013). Whatever happened to…? 'Personalized learning' as a case of policy dissipation. *Journal of Education Policy, 28*(23), 322–338. https://doi.org/10.1080/02680939.2012.724714

Maguire, M., Braun, A., & Ball, S. (2015). 'Where you stand depends on where you sit': The social construction of policy enactments in the (English) secondary school. *Discourse: Studies in the Cultural Politics of Education, 36*(4), 485–499. https://doi.org/10.1080/01596306.2014.977022

McKay, A. W., & Sutherland, L. (2020). *Teachers and the law: Diverse roles and new challenges* (4th ed.). Emond Montgomery Publications Limited.

Nilsen, P., Stahl, C., Roback, K., & Cairney, P. (2013). Never the twain shall meet? – A comparison of implementation science and policy implementation research. *Implementation Science, 8*(63), 1–12. https://doi.org/10.1186/1748-5908-8-63

Pollock, K., Wang, F., & Hauseman, D. C. (2017). Complexity and volume: In inquiry into factors that drive principals' work. In K. Leithwood, J. Sun, & K. Pollock (Eds.), *How school leaders contribute to student success: The four paths framework* (pp. 209–238). Springer International. https://doi.org/10.1007/978-3-319-50980-8_10

Pont, B. (2018). A comparative view of education system reform: Policy, politics, and people. In H. J. Malone, S. Rincón-Gallardo, & K. Kew (Eds.), *Future directions of educational change: Social justice, professional capital, and systems change* (pp. 171–187). Routledge.

Reckhow, S., Tompkins-Stange, M., & Galey-Horn, S. (2021). How the political economy of knowledge production shaped education policy: The case of teacher evaluation in federal policy discourse. *Educational Evaluation and Policy Analysis, 43*(3), 472–494.

Spillane, J. (2017). Leadership and learning: Conceptualizing relations between school administrative practice and instructional practice. In K. Leithwood, J. Sun, & K. Pollock (Eds.), *How school leaders contribute to student success: The four paths framework* (pp. 49–67). Springer International. https://doi.org/10.1007/978-3-319-50980-8_4

Starr, K. (2019). *Education policy, neoliberalism, and leadership practice: A critical analysis.* Routledge.

Teodorović, J., Stanović, D., Bodroža, B., Milin, V., & Đeric, I. (2016). Education policymaking in Serbia through the eyes of teachers, counsellors and principals. *Educational Assessment, Evaluation and Accountability, 28*(4), 347–375. http://doi.org/10.1007/s11092-015-9221-x

Tuytens, M., & Devos, G. (2009). Teachers' perception of the new teacher evaluation policy: A validity study of the policy characteristics scale. *Teaching and Teacher Education, 25*, 924–930. http://doi.org/10.1016/j.tate.2009.02.014

United Nations Educational, Scientific and Cultural Organization (UNESCO). (2021). *Guidelines to strengthen the right to education in national frameworks.* Author.

Viennet, R., & Pont, B. (2017). *Education policy implementation: A literature review and proposed framework.* OECD Education Working Paper No. 162. OECD Publishing. https://doi.org/10.1787/fc467a64-en

Ward, S. C., Bagley, C., Lumby, J., Hamilton, T., Woods, P., & Roberts, A. (2016). What is 'policy' and what is 'policy response'? An illustrative study of the implementation of the leadership standards for social justice in Scotland. *Educational Management Administration & Leadership, 44*(1), 43–56. http://doi.org/10.1177/1741143214558580

Williams, M. A. (2018). *Complexity and coherence: A mixed methods study of educational leadership and the development of leadership standards in Nova Scotia.* (Unpublished doctoral dissertation). St. Francis Xavier University.

Wisman, R. A., & Ingle, W. K. (2021). Actors, interests, and actions in shaping state education policy. In A. Urick, D. DeMatthews, & T. G. Ford (Eds.), *Maximizing the policy relevance of research for school improvement* (pp. 43–74). Information Age Publishing Inc.

Wu, X., Ramesh, M., Howlett, M., & Fritzen, S. A. (2018). *The public policy primer: Managing the policy process* (2nd ed.). Routledge.

Yoo, J. (2019). The impact of conflict among political actors on implementing South Korea's new teacher evaluation policy: A case study with implications for education policymaking. *Studies in Educational Evaluation, 61*, 94–104. http://doi.org/10.1016/j.stueduc.2019.03.006

Young, J., Levin, B., & Wallin, D. (2007). *Understanding Canadian schools: An introduction to educational administration* (4th ed.). Nelson.

Chapter 6

The Roles of Educational Leaders in the Policy Process

Introduction

As stewards, champions and trailblazers of education, educational leaders play pivotal roles in the evolution of schools and school systems. The work of educational leaders has garnered increased prominence in recent years as mounting evidence has shown that educational leadership matters (Grissom et al., 2021; Hitt & Tucker, 2016; Leithwood, 2017; Leithwood et al., 2020; Robinson, 2018, 2019). School, district and system leaders play vital roles in all aspects of education, including the policy process. As key policy actors, educational leaders make major contributions to policy development, implementation, monitoring and evaluation. A symbiotic relationship exists between leaders and policies in that educational leaders *shape* and are *shaped by* the policies that govern their work. This is because educational leaders are not merely passive recipients and implementers of external policy decisions, but active architects of the policy process, especially at the institutional level (Bell & Stevenson, 2006). The practice of educational leadership is embedded in legal and policy frameworks of education, enacted in classrooms, schools and education systems, and enriched by the diverse contexts in which educational leaders work (Bush, 2019; Campbell & Fullan, 2019; Leithwood, 2013, 2017; Robinson, 2019). This chapter examines the leadership of education policy, including leaders' roles and responsibilities, the barriers that they encounter and the supports that they employ to advance education policy in contemporary schools and education systems.

Educational Leadership

Multiple studies have confirmed the significant impact of educational leadership on student learning and improved student outcomes (e.g. Grissom et al., 2021; Hitt & Tucker, 2016; Leithwood, 2017; Leithwood et al., 2020; Pont, 2020). Overall, research has shown that school leaders support student learning mainly through leadership activities and the exertion of influence. In particular, school leaders enhance student learning by building school capacity, and revamping structural, sociocultural and relational processes to advance professional learning communities and strengthen the quality of teaching and learning (Gu et al., 2018). In fact, educational leadership is widely recognized as second only to classroom teaching among the school-based factors that influence student learning (Grissom et al., 2021; Leithwood, 2017; Leithwood et al., 2020; Pont, 2020).

Educational leadership, which is rooted in business models of management (Bush, 2019, 2020), was initially focused on the administration of school finances, facilities, human resources and operations. However, it has expanded beyond management duties to encompass key leadership functions, such as setting school and district priorities, creating inclusive learning environments, supporting teaching and learning, building positive relationships and partnerships, and leading educational change focused on student learning, well-being, and success (Bush, 2019, 2020; Leithwood, 2017; Robinson, 2018, 2019).

Educational leadership has been variously defined in the literature as different theories, conceptualizations and practices of educational leadership have continued to evolve over time (Spillane, 2017). However, one common thread that unites many definitions is their shared emphasis on the exertion of leader influence (Bush, 2020). For example, Green (2017) defines leadership as a process whereby leaders use their influence to give purpose to the combined efforts of the members of an organization while encouraging them to work together in an atmosphere of mutual respect and trust. In a similar vein, Bush (2019, 2020) describes educational leadership as the exertion of influence by leaders who act in harmony with their personal and professional values to lead advancement towards a vision of clearly defined goals for educational improvement. In this chapter, educational leadership is defined as the exertion of influence by educational leaders at all levels of education to efficiently manage schools and education systems, effectively lead progressive change, and equitably advance teaching, learning and the success of all students.

Educational Leaders

Many different descriptions of educational leaders are found in the literature (e.g. Brien & Williams, 2009; Bush, 2019; Fiore, 2004; Sun & Leithwood, 2012). Simply put: 'leaders are those who influence and mobilize others in the pursuit of a goal' (Hitt & Tucker, 2016, p. 533). Educational leaders translate theory, policy, research and standards into action (Galloway & Ishimaru, 2015) by exerting control, authority and/or influence over people and circumstances (Duffy & Hampton, 2003). The characteristics, dispositions and qualities of educational leaders evolve over time and are socially constructed through the interaction of leaders' life experiences with their knowledge and work (Gurr, 2017). Multiple variables impact educational leaders and their leadership, including legal regulations; governance structures; professional norms and standards; personal beliefs, values and expectations; multi-tiered policy frameworks; and school and community contexts (Bush, 2019, 2020; Campbell & Fullan, 2019; Leithwood, 2017; Robinson, 2018, 2019; Sun & Leithwood, 2012).

As Pollock et al. (2017) point out, schools do not exist in a vacuum, but are part of larger systems, including school districts and national, provincial, and state education systems. Thus, educational leaders serve at different levels of education, most commonly at the school, district and system levels (Fiore, 2004). The various titles that are assigned to educational leaders at different levels of education reflect the administrative hierarchies enshrined in collective agreements, policies and legislation (Brien & Williams, 2009; Fiore, 2004).

In this chapter, school leaders include educators who hold formal leadership positions at the school level, including principals, vice-principals and head teachers. District leaders include educators who hold formal leadership positions in school districts, including consultants, coordinators, directors, superintendents and assistant superintendents. System leaders include district leaders as well as individuals who hold formal leadership positions in provincial, state and national ministries and departments of education, including consultants, coordinators, directors, executive directors, education officers, secretaries, permanent secretaries, ministers and deputy ministers.

Educational Leaders and Policy

Educational leaders interact with education policies in numerous ways (Bell & Stevenson, 2006; Berkovich, 2018; Gu et al., 2018; Pollock et al., 2017; Starr, 2019). Rather than simply digesting and implementing education policies, educational leaders engage in disputes, negotiations and compromises as various policy actors attempt to secure their frequently conflicting policy objectives (Bell & Stevenson, 2006). As a result, educational leaders are faced with the daunting task of simultaneously making sense of the policies that come down from above, while responding to the competing aspirations and demands of policy actors from below. As various individuals and groups exert pressure to shape education policy, educational leaders are often caught in the middle between internal and external pressure for and against policy change. As pressures mount, educational leaders secure or resist policy changes amid ongoing power struggles between themselves and policy actors within and outside education systems. Thus, power and the establishment and maintenance of complex balances of power between educational leaders and other policy actors are integral to the policy process in education (Bell & Stevenson, 2006).

School Leaders

School leadership is conceptualized, labelled and enacted in various ways in accordance with the diverse languages, customs, cultures and education governance structures found in different countries (Brien & Williams, 2009; Fiore, 2004; Pont, 2020). Pont (2020, p. 155) describes school leadership as 'the persons or teams that direct, manage or lead education institutions at primary and secondary levels'. Included among the various titles assigned to school leaders are administrator, director, rector, principal, vice-principal and head teacher. While their titles vary, the organizational, pedagogical and fiscal responsibilities of school leaders often overlap from one jurisdiction to the next. Over the past three decades, the focus of school leadership has gradually shifted from administrative and bureaucratic functions to greater collaboration with teachers and stakeholders as part of school improvement initiatives. This reorientation of roles and responsibilities has been shaped by successive changes in the legal, policy and governance frameworks which frame school leaders' work (Pont, 2020).

School leaders play pivotal roles in the interpretation and implementation of national, provincial, state, district and school policies (Bell & Stevenson, 2006). In their roles as policy interpreters, translators and implementers, school leaders often encourage and empower teachers, including those just beginning their careers, to develop and exercise agency in policy implementation (Sullivan & Morrison, 2014). School leaders create favourable conditions for policy enactment by interpreting policies, translating them into action, leading and supporting teachers with implementation, and reconciling policy mandates with teachers' expectations (Vekeman et al., 2015). School leaders also support policy enactment by building internal school capacity for improvement, which is not a straightforward nor linear process (Gu et al., 2018).

Mizrahi-Shtelman (2021) argues that the role of the school leader exemplifies the mounting tensions experienced by leaders as the field of education becomes increasingly complex. Competing demands from stakeholders, community agencies, local and national governments, and international organizations all add to the growing pressures on school leaders. In addition, their precarious positions as the heads of schools who are also district and government officials place school leaders at the nexus of education systems, school districts, and schools. As a result, school leaders sit at the top of school hierarchies but are responsible for the implementation of policies that emanate from the upper echelons of education systems. They are expected to respond to local needs and build positive school cultures while enacting policies that they did not co-create or endorse. Moreover, school leaders are required to wear many hats and account for multiple facets of student well-being and academic success. Thus, school leaders juggle myriad roles and responsibilities that are framed by the norms, rules and policies that govern their work (Mizrahi-Shtelman, 2021).

Individual, social and structural factors also impact policy implementation by teachers and school leaders (Bergmark & Hansson, 2021). Individual factors include how teachers and school leaders learn about, negotiate, interpret and make sense of education policies based on their knowledge, beliefs and experiences. Social factors centre around social interactions, collegial conversations and professional learning opportunities wherein teachers and school leaders connect policies with their daily practice and exchange ideas and information. Structural factors include supports, processes and procedures for policy implementation that shape the policy responses of teachers and school leaders. Policy implementation is impacted by the kind of structural supports provided, the level of teacher and school leader involvement in policy decisions, the type of organizational changes enacted during the implementation process, and the creation of supportive policy environments by school leaders. Therefore, school leaders play decisive roles in policy implementation (Bergmark & Hansson, 2021).

School leaders advance policy implementation by understanding teachers' personal beliefs, perspectives and backgrounds, encouraging teacher participation in policy initiatives, buffering teachers from external demands, building social networks and securing essential supports for policy implementation (Bergmark & Hansson, 2021). They also adapt policies to school environments by prioritizing some parts of policies and downplaying others. Thus, school leaders function as gatekeepers, buffers, enablers and/or facilitators in collaboratively leading policy implementation in their schools. District leaders also advance policy implementation in schools by providing teachers and school leaders with various resources and supports (Bergmark & Hansson, 2021).

District Leaders

The vital role of school districts in policy implementation has garnered increased recognition in recent years (DuFour & Marzano, 2011; Leithwood, 2013; Tichnor-Wagner, 2019; Woulfin et al., 2016). District leaders play key roles in interpreting state-level education policies and shaping their implementation, and supporting improvement and reform efforts (Woulfin et al., 2016). District leaders advance policies and reforms by creating the conditions necessary for student and teacher success in the classroom. Additionally, they work with district staff to translate policies and regulations into practice in a manner that is aligned with school contexts and district priorities. Moreover, district leaders support successful reforms and policy initiatives by fostering coherence between new and existing policies, and co-occurring educational reforms. Thus, district leaders serve as key intermediaries who interpret, frame and implement education policies through various means (Leithwood, 2013; Woulfin et al., 2016).

District leaders promote policy development and implementation in various ways (Tichnor-Wagner, 2019). For instance, school districts may enact new policies that complement anticipated national or regional policy initiatives. District leaders also create conditions that are conducive to policy implementation by creating coherence, generating positive will, building capacity and re-orienting the district. Because school districts are located at the critical juncture between top-down national, provincial and state policies, and bottom-up school policies, district leaders strive to create coherence between multiple levels of education policy that are layered on top of each other (Tichnor-Wagner, 2019).

During policy implementation, district leaders make sense of policy concepts and the conflicting policy messages that they receive from many sources, including school board members, government administrators and policy actors outside the education system (Woulfin et al., 2016). In addition, they strategically frame and communicate key policy messages to school-based educators. Skilled district leaders also support successful policy implementation by acting proactively to anticipate changes, develop organizational capacity and readiness for pending changes, and assist schools and districts with the absorption of new innovations into existing structures, programs and policies (Durand et al., 2016).

District leaders employ multiple strategies to guide their districts through large-scale educational changes and reforms (Durand et al., 2016). For example, they support the development and attainment of school goals and strategies through the allocation of a wide range of human, financial and material resources (Honig & Hatch, 2004). In addition to updating schools on evidence-based practices, district leaders organize and fund professional development on those practices. Additionally, district leaders continuously seek and utilize pertinent school information to guide policy development, align resource allocations with school policy goals and support their achievement (Honig & Hatch, 2004). Very importantly, district leaders support policy implementation by developing organizational structures, facilitators, and strategies for innovation that help build school readiness and capacity for policy change (Durand et al., 2016). At the same time, they foster the progressive development of educators' competencies and commitments, and build trust within schools and between school leaders and district leaders to support policy implementation (Durand et al., 2016).

System Leaders

System leaders, who often have specific spheres of responsibility, such as curriculum, human resources, finance and/or special education, are responsible for the general oversight of the operation of an education system and the results produced (Fiore, 2004). The actions, practices and priorities of system leaders significantly impact the work of school leaders and teachers (Epstein et al., 2011; Wahlstrom et al., 2010). Successful system leaders exert this influence by (a) guiding the development and implementation of curriculum and learning standards; (b) addressing local needs and priorities; and (c) playing a significant role in instructional improvement. They also establish clear expectations for principal leadership and assist principals in meeting these expectations by providing supportive supervision and professional learning opportunities that are tailored to principals' learning needs (Epstein et al., 2011).

In addition, system leaders play substantial roles in setting the direction for their organizations and developing policies and procedures (Sharratt & Planche, 2016). While it is true that the daily work in classrooms and schools ultimately determines the success of all education stakeholders, the level of success possible is directly impacted by the organizational structures, cultures and processes cultivated by system leaders. In collaboratively leading school and system improvement, system leaders help to link everyone involved with the mission, vision and values of their educational organizations. They support school improvement by establishing processes for data collection, analysis and information sharing. In addition, system leaders work closely with school leaders to enhance teaching, learning and student outcomes (Sharratt & Planche, 2016).

System leaders, including those in senior leadership positions, often face complex challenges because they work at the interface between education systems and external socio-political environments (Bell & Stevenson, 2006). In making pivotal decisions regarding the interpretation and implementation of externally imposed policy agendas, they must consider multiple variables, including their own personal values, stakeholders' perspectives and power, and available resources. Thus, the ability to understand, anticipate and act on policy directions is integral to their work. System leaders must understand where policies originate, what their intended outcomes are, how they impact teaching and learning, and what their intended and unintended consequences may be for students, parents and educators (Bell & Stevenson, 2006). In addition, they must identify, analyse and surmount formidable barriers that undermine education policy, including policy proliferation, policy borrowing, the gap between research and policy, the fast pace of policy change and increasingly frequent and severe crises that disrupt education around the world.

Barriers to the Leadership of Education Policy

Policy Proliferation

As the twenty-first century progresses, schools and education systems are called upon to enact an ever-increasing number of policies that impact all aspects of school life (Pont, 2018; Starr, 2019). For example, one study found that the member countries of the Organization for Economic Cooperation and Development (OECD) undertake a tremendous number of education reforms, with an average of 17 education policies per country between 2008 and 2014 (Pont, 2018). Within this timeframe, some countries adopted at least 20 education policies, while others enacted as many as 40 policies. Thus, the sheer volume of policy initiatives presents significant challenges for the educators tasked with their implementation. 'Put simply, policy shifts have become unavoidable political realities of education in many systems' (Gu et al., 2018, p. 374). Multiple policy initiatives can overwhelm the educators as they attempt to juggle the enactment of new policy reforms with the many duties associated with the everyday operation of schools and classrooms (Pont, 2018). Thus, the international trend towards policy proliferation has added to the size and complexity of teachers' and educational leaders' workloads, as has the practice of policy borrowing (Harris, 2008).

Policy Borrowing

Increasingly, policy solutions from jurisdictions with strong student performance are being borrowed and copied by other education systems in the hope of achieving similar results (Broekman, 2016; Harris, 2008; Harris et al., 2016; Wei, 2017). Cross-national comparisons of student achievement on large-scale assessments have permeated policy debates and spurred the trend towards educational policy borrowing, despite mounting evidence that no one education system has all the answers to the different challenges that education systems face (Gur et al., 2011; Harris, 2008; Rochex, 2006). As a result, multiple policies and practices have been borrowed and launched in rapid succession as nations try to compete. In the process, teachers have been placed in the policy spotlight because many governments are of the view that improving the quality of teachers will increase their competitiveness (Broekman, 2016). Despite the global trend towards policy borrowing, the fact remains that education policies cannot be simply disconnected and transplanted from the sociopolitical environments in which they were developed (Bell & Stevenson, 2006).

A variety of factors have contributed to the deleterious effects of policy borrowing (Harris, 2008). The underlying assumption that education policies can be easily transplanted from one cultural context to another is fundamentally flawed. In reality, achieving a cultural fit between policies and the new cultural contexts in which they are implemented entails significant adaptation, adjustment and modification. Another associated challenge is that policy borrowing has contributed to the unintentional replication of failed policy initiatives that appeared promising at the outset in one jurisdiction but faltered over time. Additionally, unrealistic goals and short timelines for the implementation of borrowed policies lead to failure because quick fixes don't work in education (Harris, 2008).

Very importantly, policy borrowing flies in the face of research that confirms the importance and influence of contextual and cultural differences in policy implementation (Harris, 2008; Harris et al., 2016; Wei, 2017). Despite considerable research evidence to the contrary, many policymakers persist in turning to the lessons learned in high performing education systems when developing policy initiatives of their own. As a result, educational leaders are often placed in the unenviable position of attempting to implement education policies from afar that are ill-suited to their students, teachers and school communities. This tendency towards policy borrowing in contravention of research findings is indicative of another barrier to education policy, the persistent divide between research and policy in educational policymaking.

Gap Between Research and Policy

While education policy and system reforms have become global government priorities, major gaps persist between educational research and education policy (Pont, 2018). Educational policymaking has accelerated in areas ranging from vocational education and tertiary education to governance, equity and school improvement, but research findings and expectations remain frequently underutilized in the actual practice of policymaking (Pont, 2018; Urick et al., 2021). Generally speaking, local, provincial and state, and national policymakers do not sufficiently utilize educational research to inform their decisions (Urick et al., 2021).

The relegation of educational research to the periphery of policymaking has serious ramifications for policy development and implementation (Urick et al., 2021). Although research has demonstrated the efficacy of evidence-based policy reforms that are grounded in long-term visions of educational advancement for all students, tailored to diverse policy contexts, and focused on implementation, many policy reforms continue to be political, short-lived and lacking in coherence and evaluation (Pont, 2018). To break this pattern, concerted efforts are required on the part of researchers, policymakers and educational leaders to bridge the research-policy gap and address other major barriers to education policy going forward (Urick et al., 2021). Key among these barriers is the escalating pace of policy change.

Fast Pace of Policy Change

While all nations are understandably eager to improve their education systems, fast-paced reforms and heightened demands for increased school and system performance have intensified the pressure on educators and undermined successful change (Harris & Jones, 2020a). In response to mounting pressure, policymaking mechanisms have generated successive, mandated changes and policies that have placed undue stress for change on everyone involved, including teachers and students. As the production, revision and expansion of education policies continues apace, overloaded educators experience change fatigue as they struggle to enact multiple policies in rapid succession. Thus, although transformation and change are fundamental to school and system improvement, fast-paced changes and associated workloads can overwhelm teachers and school leaders. Over time, educators' well-being may suffer as they attempt to implement new policies and programs on top of the complex, daily work of educating children (Harris & Jones, 2020a).

Consistent with these findings, Starr (2019) notes that education policies often come and go in flurries of activity, especially when incoming governments change the education policies of their predecessors and embark on new policy agendas. As a result, education policy is in a state of constant flux which makes full implementation impossible. Moreover, the uncertainty, complexity and fluidity of policy change is exacerbated by short-term governments and frequently changing business models. As a result, constant change is the new norm in education and the mounting pressure for change makes the governance, leadership, and management of education more complex and demanding. In addition, the growing tendency towards multiple, simultaneous change initiatives has placed considerable strain on teachers and educational leaders. As Starr (2019, p. 162) points out, 'the major issue in education is that change of any magnitude occurs amidst many other changes-imposed and created'. Adding to this complexity, major crises at home and abroad have forced teachers and educational leaders to abandon longstanding policy processes, amid increasingly volatile conditions.

Crises

In the twenty-first century, education has been seriously and repeatedly disrupted by natural disasters, extreme weather events, armed conflicts, the COVID-19 pandemic, and other short-term and long-term crises that have negatively impacted students, parents, and educators (Farhadi & Winton, 2022; Grissom & Condon, 2021; Harris & Jones, 2020b; UNESCO, 2021). As contemporary educational leaders cope with successive crises, they face innumerable challenges in leading schools and education systems within increasingly unstable contexts (Grissom & Condon, 2021; Harris & Jones, 2020b). Amid this volatility and flux, the urgency and seriousness of educational policy decisions have intensified (Grossman et al., 2021).

In addition, the COVID-19 pandemic exposed, highlighted and exacerbated existing policy problems and inequities in many public services, including education (Capano et al., 2022; Patrick et al., 2021; UNESCO, 2021). As a global crisis, the COVID-19 pandemic also disrupted and undermined policy processes in profound ways, including the alteration of established policy paradigms and practices across nations and government sectors (Capano et al., 2022). Consequently, teachers, educational leaders and policymakers faced relentless public pressure to make hasty and momentous policy decisions amid the political turmoil, rapidly changing medical information and sharply divided public opinions surrounding the pandemic.

Some of the most contentious and impactful education policy decisions during the pandemic surrounded school closure and reopening (Farhadi & Winton, 2022; Grossman et al., 2021). As countries mandated partial and full societal lockdowns beginning in March 2020, governments and education systems handled school closures and reopenings very differently (Grissom & Condon, 2021). In Michigan, the pandemic triggered momentous and rapid policy decisions by state governments and local school districts regarding school closure and school reopening (Grossman et al., 2021). Amid the polarized political context in the United States, partisan politics and union influences impacted the pandemic policy decisions of school districts such that school opening decisions split along party lines. In Ontario, Canada, teachers had to navigate a plethora of policy changes, as schools were closed, online learning was implemented, examinations were suspended, schools reopened, school timetables were altered, and blended and asynchronous learning were introduced in rapid succession (Farhadi & Winton, 2022). Similarly, teachers in Tennessee had to quickly switch to remote learning during the Spring of 2020 when schools were closed (Patrick et al., 2021).

As educators everywhere navigate the pandemic, extreme weather events, natural disasters, and other short-term and long-term crises, the need for innovative policy solutions and flexible policy supports has never been greater (UNESCO, 2021). In addition, strong supports and skilled leadership are required to stabilize and mobilize education policies for the benefit of students, teachers and parents during challenging times.

Supports for the Leadership of Education Policy

The leadership of education policy is enabled by a wide range of leadership practices. A practice is a cluster of activities that (a) is enacted by individuals or groups; (b) reflects the specific circumstances in which they find themselves; and (c) targets shared outcomes (Leithwood, 2017). Research into the relationship between leadership practices and student outcomes has identified several evidence-based practices for supporting student success (e.g. Grissom et al., 2021; Leithwood, 2013, 2017; Leithwood et al., 2020; Robinson, 2018, 2019). In Canada, the Ontario Leadership Framework is an integrated model of successful leadership practices for school and district leaders aimed at improving the quality of teaching and learning, and creating organisational conditions that support improvements (Leithwood, 2017). The model is comprised of 21 successful leadership practices grouped into five domains:

(1) Set directions;
(2) Build relationships and develop people;
(3) Develop the organisation to support desired practices;
(4) Improve the instructional programme; and
(5) Secure accountability.

(Leithwood, 2017, p. 35)

These and other leadership practices that support teaching, learning, and student success are also integral to successful policy initiatives, including setting direction, upholding values, building trust, using a systems approach, crafting coherence, brokering, bridging and buffering.

Setting Direction

Setting direction is a collaborative endeavour in which educational leaders and stakeholders come together to identify priorities and develop strategies for achieving them (Leithwood, 2013, 2017, 2020). By collaboratively setting direction, educational leaders chart a course for their districts and schools to follow in enabling all students to reach their full potential as learners (Campbell & Fullan, 2019). Setting direction involves translating concepts of student learning into actions, including the development and implementation of readily understandable and easily measurable policies, strategic goals and implementation indicators. These actions are crucial to enhancing the quality of education for all students and improving student outcomes (Campbell & Fullan, 2019; Leithwood, 2013, 2017, 2020).

The collaborative process of setting direction is accomplished by building a shared vision to work towards, identifying specific goals, promoting high expectations for all students, and clearly communicating the vision, goals and expectations to everyone involved (Leithwood, 2013, 2017). To achieve these aspirations, it is incumbent upon educational leaders to develop policies that (a) dovetail with the vision, goals and expectations that have been set; and (b) uphold the direction of schools and education systems in a cohesive and consistent manner. Educational leaders set and pursue direction in a variety of ways, including the promotion of shared values.

Upholding Values

One of the main roles of educational leaders is establishing, modelling, and upholding their values and moral purpose when leading policy initiatives in their daily work (Robinson, 2018). Values are 'those beliefs and principles that individuals hold most dear' (Bell & Stevenson, 2006, p. 23). At its' core, educational leadership is values-laden, guided by the character of educational leaders, and shaped by the multi-layered education contexts in which they work.

> Educational leadership is a moral endeavour. It combines excellent management to ensure that the organization works effectively and efficiently with creative, proactive, and transformative efforts to ensure that it is fulfilling its critical democratic goals in an equitable and socially-just fashion. Educational leadership is grounded in a strong sense of moral purpose, clear goals, and strong personal values.
> (Shields, 2015, p. 83)

As school leaders shape the policy agendas of their schools, they are influenced by their own personal values and those of other members of the school community (Bell & Stevenson, 2006). Values also underpin school leaders' work in aligning school policies with external policies from other levels of education. Values are continually moulded, revised and revamped within the multi-layered contexts in which they exist. By serving as moral compasses, values assist students, parents and educators with navigating contested issues in education (Bell & Stevenson, 2006), and building positive relationships and trust (Robinson, 2018, 2019).

Building Trust

Although trust in education is conceptualized in different ways, many definitions centre around a belief by teachers that all members of school communities (including colleagues, students and parents) support school goals for student learning and work collaboratively to achieve them (Leithwood, 2017; Tschannen-Moran & Gareis, 2017). Cultivating a climate of trust in schools and education systems helps build positive relationships and nurturing learning environments that promote student curiosity and a love of learning (Tschannen-Moran & Gareis, 2017). Moreover, because teacher trust is vital to successful schools, the fostering of positive relationships and trust is essential in advancing policy initiatives and improvement efforts (Lawson et al., 2017). Trust paves the way for dramatic and sudden policy changes because it supports collegiality and collective effort, instead of reinforcing professional isolation.

Trust is produced and experienced by educators in schools and district offices through their interpersonal interactions and relationships (Lawson et al., 2017). It is reliant upon the mutual confidence of educational colleagues in their shared dependability, kindness, honesty, competence and professionalism. Communication is also indispensable when building and maintaining trust in schools and school districts. In particular, communication systems that facilitate intraschool and school-district communication and provide opportunities for discourse foster trust and organizational change. Therefore, trust is dependent upon and supportive of communication, which in turn nurtures and reinforces positive relationships (Lawson et al., 2017). When combined, trust, communication and relationships assist schools and school districts with the adoption and implementation of innovative policies and practices (Lawson et al., 2017; Malloy & Leithwood, 2017; Robinson, 2018, 2019).

Educational leaders play major roles in building and sustaining trust (Lawson et al., 2017; Robinson, 2011, 2018). School leaders build trust by acting with integrity, modelling values, beliefs and practices, dealing with others fairly, and involving others in decision-making (Gurr, 2017). At the district level, superintendents develop trust by demonstrating kindness, integrity, competence and openness. In their research into the impact of trust, communication and relationships on policy implementation, Lawson et al. (2017) found that strong trust and communication between district leaders and school principals, and positive relationships between district leaders and front-line professionals, especially teachers, facilitated the implementation of policy innovations. Another leadership practice that supports policy innovations and educational change is the use of a systems approach.

Using a Systems Approach

A systems approach is grounded in the belief that the diverse contexts, physical facilities, administrative structures, interpersonal relationships, internal processes and ways of working in education systems collectively impact student outcomes (Campbell & Fullan, 2019). Accordingly, systems thinking is the process of understanding how the people, structures, programmes, processes, and policies of an education system work together to achieve desired results (Bernhardt, 2017; Leithwood, 2013). By using a systems approach, educational leaders look beyond their individual roles and responsibilities to consider the many interactive factors that impact individual actions and organisational outcomes (Bernhardt, 2017, 2018; Campbell & Fullan, 2019; Forman et al., 2018; Leithwood, 2013). When employing a systems approach, educational leaders support policy implementation by addressing multiple variables, including the multi-layered contexts of schools and the interpersonal relationships between members of school communities. They also support policy implementation by aligning policies with education priorities, structures and processes, and ensuring that policies are enacted in tandem with other educational initiatives in an aligned and coherent way (Bernhardt, 2017, 2018; Campbell & Fullan, 2019; Forman et al., 2018; Leithwood, 2013).

Alignment occurs when the main structures, processes, and priorities of an education system are in sync, including goals, finances, legislation, policies, procedures, administrative structures and human resources (Campbell & Fullan, 2019). Coherence is the subjective side of alignment, whereby the members of a school system reach common understandings and shared commitments that guide their work. Coherence requires leaders and teachers to collaborate in identifying problems in practice, implementing solutions, evaluating the impact of their efforts and making adjustments to improve student outcomes. Thus, coherence is the collective capability of the members of an education system to connect and align the requisite resources for implementing change (Forman et al., 2018). Crafting coherence is one the main strategies that educational leaders employ to advance and sustain policy initiatives.

Crafting Coherence

Policy coherence is 'an ongoing process whereby schools and school district central offices work together to help schools manage external demands' (Honig & Hatch, 2004, p. 26). Even when they are complementary with each other and with school priorities, the implementation of multiple policies presents many challenges for schools (Stosich, 2018). Through negotiation, school and district leaders match external policy demands with a school's goals and strategies to advance the realization of school priorities. Thus, crafting coherence is an interpersonal endeavour in which the ongoing interactions between students, teachers, school structures and educational programs support unity of purpose in the attainment of school goals and strategies (Honig & Hatch, 2004).

Crafting coherence is a context-bound process as teachers and leaders make sense of education policies and evaluate how they dovetail with a school's unique culture, operations, aspirations and tenets of professionalism (Honig & Hatch, 2004). School leaders act as informed judges and interpreters of external demands, and district leaders interpret and support school decisions. The establishment of collective decision-making structures and the management of information are integral to the development of school goals and strategies, and their alignment with education policies. By working in tandem, school and district leaders align and integrate school goals and policies with district goals and policies to ensure a coordinated and integrated approach to policy implementation (Honig & Hatch, 2004).

District leaders craft coherence by adapting external policy mandates to fit district visions and goals, aligning policy supports and resources, and forging strong internal connections between district departments (Tichnor-Wagner, 2019). They build good will and capacity for policy implementation by demonstrating positive attitudes, securing stakeholder support, obtaining essential supports and sponsoring professional learning opportunities for school personnel. As well, district leaders support policy implementation by re-orienting their organizations towards well-defined visions, and renewing district cultures, structures and processes to realize the visions. Through visionary leadership, the provision of resources to school personnel, and the assignment of supporting roles to district staff, district leaders create enabling conditions for policy implementation (Tichnor-Wagner, 2019). In addition, both district and school leaders employ various strategies to craft coherence within and between the different levels of education systems, including brokering, bridging and buffering (Durand et al., 2016; Honig & Hatch, 2004; LeChasseur et al., 2018; Tichnor-Wagner, 2019).

Brokering
School leaders utilize brokering to ease multiple, competing pressures on school staff and defuse stressful situations (LeChasseur et al., 2018). With brokering, principals create compromises between multiple policy demands and competing policy agendas to ease the pressure that school staff feel to implement numerous policies all at once. To do this, principals identify which policy initiatives merit immediate and concentrated attention, and which initiatives may be put on the back burner. In this way, school leaders use brokering to arrive at pragmatic solutions for moving forward that lessen the burden on teachers to meet the many expectations that are placed upon them.

Bridging
School leaders use bridging to build partnerships with education stakeholders and community agencies. These partnerships enhance school access to funding sources, professional networks and stakeholder groups that support their policy goals (Honig & Hatch, 2004). In addition, school leaders utilize bridging to intervene early in policy initiatives by lobbying policymakers to influence the design of policies and programs. By acting early, school leaders shape external policy demands and their compliance with them.

District leaders also build bridges by (1) creating and maintaining trust through communication with school leaders and teachers; (2) providing clear and consistent messages that affirm teachers' and school leaders' capabilities and expertise; (3) using district resources creatively; and (4) permitting adjustments and adaptions as policy implementation unfolds (Durand et al., 2016).

Buffering
With buffering activities, school leaders do not summarily dismiss external demands but strategically curtail school engagement with them (Honig & Hatch, 2004). Examples of buffering include setting aside time for the incubation of new ideas and innovations, ignoring negative feedback that may derail school decision-making, restricting school interactions with outside entities and limiting school participation in multiple initiatives (Honig & Hatch, 2004).

District leaders also buffer educators from competing policy demands by prioritizing and protecting the instructional core of teaching and learning, and supporting flexible implementation schedules and school timetables (Durand et al., 2016). In all of their efforts to support the successful implementation of education policy and educational change, district leaders collaboratively develop and strive towards an aligned vision for their district that is clearly and consistently communicated to everyone involved through the use of a common vocabulary.

Conclusion

Educational leaders at the school, district and system levels are key policy actors who play crucial roles in all phases of the policy process. They implement a wide range of leadership practices to overcome entrenched barriers to education policy, and support teachers, students, parents and education stakeholders with the collaborative development and implementation of education policies for the benefit of everyone involved. In so doing, they advance core values and policy goals, and systematically build the capacity of schools and education systems for successful policy implementation, which is the focus of Chapter 7.

References

Bell, L., & Stevenson, H. (2006). *Education policy: Process, themes and impact.* Routledge.

Bergmark, U., & Hansson, K. (2021). How teachers and principals enact the policy of building education in Sweden on a scientific foundation and proven experience: Challenges and opportunities. *Scandinavian Journal of Educational Research, 65*(3), 448–467. https://doi.org/10.1080/00313831.2020.1713883

Berkovich, I. (2018). *Education policy, theories, and trends in the 21st century: International and Israeli perspectives.* Springer. https://doi.org/10.1007/978-3-030-63103-1

Bernhardt, V. L. (2017). *Measuring what we do in schools: How to know if what we are doing is making a difference.* ASCD.

Bernhardt, V. L. (2018). *Data analysis for continuous school improvement* (4th ed.). Routledge.

Brien, K., & Williams, R. (2009). Redefining educational leadership for the twenty-first century. In T. G. Ryan (Ed.), *Canadian educational leadership* (pp. 7–44). Detselig.

Broekman, A. (2016). The effects of accountability: A case study from Indonesia. In J. Evers & R. Kneyber (Eds.), *Flip the system: Changing education from the ground up* (pp. 48–67). Routledge.

Bush, T. (2019). Models of educational leadership. In T. Bush, L. Bell, & D. Middlewood (Eds.), *Principles of educational leadership and management* (3rd ed., pp. 4–17). SAGE Publications Ltd.

Bush, T. (2020). *Theories of educational leadership and management* (5th ed.). SAGE.

Campbell, D., & Fullan, M. (2019). *The governance core: School boards, superintendents, and schools working together.* Corwin.

Capano, G., Howlett, M., Jarvis, D. S., & Ramesh, M. (2022). Long-term policy impacts of the coronavirus: Normalization, adaptation, and acceleration in the post-COVID state. *Policy and Society, 41*(1), 1–12. https://doi.org/10.1093/polsoc/puab018

Duffy, F. M., & Hampton, E. E. (2003). Dancing on ice: Navigating rapid, complex, nonlinear change to create and sustain systemic school improvement. In F. M. Duffy (Ed.), *Courage, passion and vision: A guide to leading systemic school improvement* (pp. 57–98). Scarecrow Press.

DuFour, R., & Marzano, R. J. (2011). *Leaders of learning: How district, school and classroom leaders improve student achievement*. Solution Tree Press.
Durand, F. T., Lawson, H. A., Campbell Wilcox, K., & Schiller, K. S. (2016). The role of district office leaders in the adoption and implementation of the common core state standards in elementary schools. *Educational Administration Quarterly*, *52*(1), 45–74. http://doi.org/10.1177/0013161X15615391
Epstein, J. L., Galindo, C. L., & Sheldon, S. B. (2011). Levels of leadership: Effects of district and school leaders on the quality of school programs and family and community involvement. *Educational Administration Quarterly*, *47*(3), 462–495. https://doi.org/10.1177/0013161X10396929
Farhadi, B., & Winton, S. (2022). Ontario teachers' policy leadership during the COVID-19 pandemic. *Canadian Journal of Educational Administration and Policy*, *200*, 49–62. http://doi.org/10.7202/1092707ar
Fiore, D. J. (2004). *Introduction to educational administration: Standards, theories, and practice*. Eye on Education.
Forman, M. L., Stosich, E. L., & Bocala, C. (2018). *The internal coherence framework: Creating the conditions for continuous improvement in schools*. Harvard Education Press.
Galloway, M. K., & Ishimaru, A. M. (2015). Radical recentering: Equity in educational leadership standards. *Educational Administration Quarterly*, *5*(3), 372–408. https://doi.org/10.1177/0013161X15590658
Green, R. L. (2017). *Practicing the art of leadership: A problem-based approach to implementing the professional standards for educational leaders* (5th ed.). Pearson.
Grissom, J. A., & Condon, L. (2021). Leading schools and districts in times of crisis. *Educational Researcher*, *50*(5), 315–324. https://doi.org/10.3102/0013189X21102311
Grissom, J. A., Egalite, A. J., & Lindsay, C. A. (2021). *How principals affect students and schools: A systematic synthesis of two decades of research*. The Wallace Foundation.
Grossmann, M., Reckhow, S., Strunk, K. O., & Turner, M. (2021). All states close but red districts reopen: The politics of in-person schooling during the COVID-19 pandemic. *Educational Researcher*, *50*(9), 637–648. https://doi.org/10.3102/0013189X211048840
Gu, Q., Sammons, P., & Chen, J. (2018). How principals of successful schools enact education policy: Perceptions and accounts from senior and middle leaders. *Leadership and Policy in Schools*, *17*(3), 373–390. https://doi.org/10.1080/15700763.2018.1496344
Gur, B. S., Celik, Z., & Ozoglu, M. (2011). Policy interpretations for Turkey: A critique of the interpretation and utilization of PISA results in Turkey. *Journal of Education Policy*, *27*(1), 1–21. https://doi.org/10.1080/02680939.2011.595509
Gurr, D. (2017). A model of successful school leadership from the international successful school principalship project. In K. Leithwood, J. Sun, & K. Pollock (Eds.), *How school leaders contribute to student success: The four paths framework* (pp. 15–30). Springer. https://doi.org/10.1007/978-3-319-50980-8_2
Harris, A. (2008). Big change question: Does politics help or hinder educational change? *Journal of Educational Change*, *10*, 63–67. https://doi.org/10.1007/s10833-008-9093-7

Harris, A., & Jones, M. S. (2020a). *System recall*. Corwin.

Harris, A., & Jones, M. (2020b). COVID 19 – School leadership in disruptive times. *School Leadership & Management*, *40*(4), 243–247. http://doi.org/10.1080/13632434.2020.1811479

Harris, A., Jones, M., & Adams, D. (2016). Qualified to lead? A comparative, contextual and cultural view of educational policy borrowing. *Educational Research*, *58*(2), 166–178. https://doi.org/10.1080/00131881.2016.1165412

Hitt, D. H., & Tucker, P. D. (2016). Systematic review of key leader practices found to influence student achievement: A unified framework. *Review of Educational Research*, *86*(2), 531–569. https://doi.org/10.3102/0034654315614911

Honig, M. I., & Hatch, T. C. (2004). Crafting coherence: How schools strategically manage multiple, external demands. *Educational Researcher*, *33*(8), 16–30. https://doi.org/10.3102/0013189X033008016

Lawson, H. A., Durand, F. T., Campbell Wilcox, K., Gregory, K. M., Schiller, K. S., & Zuckerman, S. J. (2017). The role of district and school leaders' trust and communications in the simultaneous implementation of innovative policies. *Journal of School Leadership*, *27*(1), 31–67. https://doi.org/10.1177/105268461702700102

LeChasseur, K., Donaldson, M., Fernandez, E., & Femc-Bagwell, M. (2018). Brokering, buffering, and the rationalities of principal work. *Journal of Educational Administration*, *56*(3), 262–276. https://doi.org/10.1108/JEA-10-2016-0129

Leithwood, K. (2013). *Strong districts and their leadership*. A Paper Commissioned by The Council of Ontario Directors of Education and the Institute for Educational Leadership.

Leithwood, K. (2017). The Ontario leadership framework: Successful school leadership practices and personal leadership resources. In K. Leithwood, J. Sun, & K. Pollock (Eds.), *How school leaders contribute to student success: The four paths framework* (pp. 31–43). Springer. https://doi.org/10.1007/978-3-319-50980-8_3

Leithwood, K., Harris, A., & Hopkins, D. (2020). Seven strong claims about successful school leadership revisited. *School Leadership & Management*, *40*(1), 5–22. http://doi.org/10.1080/13632434.2019.1596077

Malloy, J., & Leithwood, K. (2017). Effects of distributed leadership on school academic press and student achievement. In K. Leithwood, J. Sun, & K. Pollock (Eds.), *How school leaders contribute to student success: The four paths framework* (pp. 69–91). http://doi.org/10.1007/978-3-319-50980-8_5

Mizrahi-Shtelman, R. (2021). Role identity and sensemaking as institutional mechanisms for policy translation: The case of school principals and education reforms in Israel. *Leadership and Policy in Schools*, *20*(2), 203–221. https://doi.org/10.1080/15700763.2019.1638422

Patrick, S. K., Grissom, J. A., Colby, S. W., & Newsome, U. W. (2021). Broadband access, district policy, and student opportunities for remote learning during COVID-19 school closures. *AERA Open*, *7*(1), 1–22. https://doi.org/10.1177/23328584211064298

Pollock, K., Wang, F., & Hauseman, D. C. (2017). Complexity and volume: In inquiry into factors that drive principals' work. In K. Leithwood, J. Sun, & K. Pollock (Eds.), *How school leaders contribute to student success: The four paths framework* (pp. 209–238). Springer. https://doi.org/10.1007/978-3-319-50980-8_10

Pont, B. (2018). A comparative view of education system reform: Policy, politics, and people. In H. J. Malone, S. Rincón-Gallardo, & K. Kew (Eds.), *Future directions of educational change: Social justice, professional capital, and systems change* (pp. 171–187). Routledge.

Pont, B. (2020). A literature review of school leadership policy reforms. *European Journal of Education, 55*(2), 154–168. https://doi.org/10.1111/ejed.12398

Robinson, V. (2011). *Student-centered leadership*. John Wiley & Sons, Inc.

Robinson, V. (2018). *Reduce change to increase improvement*. Corwin.

Robinson, V. (2019). Excellence in educational leadership: Practices, capabilities, and virtues that foster improved student outcomes. In T. Bush, L. Bell, & D. Middlewood (Eds.), *Principles of educational leadership and management* (3rd ed., pp. 73–91). SAGE Publications Ltd.

Rochex, J. Y. (2006). Chapter 5: Social, methodological, and theoretical issues regarding assessment: Lessons from a secondary analysis of PISA 2000 literacy tests. *Review of Research in Education, 30*(1), 163–212. https://doi.org/10.3102/0091732X030001163

Sharratt, L., & Planche, B. (2016). *Leading collaborative learning: Empowering excellence*. Corwin.

Shields, C. (2015). What is educational leadership? In D. Griffiths & J. P. Portelli (Eds.), *Key questions for educational leaders* (p. 83). Word and Deed.

Spillane, J. (2017). Leadership and learning: Conceptualizing relations between school administrative practice and instructional practice. In K. Leithwood, J. Sun, & K. Pollock (Eds.), *How school leaders contribute to student success: The four paths framework* (pp. 49–67). Springer International. https://doi.org/10.1007/978-3-319-50980-8_4

Starr, K. (2019). *Education policy, neoliberalism, and leadership practice: A critical analysis*. Routledge.

Stosich, E. L. (2018). Principals and teachers "craft coherence" among accountability policies. *Journal of Educational Administration, 56*(2), 203–219. https://doi.org/10.1108/JEA-10-2016-0124

Sullivan, A. M., & Morrison, C. (2014). Enacting policy: The capacity of school leaders to support early career teachers through policy work. *Australian Educational Researcher, 41*(5), 603–620. https://doi.org/10.1007/s13384-014-0155-y

Sun, J., & Leithwood, K. (2012). Transformational school leadership effects on student achievement. *Leadership and Policy in Schools, 11*(4), 418–451. https://doi.org/10.1080/15700763.2012.681001

Tschannen-Moran, M., & Gareis, C. R. (2017). Principals, trust, and cultivating vibrant schools. In K. Leithwood, J. Sun, & K. Pollock (Eds.), *How school leaders contribute to student success: The four paths framework* (pp. 153–174). Springer. https://doi.org/10.1007/978-3-319-50980-8_8

Tichnor-Wagner, A. (2019). District agency in implementing instructional reform: A comparative case study of global education. *Journal of Educational Change, 20*(4), 495–525. https://doi.org/10.1007/s10833-019-09346-2

United Nations Educational, Scientific and Cultural Organization (UNESCO). (2021). *Guidelines to strengthen the right to education in national frameworks*. Author.

Urick, A., DeMatthews, D., & Ford, T. G. (2021). Introduction. In A. Urick, D. DeMatthews, & T. G. Ford (Eds.), *Maximizing the policy relevance of research for school improvement* (pp. 1–12). Information Age Publishing Inc.

Vekeman, E., Devos, G., & Tuytens, M. (2015). The influence of teachers' expectations on principals' implementation of a new teacher evaluation policy in Flemish secondary education. *Educational Assessment, Evaluation and Accountability*, 27(2), 129–151. https://doi.org/10.1007/s11092-014-9203-4

Wahlstrom, K. L., Louis, K. S., Leithwood, K., & Anderson, S. E. (2010). *Investigating the links to improved student learning: Executive summary of research findings*. Learning from Leadership Project: The Wallace Foundation.

Wei, W. (2017). Educational policy borrowing: Professional leadership standards for school leaders in China. *Chinese Society and Education*, 50(3), 181–202. https://doi.org/10.1080/10611932.2017.1331012

Woulfin, S. L., Donaldson, M. L., & Gonzales, R. (2016). District leaders' framing of educator evaluation policy. *Educational Administration Quarterly*, 52(1), 110–143. https://doi.org/10.1177/0013161X15616661

Chapter 7

Policy Implementation

Introduction

Policy implementation is the critical juncture in the policy process where education theory, research, governance and innovation are translated into practice in the daily work of educators. Achieving the major transformation from policy statements to professional practices requires adequate time, resources and supports. It also requires the experience, expertise and engagement of teachers, educational leaders and education stakeholders who collectively make policy come to life in schools and classrooms (Bell & Stevenson, 2006; Darling-Hammond et al., 2017; Farhadi & Winton, 2022; Leithwood, 2017). Policy implementation is a complex process that is shaped by interconnected variables, constrained by persistent barriers, and enabled by coordinated supports. Most importantly, policy implementation is about people – the students, teachers, educational leaders and stakeholders at the centre of the process who enact policies to enhance education. This chapter examines key facets of policy implementation, including the policy implementers, contexts, barriers and supports that shape how the process unfolds.

Policy Implementation and Enactment

The process of translating policy into practice into schools, classrooms and education systems is variously referred to as policy implementation and policy enactment (Ball, 2015; Ball et al., 2011; Bell & Stevenson, 2006; Berkovich, 2018; Braun et al., 2011; Maguire et al., 2013, 2015; Wu et al., 2018). While both terms are used throughout this chapter to describe the translation of policy into practice, they are described differently in the literature.

Policy implementation occurs at the point in the policy process at which the ideas embedded in policy decisions and plans are translated into actions by policy implementers (Wu et al., 2018). In Fullan's (2016) view, implementation is the process of putting ideas, programmes, policies, and/or structures into practice that are new to the people implementing them. Through policy implementation, specific policy objectives are translated into concrete actions and changes in schools and classrooms (OECD, 2020; Wu et al., 2018). In contrast, *policy enactment* is described as a creative, sophisticated, complex and iterative process whereby diverse policy actors interpret policies and translate them into action in the dynamic contextual, historical, and psychosocial environments of schools (Ball et al., 2011; Braun et al., 2011).

During policy enactment, teachers, school leaders and other policy actors interpret and translate abstract policy ideas into practices as they read, discuss and debate the policies they are tasked with implementing (Ball et al., 2011; Braun et al., 2011; Maguire et al., 2015). Therefore, policy enactment centres around processes of interpretation and recontextualization, including various interpretations and reinterpretations as polices are read, debated and responded to in different ways by policy actors (Braun et al., 2011). While policy implementation and policy enactment are differentiated in the literature on the basis of their complexity, they both serve the same basic function: converting policies into practices on the ground. This conversion is accomplished by diverse policy implementers.

Policy Implementers

In education, policy implementers are the policy actors (including teachers, students, parents and educational leaders) who put education policies into practice every day (Berkovich, 2018; Viennet & Pont, 2017; Wu et al., 2018). Contemporary approaches to policy implementation view policy implementers holistically and take into account the complex networks, relationships, and interconnections that frame their work (Nilsen et al., 2013). As Hardy and Melville (2019, p. 4) point out, 'different actors respond differently to the particular policy conditions within which they find themselves'. As teachers and other policy implementers enact education policies, they complete a series of interconnected activities, including policy interpretation and translation (Hardy & Melville, 2019).

Policy Interpretation

Interpretation is an initial reading of policy in an effort to make sense of it (Ball et al., 2011; Maguire et al., 2013, 2015). Interpretation occurs within school communities as teachers evaluate the importance of different policies, determine the actions required of them and estimate the consequences of enacting or ignoring policies. Interpretation occurs during staff meetings, working groups and professional conversations as teachers discuss and debate the value of policies and the impact of policies on their daily work (Maguire et al., 2015).

Policy Translation

Translation is the iterative process of putting policies into action. Through this process, policies are transformed into concepts, materials, practices, procedures and orientations that are enacted in diverse schools and classrooms (Ball et al., 2011; Maguire et al., 2013, 2015). Policy translation may occur through planned events, such as department meetings, and through the everyday exchanges that take place in school hallways and classrooms. In this way, the language of policy is decoded into the language of practice, words are transformed into actions and abstract concepts are converted into practical processes and procedures. In essence, interpretation is about strategy and translation is about tactics, and the two are often closely intertwined in practice, at all levels of education (Ball et al., 2011).

Levels of Policy Implementation

Policy implementation occurs within and between successive levels of education hierarchies (Coburn, 2016; Nilsen et al., 2013). At the school, district and system levels, the space for policy interpretation, translation and enactment varies from one policy to the next, and from one person to the next, and is influenced by a variety of factors. For example, Ward and Parr (2011) argue that national education policies are implemented at three distinct levels. At the first level, strategic policies provide high level statements of policy purposes and goals. These visionary, theoretical policies describe desired ends and provide guiding principles rather than practical suggestions. At the second level, operational policies are more practical in nature and focused on the means by which policy purposes and goals may be fulfilled. These policies are developed and funded by ministries of education to advance their strategic priorities. Both strategic and operational policies are implemented at the third level of schools and classrooms. The extent to which the policies are implemented in practice depends in large part on the willingness of the educators involved. In addition, the degree of coherence and alignment within and between education policies and implementation activities impact the extent to which policies are translated into practice. Thus, multiple, interconnected factors at all levels of education shape policy implementation (Ward & Parr, 2011).

Factors That Influence Policy Implementation

Many different variables influence policy implementation (Bergmark & Hansson, 2021; Maguire et al., 2013, 2015; OECD, 2020; Viennet & Pont, 2017). Specifically, variations in the types of policies that are ratified, the levels of education at which they are produced and interpreted, and the perspectives, values, positions, experiences and contexts of policy actors all contribute to the complexity and variability of policy enactment. Policy implementation is also impacted by the kind of structural supports provided, the level of teacher and school leader involvement in policy decisions, the type of organizational changes enacted during the implementation process, and the creation of supportive policy environments by school leaders (Bergmark & Hansson, 2021). Given the increased complexity of policymaking and the multiplicity of variables in play, education policymakers must consider numerous factors when devising coherent implementation strategies (OECD, 2020). These factors include politics, policy contexts, teacher careers stages, teacher subject specialties and positions, and time and space.

Politics

The influence of politics on policy implementation is powerful and far-reaching (Bell & Stevenson, 2006; Berkovich, 2018; Greene & McShane, 2018; Harris & Jones, 2020; Starr, 2019; Wu et al., 2018). Government policymaking at the legislative level is characterised by instrumentality, hierarchy and the relegation of teachers and other school professionals to the role of implementers in the policy process (Maguire et al., 2015). As governments are formed by different political parties, each successive government produces its own slate of education policies and passes them down to schools with the assumption that schools will respond quickly to these constantly shifting policy requirements (Maguire et al., 2013; Starr, 2019). During legislative sessions, waves of new education policies, regulations and programs are enacted by governments and trickle down through government departments, ministries of education, school districts and schools to eventually reach classrooms (Greene & McShane, 2018).

Thus, education policy is fundamentally political in nature, and politics is about interests, persuasion, consequences and pressure (Greene & McShane, 2018). Political pressure, budget cuts and changes in government can prompt district and system leaders to adopt or abandon policies because, at the end of the day, the ultimate control over education policy rests with elected government officials (Greene & McShane, 2018). In addition to the impact of shifting political sands, policy contexts exert considerable influence over policy implementation (Braun et al., 2011).

Policy Contexts

The multi-layered historical, geographical, political, economic, cultural and technological contexts of education impact policy processes and outcomes at all levels of education (Braun et al., 2011; Harris et al., 2016; Starr, 2019). Nilsen et al. (2013, p. 6) define context as 'the social environment in which implementation takes place'. In their view, contexts encompass various influences on the implementation process whose impact is beyond the control of the implementers. Similarly, Braun et al. (2011, p. 585) argue that '... policies are intimately shaped and influenced by school-specific factors'. Therefore, translating policies into practice is a creative, complex and constrained process in which policies are variously contested and interpreted as they are enacted in novel and creative ways in diverse school and classroom contexts (Braun et al., 2011). Consistent with these findings, Harris and Jones (2020, p. 49) state that 'the policy context in which students, teachers, and school leaders find themselves is a critical determinant of their success or failure'. Accordingly, contexts and cultures are influential variables in improvement efforts at the classroom, school and system levels.

Schools have varying capacities for policy enactment and respond to policies differently based on the cultures, limitations and resources of their school contexts. For example, Braun et al. (2011) found that schools have variable histories, physical plants, staffing complements, leadership capacities, budgetary constraints, and teaching and learning strengths and challenges. As a result, even when schools appear similar from the outside, their contextual differences shape the variable capacities of schools for coping with and responding to policies. Specifically, the situated, professional, material and external contexts that frame schools shape their policy capacities and responses in various ways (Braun et al., 2011).

Situated contexts include a school's history, setting, geographical location and student body (Braun et al., 2011). Schools may be urban or rural, serve different cultural and linguistic groups, and cover catchment areas that encompass diverse communities of varying size. In addition, schools serve students from different economic backgrounds who live in farming and fishing villages, manufacturing and mining towns, and large cities that are centres for health, education and government services. Schools also have distinctive histories and reputations that impact how they are perceived, in their own locales and further afield (Braun et al., 2011).

Professional contexts encompass more intangible variables, including teachers' values, attitudes and experiences with policy implementation in their respective schools (Braun et al., 2011). Given the diversity of teacher values, attitudes and experiences found in every school, professional contexts vary within and between schools. In some cases, separate departments in the same school may operate as autonomous units, and part-time and full-time teachers may have very different interactions with education policy (Braun et al., 2011).

Material contexts include the physical aspects of schools, such as buildings, budgets, staffing and technology (Braun et al., 2011). The age, layout, capacity, square footage and quality of the facilities and equipment in school buildings may significantly influence policy enactment. Variations in school budgets, due to disparities in school size, student enrolment, funding formulas and subsidies, also impact the capacity of schools to implement policies. Stable school staffs support policy implementation, but frequent staff turnover is an unfortunate reality in many schools that struggle to attract and retain competent teachers due to their geographic locations, local housing costs and limited transportation links (Braun et al., 2011).

External contexts include the outside pressures and expectations placed on schools, including comparisons of student performance on national and international tests of student achievement (Braun et al., 2011; Gur et al., 2011; Rochex, 2006). The publication of comparative tables of student grades and school rankings, such as the provincial assessments in Canada, the Ofsted ratings and league tables in Britain, and the international Programme for International Student Assessment (PISA) rankings, place constant pressure on schools to improve student performance, and spur governments to enact successive policy reforms (Gur et al., 2011; Rochex, 2006). The teachers at the receiving end of this barrage of policy changes vary in their responses to external policy demands, and their capacity for policy implementation (Braun et al., 2011).

Policy Capacity

Policy capacity, which centres around the ability of individuals and organizations to enact change, is essential to successful policy implementation (Cobb et al., 2013; OECD, 2020; Wu et al., 2018). In recent decades, there has been a growing recognition of the importance of policy capacity at all levels of education systems and among policy actors, including teachers and educational leaders. This heightened awareness has spawned capacity-building initiatives around the world, including professional development programs aimed at strengthening the knowledge, skills and resources of policy actors. These efforts are well-founded in that policy capacity encompasses a wide range of capabilities (Cobb et al., 2013; Wu et al., 2018). For example, Wu et al. (2018) describe nine components of policy capacity, including domain knowledge, research skills, visionary leadership, strategic management skills, networking skills, data collection and analysis processes, and intergovernmental and interagency coordination. In addition to policy capacity, other variables influence policy implementation, including teachers' career stages, teaching specialties, formal positions, as well as the time and space available to them to fulfil their policy obligations.

Teacher Career Stages

Differences in teacher subject specialties, positions and career stages impact policy enactment, as described by Maguire et al. (2015). For example, new, inexperienced teachers who are at the start of their careers and are consumed by the demands of their classrooms are often more preoccupied with survival than policy implementation. For beginning teachers, policies may seem distant, invisible and unrelated to the immediate, pressing concerns that they face. From their standpoint, policies appear to come at them from the school, district and/or government levels, and policy work consists of muddling through as best they can while focusing on their daily work. In contrast, more experienced senior teachers, department heads and school leaders are called upon to comply with policy directives and demonstrate how policies are implemented in practice (Maguire et al., 2015).

Teaching Specialties and Positions

The different teaching specialities and positions within schools also affect policy interpretation and enactment in areas such as student discipline (Maguire et al., 2015). For example, school discipline policies may be interpreted and implemented differently by teachers of various subjects because behaviour that is acceptable in drama and physical education classes may not be deemed appropriate in science laboratories. Moreover, school counsellors and school administrators may approach student discipline policies very differently due to dissimilarities in their positions, education, experience, values and/or professional responsibilities. Within school departments, teachers of the same subjects may also interpret and enact discipline policies differently because they hold contrasting beliefs, values and orientations to the complex issues surrounding student behaviour. Thus, policy enactment varies among educators in accordance with their teaching experience, subject specialties, and personal beliefs and values (Maguire et al., 2015).

Time and Space

Time and space impact every aspect of teaching practice, including policy implementation. Specifically, the ever-present constraints on time and space in schools influence where teachers stand in relation to education policies, which policies are enacted, and which policies are left to the wayside (Maguire et al., 2015). As Braun et al. (2011) point out, policies literally move through the different spaces in schools as they are enacted and the physical location of school departments, programmes and personnel impact can increase or lower the visibility of policy enactment. For example, the low visibility of school programmes that are located in remote sections of schools can lessen the pressure on teachers in those locations for policy enactment (Maguire et al., 2015).

School timetables and calendars are also impactful because policy implementation spans different terms, semesters, examination periods, holidays, and school events that compete for the limited time available in the school day and the school year (Maguire et al., 2015). Annual rituals and rites of passage, such as school start-up, the arrival and departure of students and staff, and graduation ceremonies punctuate the annual cycles of schools. Policy enactment may be strong at the start of the school year but subsequently taper off because schools are 'real-time' institutions where people get tired and pay different levels of attention to different policies at different times in the school year (Maguire et al., 2015). Inadequate time, along with other formidable barriers, undermines the successful and sustainable implementation of education policies.

Barriers to Policy Implementation

Despite the worldwide proliferation of education policies, they are not always translated into desired actions, results and outcomes in schools (Fullan, 2016; Harris & Jones, 2020; OECD, 2020; Robinson, 2018; Starr, 2019; Viennet & Pont, 2017). In light of the serious ramifications of policy failure, including the erosion of public trust and the waste of public resources, policy implementation has assumed greater prominence among governments, researchers and international organizations. Accordingly, increased attention is being paid to the causes of policy failure, strategies for preventing them, and ways of overcoming them (Hudson et al., 2019). In their research into policy failure and impediments to policy implementation, Hudson et al. (2019) identified four main barriers, as described below.

Overly Optimistic Expectations

Overly optimistic expectations include the overestimation of policy benefits and the underestimation of the time, costs, challenges, risks and complexities involved (Hudson et al., 2019). Overly optimistic expectations may result from failing to fully appreciate the complexity of policy implementation, relying on insufficient data and evidence, misreading divergent stakeholder viewpoints, boosting the prospects of vested interests, and promoting the short-term recognition of decision-makers. Additional challenges include the uneven distribution of costs and benefits over time, long time lags between policy implementation and the achievement of policy outcomes, the politically contentious nature of many government policy initiatives, and the difficulties associated with initiatives that span multiple, siloed government departments.

Implementation in Dispersed Governance

Implementation in dispersed governance refers to policies that are formulated nationally but implemented locally at different levels of government (Hudson et al., 2019). Dispersed governance can impede policy implementation because national policies may be variously interpreted and enacted as they are tailored to different school, district and system contexts. Policy implementation may be especially fragmented when different levels of government have independent political authority. Even when governance is centralized rather than dispersed, policy implementation is highly reliant upon and influenced by local contexts. Therefore, it is incumbent upon centralized policymakers to consider the engagement of multiple stakeholders, and recognise that policy interventions that are successful in one locale are not necessarily well suited to others. Moreover, policymakers require an accurate grasp of the realities confronting frontline workers and the collective impact of these workers in shaping and reshaping policy intentions (Hudson et al., 2019).

Inadequate Collaborative Policymaking

Inadequate collaborative policymaking refers to centralized policy development in siloed government departments in the absence of authentic consultation, communication, collaboration, and partnership with educators and stakeholders (Hudson et al., 2019). The failure to build collaborative structures and processes for communication, problem-solving and the resolution of stakeholder differences during policy design and development may significantly impede implementation. Policy design requires continual communication and collaboration with multiple stakeholders at the central, regional and local levels, including managerial and frontline staff and partner agencies. In particular, the end-users of policy are key actors in the implementation process. Therefore, a collaborative and integrated process of policy design, development and implementation is essential (Hudson et al., 2019).

Vagaries of the Political Cycle

Vagaries of the political cycle refers to the general political preference for policies that are quickly developed and enacted and produce immediate results, rather than long-term policies that require sustained stakeholder consultation, implementation and accountability for the results achieved (Hudson et al., 2019). In many cases, politicians' terms in office are short, such that they are not held accountable for the results of their policy initiatives. Because politicians are more likely to get credit for policies passed than implementation problems avoided, policies that can be pushed through quickly during their terms in office are more attractive. As a result, policies may be enacted in rapid succession without sufficient attention to the policy process, actors and contexts involved in implementation (Hudson et al., 2019).

Starr (2019) also found that changes in government exert a destabilizing influence, as new governments are sworn in and cancel the education policies of their predecessors in order to promote their own short-term agendas for educational change. As education policies are quickly replaced by new versions, full implementation becomes impossible and the potential impact of policies is curtailed. The uncertainty, complexity and fluidity produced by fluctuating policy agendas make the leadership, management and governance of education more demanding, challenging and risky (Hudson et al., 2019). In addition, political instability, sudden shifts in policy direction and the frequent abandonment of policy initiatives also undermine policy implementation by contributing to teacher and leader cynicism and weariness with successive educational reforms (Teodorović et al., 2016). While these and other barriers to policy implementation are daunting, several supports have proven effective in preventing and overcoming them.

Supports for Policy Implementation

A variety of implementation supports are vital to successful policy implementation because the diversity of educational policies and contexts necessitate different approaches to implementation (Teodorović et al., 2016; Viennet & Pont, 2017). In essence, policy implementation depends to a large extent on the appropriateness of the policy instruments or mechanisms that are utilized to put it into practice. Moreover, a blend of policy instruments often yields more positive outcomes than single supports (Cobb et al., 2013). Instead of pre-packaged, ready-made, policy supports, there is a need for customized policy supports that are tailored to the specific goals and objectives of individual policies and their unique implementation contexts. As Teodorović et al. (2016, p. 363) point out, 'no education policy lives in a vacuum; it is always conditioned by the context in which it is initiated and implemented and which it, in turn, influences'. Successful policy implementation also requires effective communication, efficient problem-solving, timely feedback and the clear division of educators' roles and responsibilities by educational leaders at the school and system levels (Teodorović et al., 2016).

Policy implementation is also enabled by key design features, including policy function, scope, intensity and reach (Cobb et al., 2013). Coherence and alignment are also influential: policies characterized by coherence and alignment with existing policies and practices in schools and districts have greater chances of success (Campbell & Fullan, 2019; Cobb et al., 2013; Quinn & Fullan, 2018; Robinson, 2018). Additional supports for policy implementation include sustained stakeholder involvement; stable policy environments; effective communication strategies; and the beliefs, attitudes and motivations of policy implementers (Cobb et al., 2013). Individually and in combination, all of these supports build the capacity of educators, schools and education systems to complete policy implementation.

Policy Support Programs

To strengthen policy implementation, policymakers require a deep understanding how policy moves through the preparation, tracking, support and review phases of policy implementation, and how implementation can be enabled at each point along the way (Hudson et al., 2019). The development of policy support programs that address each phase of the implementation process can support the process in a variety of ways.

Preparation

In the preparation phase, policymakers need to fully appraise the practicalities of implementation by carefully scrutinizing policy proposals from the outset and ensuring robust policy design (Australian Government, 2014; Hudson et al., 2019). At this point in the implementation process, policymakers must guard against the causes of flawed policy design, such as superficial understandings of policy problems, inadequate information about implementation contexts, nebulous and/or conflicting policy goals, deficient policy evidence and insufficient political backing (Hudson et al., 2019). Key implementation supports at this phase include

- the creation of collaborative policy design forums that promote consensus;
- policy design assurance frameworks that address risks and challenges;
- robust implementation statements that articulate clear expectations; and
- adequate implementation funding and resources that set the stage for success from the outset (Australian Government, 2014; Hudson et al., 2019).

Policy Tracking

During the policy tracking phase, mechanisms and procedures are established for tracking the progress of policy implementation (Hudson et al., 2019). The effectiveness of tracking measures hinges upon several key practices, including (a) focusing on a few policy priorities that are supported by adequate funding; (b) amassing quality data and evidence for measuring progress; (c) creating mutually agreed upon and feasible policy targets; (d) actively and authentically engaging stakeholders; and (e) building effective communication channels.

As the tracking phase unfolds, key implementation supports include the creation of intermediary bodies that bridge policymaking and policy implementation, two-way communication between policy implementers and policymakers, consensus on policy targets and timelines, and realistic expectations and indicators of success that reflect the complexity of the policy problems that educators face (Hudson et al., 2019).

Implementation Support

In the implementation support phase, various mechanisms are established to enable and sustain policy implementation. The effective identification, creation and enactment of essential policy supports requires the input, experience and expertise of multiple policy actors, including policymakers, administrators and frontline workers (Australian Government, 2014; Hudson et al., 2019). Because teachers, educational leaders and support staff know more about the local contexts and challenges of policy implementation than national policymakers, implementation support mechanisms must tap into experience and expertise of front line personnel. This entails appraising the local capacity for policy implementation by identifying what is working well, areas for improvement and strategies for capacity-building. In some jurisdictions, arm's-length bodies have been created that work alongside governments to support policy implementation and system change (Hudson et al., 2019).

At this juncture in the policy implementation process, key supports include the creation and maintenance of common ground between policymakers and stakeholders, policymaker appreciation of the tensions and dilemmas experienced by frontline workers, recruitment and professional development of skilled policy implementers, and the provision of ongoing support for problem-solving and capacity-building as implementation unfolds (Hudson et al., 2019).

Policy Review

During the review phase, which is the last point in the policy implementation process, an assessment is conducted to determine the extent to which policy objectives were realized (Hudson et al., 2019). Key topics of investigation include whether the policy problem was accurately identified, all policy components were addressed, essential data was collected and policy expectations were met. In addition, reviewers scrutinize the implementation process for lessons learned that may inform future policy initiatives (Australian Government, 2014). Another vital focus of implementation reviews is the critical evaluation of the policy supports that were enacted. Reviewers may query the extent to which implementation supports promoted policy legitimacy, built stakeholder support, addressed the complexity of policy implementation, and contributed to the achievement of policy objectives (Hudson et al., 2019). In this final phase, policy implementation is supported by short-, medium- and long-term benchmarks for appraising progress, the utilization of action research in formative and summative evaluations of the implementation process, and sustained political support for long-term, complex policies.

In summary, policy support programs provide a wide range of implementation supports. Policy implementation frameworks also provide useful guidelines, strategies and supports that may be customized to diverse schools and education systems.

Policy Implementation Frameworks

The various frameworks for policy implementation found in the literature reflect different philosophies, theories and contexts of education. The Australian Government (2014) developed a comprehensive framework for the implementation of government policy, including education policy, that highlighted the importance of essential preconditions and capabilities and described six interconnected building blocks of implementation: engaging stakeholders; planning; securing resources; monitoring, review and evaluation; governance; and risk management. Barnett (2021) advocated a policy implementation framework centered on principal capabilities in autonomy, knowledge and accountability that are essential to effective policy implementation in schools. Viennet and Pont's (2017) intricate policy implementation framework, which is composed of four components (smart policy design; inclusive stakeholder engagement; conducive institutional, policy and societal context; coherent implementation strategy) was subsequently refined and elaborated upon (Gouedard, 2021; OECD, 2020).

OECD Policy Implementation Framework

The OECD (2020) proposed a policy implementation framework for education based on international research, national practices and the experience of OECD representatives in working with countries around the world on education policies and reforms. Within this framework, policy refers to governmental action aimed at addressing an issue or initiating improvement in education. The aim of the framework is to encourage policymakers to look at policymaking from the perspectives of change and implementation rather than concentrating solely on policy design. By shifting the focus from policy design to the entire policy process, and promoting broad stakeholder engagement in all phases of the cycle, the framework supports the successful adoption and long-term sustainability of education policies.

The proposed framework is an informative resource for educators, policymakers, and stakeholders as they strive to move education policy from paper to action (OECD, 2020). By balancing top-down and bottom-up implementation strategies, the framework is adaptable to diverse and complex policy environments. In essence, the framework asserts that an effective policy implementation strategy requires the coherent alignment and enactment of three interactive dimensions: (1) smart policy design; (2) inclusive stakeholder engagement; and (3) conducive environments. To assist policymakers in planning new policies and assessing the impact of existing policies on educational change, the framework describes the key elements of each dimension and provides guiding questions for each one.

Smart Policy Design

Smart policy design refers to policies that are guided by a vision and supported by pertinent policy tools and resources that closely match the policy objectives (OECD, 2020). Smart policy design guides stakeholders and impacts all aspects of the implementation process, including the extent to which education policies result in desired change. The quality of policy design is influenced by the policy vision, accompanying policy tools, and available resources.

Policy visions articulate aspirations for educational enhancements, guide policy decisions and orient policies toward targeted educational change (OECD, 2020). These visions may be driven and shaped by different variables in educational contexts, including scientific research, social change, political will and political cycles. The importance of a clear, consensual vision to successful policy implementation and educational change cannot be overstated. A clear vision, collaboratively developed and agreed to by multiple stakeholders, should be established in order to ensure common understandings of the policy and its objectives, and promote policy coherence (OECD, 2020). Policy tools and resources are also invaluable implementation supports.

Policy tools are multiple levers or actions that policymakers employ to achieve specific policy objectives (OECD, 2020). For example, to achieve the policy objective of increasing the attractiveness of the teaching profession, policymakers may undertake a range of actions, including reviews of teachers' salaries, teacher preparation programs, recruitment and hiring, and career paths. The choice of different actions aimed at the achievement of policy objectives impacts policy implementation. Different policy tools are selected on the basis of research, evidence and their suitability for the policy objectives and contexts at hand. Policy resources include the time, funding, equipment, facilities and personnel that support the implementation and sustainability of education policies. If any of these resources are inadequate, policy implementation may be compromised. When shortages arise, actions should be undertaken to secure the resources necessary to ensure successful policy implementation (OECD, 2020).

Inclusive Stakeholder Engagement

Inclusive stakeholder engagement is characterized by the effective communication of policy goals and objectives, and the active engagement of various stakeholders whose roles and responsibilities in policy implementation are clearly defined and transparent to everyone involved (OECD, 2020). Stakeholders are individuals, groups of individuals, or organizations that have a vested interest in, are directly affected by, and/or wield an explicit influence over the sphere of education associated with a specific policy. Because stakeholder perspectives and behaviours shape education policies and profoundly influence all phases of the policy process, active stakeholder engagement is vital to successful policy implementation. Inclusive stakeholder engagement empowers individuals, groups, and organizations to share their visions of education, communicate their interests and priorities, and contribute to policy design and implementation in meaningful ways within their local contexts. The essential elements of inclusive stakeholder engagement include communication, involvement and transparency.

Involvement refers to the opportunities that stakeholders have to influence policy design and implementation (OECD, 2020). Stakeholder involvement supports sound policy design, the achievement of consensus among diverse participants, and the mediation of competing viewpoints and priorities. The level of involvement is determined by government efforts to engage stakeholders and by stakeholders' willingness and capacity to participate. Stakeholders may be engaged in a variety of ways, including public consultations, committee meetings, polls, surveys, online forums and publications.

Transparency in stakeholder engagement refers to clear, consistent and open communication of key aspects of the policy implementation process, including the specific roles and responsibilities of policymakers and stakeholders, the procedures that are followed, and the mechanisms that are put in place to regularly monitor, evaluate and report progress in an accountable and forthright manner (OECD, 2020). Transparency builds trust among stakeholders, encourages stakeholder participation, supports evidence-informed decisions, and promotes ongoing adjustments to policy implementation as it unfolds.

Conducive Environments

In conducive environments, education policies are aligned within legal and policy frameworks, adapted to the capacities of teachers and educational leaders who implement them, and tailored to the political, institutional and socio-economic contexts in which implementation takes place (OECD, 2020). Conducive environments are comprised of supportive governance structures, institutional settings, socio-economic conditions and international trends in education. Conducive environments also encompass a variety of contextual factors that comprise the national, district and school settings of policy implementation, such as demographics, political climates, and school and system capacities for educational change. Therefore, institutions, policy capacity and policy alignment figure prominently in conducive environments (OECD, 2020).

Institutions include the explicit and implicit rules, norms and strategies that impact individual behaviours and decision-making processes at different levels of education (OECD, 2020). Explicit rules include education governance systems comprised of legislation, policies and governing bodies that underpin the administration of education systems. Implicit rules refer to the leadership styles of system leaders, the guiding principles that mould educator and stakeholder behaviour, and the levels of trust among individuals and within educational institutions. These and other institutional factors merit careful consideration because they may significantly enhance or constrain policy implementation.

Policy capacity refers to the knowledge, skills and competencies that policy implementers at different levels of an education system require to successfully implement a policy (OECD, 2020). Key among them are the capacity of teachers and school leaders to shape, monitor, and adjust policy implementation at the school and classroom levels. System leaders play pivotal roles in supporting teachers and administrators in this vital work by initiating, aligning, coordinating and resourcing policy frameworks. Without strong system support, schools may not receive the necessary resources for successful implementation. To address shortfalls in teacher and leader capacity for policy implementation, professional development may be provided that enables the acquisition of requisite knowledge, skills and competencies (OECD, 2020).

Policy alignment occurs when complementary education policies have compatible goals and are integrated in cohesive policy frameworks rather than being enacted singly (OECD, 2020). When designing and implementing education policies, it is important to bear in mind that they are not developed in isolation and must fit into existing legal and policy frameworks. In addition, education policies must uphold the visions and priorities of the education systems, districts and schools in which they are embedded. Therefore, whole-system approaches to policy alignment are recommended, including building on existing policies and integrating new policies to promote aligned and coherent policy implementation (OECD, 2020).

Coherence is essential when weaving the components of the policy implementation framework together to form a coherent implementation strategy (OECD, 2020; Viennet & Pont, 2017). Rather than enacting disjointed measures and isolated actions, the creation of a coherent implementation strategy ensures that education policy produces desired educational change. Because unanticipated roadblocks and challenges are likely to arise during the implementation process, a strategic approach to implementation is vital. Being strategic entails (a) understanding the key dimensions of policy implementation and their interconnections; (b) carefully considering the key dimensions in decision-making; (c) building upon stakeholder engagement and valuing their collective effort; and (d) treating policy implementation as a multidimensional, cooperative endeavour rather than a linear, solo activity. In summary, a coherent policy implementation strategy may be developed by:

(1) Collaboratively developing a shared vision with stakeholders;
(2) Selecting the necessary policy tools to turn the vision into reality;
(3) Provisioning sufficient resources;
(4) Establishing a communication strategy to inform different stakeholder groups;
(5) Actively involving stakeholders in policy design;

(6) Fostering transparency;
(7) Building on existing educational institutions;
(8) Assessing and developing the capacity of frontline policy implementers; and
(9) Adopting a whole-of-system approach.

(OECD, 2020, p. 12)

In addition to coherent implementation strategies, integrated governance structures can enhance policy implementation, including coherent and aligned legal and policy frameworks.

Coherent and Aligned Legal and Policy Frameworks

Policy implementation is enhanced by the integration of the legislation, standards, policies and procedures that co-exist at the school, district and system levels, and across government departments and agencies (Campbell & Fullan, 2019; CEPPE, 2013; Williams, 2018; Williams et al., 2022). As a growing international trend, governments across the globe are enacting coherent and aligned frameworks of education laws, policies and standards that consolidate and focus multiple education initiatives on a few, concentrated priorities (CEPPE, 2013; Hitt & Tucker, 2016; Leithwood, 2017; Viennet & Pont, 2017; Williams, 2018; Williams et al., 2022).

Developing cohesive legal and policy frameworks, rather than enacting legislation and policies in isolation, enables education systems to make the crucial leap from adopting policies, laws and standards, to turning them into practice in the daily work of educators (Viennet & Pont, 2017). Moreover, coherent and aligned legal and policy frameworks support the efficient and effective coordination, planning and implementation of continuous school and system improvement. In fact, research has shown that the highest performing and improving education systems have adopted this coordinated approach (CEPPE, 2013; Viennet & Pont, 2017; Williams, 2018; Williams et al., 2022).

The need for coherent and aligned legal and policy frameworks has taken on new urgency in the wake of the COVID-19 pandemic (UNESCO, 2021). At its peak, when most schools were shut, the pandemic impacted 1.6 billion students around the globe. This worldwide disruption in education highlighted and exacerbated existing problems and inequities in education and undermined the universal right to education, especially for the most vulnerable and marginalized students. Therefore, the creation of coherent and aligned legal, institutional, and policy frameworks for education that protect the universal right to education is a pressing international matter. Specifically, strong, rights-based legal and policy frameworks are required that (a) provide solid foundations and conducive conditions for free, inclusive, equitable, and quality education; (b) bolster the continuity of learning and education during crises; and (c) reinforce the principles and fulfil the obligations associated with the universal right to education enshrined in national and international agreements and legislation (UNESCO, 2021).

Conclusion

Policy implementation is, in many ways, a fraught process that is buffeted by clashing values, priorities, and political agendas. Successful and sustainable policy implementation requires extensive time, resources, collaboration and coordination, but education policies are often disjointed, under-resourced and enacted in isolation. While formidable barriers impede policy implementation, significant progress has been made in identifying proven strategies for preventing and overcoming these barriers and bolstering implementation. This is important because successful policy implementation not just about resolving problems in education, but advancing positive change that strengthens teaching and learning for all students. The myriad interconnections between policy, reform and change are examined in Chapter 9. First, however, Chapter 8 delves deeper into the barriers to policy implementation, especially the enduring gap between theory, policy and practice in education and strategies for bridging the divide.

References

Australian Government. (2014). *Policy implementation*. Department of the Prime Minister and Cabinet.

Ball, S. J. (2015). What is policy? 21 years later: Reflections on the possibilities of policy research. *Discourse: Studies in the Cultural Politics of Education*, *36*(3), 306–313. https://doi.org/10.1080/01596306.2015.1015279

Ball, S. J., Maguire, M., Braun, A., & Hoskins, K. (2011). Policy subjects and policy actors in schools: Some necessary but insufficient analyses. *Discourse: Studies in the Cultural Politics of Education*, *32*(4), 611–624. https://doi.org/10.1080/01596306.2011.601564

Barnett, E. (2021). Towards an alternative approach to the implementation of education policy: A capabilities framework. *Issues in Educational Research*, *31*(2), 387–403.

Bell, L., & Stevenson, H. (2006). *Education policy: Process, themes and impact*. Routledge.

Bergmark, U., & Hansson, K. (2021). How teachers and principals enact the policy of building education in Sweden on a scientific foundation and proven experience: Challenges and opportunities. *Scandinavian Journal of Educational Research*, *65*(3), 448–467. https://doi.org/10.1080/00313831.2020.1713883

Berkovich, I. (2018). *Education policy, theories, and trends in the 21st century: International and Israeli perspectives*. Springer. https://doi.org/10.1007/978-3-030-63103-1

Braun, A., Ball, S. J., Maguire, M., & Hoskins, K. (2011). Taking context seriously: Towards explaining policy enactment in the secondary school. *Discourse: Studies in the Cultural Politics of Education*, *32*(4), 585–596. https://doi.org/10.1080/01596306.2011.601555

Campbell, D., & Fullan, M. (2019). *The governance core: School boards, superintendents, and schools working together*. Corwin.

Centre of Study for Policies and Practices in Education (CEPPE). (2013). *Learning standards, teaching standards and standards for school principals: A comparative study*. OECD Education Working Papers, No. 99. OECD Publishing.

Cobb, C. D., Donaldson, M. L., & Mayer, A. P. (2013). Creating high leverage policies: A new framework to support policy development. *Berkeley Review of Education, 4*(2), 265–284. https://doi.org/10.5070/B84110010

Coburn, C. E. (2016). What's policy got to do with it? How the structure-agency debate can illuminate policy implementation. *American Journal of Education, 122*(May, 2016), 465–475.

Darling-Hammond, L., Burns, D., Campbell, C., Goodwin, A. L., Hammerness, K., Low, E. L., McIntyre, A., Sato, M., & Zeichner, K. (2017). *Empowered educators: How high performing systems shape teaching quality around the world.* Jossey-Bass.

Farhadi, B., & Winton, S. (2022). Ontario teachers' policy leadership during the COVID-19 pandemic. *Canadian Journal of Educational Administration and Policy, 200*, 49–62. http://doi.org/10.7202/1092707ar

Fullan, M. (2016). *The new meaning of educational change* (5th ed.). Teachers College Press.

Gouëdard, P. (2021). *Developing indicators to support the implementation of education policies.* OECD Education Working Papers No. 255. OECD Publishing. http://doi.org/10.1787/b9f04dd0-en

Greene, J. P., & McShane, M. Q. (2018). Learning from failure. *Phi Delta Kappan International, 99*(8), 46–50.

Gur, B. S., Celik, Z., & Ozoglu, M. (2011). Policy interpretations for Turkey: A critique of the interpretation and utilization of PISA results in Turkey. *Journal of Education Policy, 27*(1), 1–21. https://doi.org/10.1080/02680939.2011.595509

Hardy, I. J., & Melville, W. (2019). Professional learning as policy enactment: The primacy of professionalism. *Education Policy Analysis Archives, 27*(90), 1–23.

Harris, A., Jones, M., & Adams, D. (2016). Qualified to lead? A comparative, contextual and cultural view of educational policy borrowing. *Educational Research, 58*(2), 166–178. https://doi.org/10.1080/00131881.2016.1165412

Harris, A., & Jones, M. S. (2020). *System recall.* Corwin.

Hitt, D. H., & Tucker, P. D. (2016). Systematic review of key leader practices found to influence student achievement: A unified framework. *Review of Educational Research, 86*(2), 531–569. https://doi.org/10.3102/0034654315614911

Hudson, B., Hunter, D., & Peckham, S. (2019). Policy failure and the policy-implementation gap: Can policy support programs help? *Policy Design and Practice, 2*(1), 1–14. https://doi.org/10.1080/25741292.2018.1540378

Leithwood, K. (2017). The Ontario leadership framework: Successful school leadership practices and personal leadership resources. In K. Leithwood, J. Sun, & K. Pollock (Eds.), *How school leaders contribute to student success: The four paths framework* (pp. 31–43). Springer. https://doi.org/10.1007/978-3-319-50980-8_3

Maguire, M., Ball, S. J., & Braun, A. (2013). Whatever happened to...? 'Personalized learning' as a case of policy dissipation. *Journal of Education Policy, 28*(23), 322–338. https://doi.org/10.1080/02680939.2012.724714

Maguire, M., Braun, A., & Ball, S. (2015). 'Where you stand depends on where you sit': The social construction of policy enactments in the (English) secondary school. *Discourse: Studies in the Cultural Politics of Education, 36*(4), 485–499. https://doi.org/10.1080/01596306.2014.977022

Nilsen, P., Stahl, C., Roback, K., & Cairney, P. (2013). Never the twain shall meet? – A comparison of implementation science and policy implementation research. *Implementation Science, 8*(63), 1–12. https://doi.org/10.1186/1748-5908-8-63

Organisation for Economic Co-operation and Development (OECD). (2020). *An implementation framework for effective change in schools.* OECD Education Policy Perspectives No. 9. OECD Publishing. https://doi.org/10.1787/b9f04dd0-en

Quinn, J., & Fullan, M. (2018). Coherence making: Whole system change strategy. In H. J. Malone, S. Rincón-Gallardo, & K. Kew (Eds.), *Future directions of educational change: Social justice, professional capital, and systems change* (pp. 223–237). Routledge.

Robinson, V. (2018). *Reduce change to increase improvement.* Corwin.

Rochex, J. Y. (2006). Chapter 5: Social, methodological, and theoretical issues regarding assessment: Lessons from a secondary analysis of PISA 2000 literacy tests. *Review of Research in Education, 30*(1), 163–212. https://doi.org/10.3102/0091732X030001163

Starr, K. (2019). *Education policy, neoliberalism, and leadership practice: A critical analysis.* Routledge.

Teodorović, J., Stanović, D., Bodroža, B., Milin, V., & Đeric, I. (2016). Education policymaking in Serbia through the eyes of teachers, counsellors and principals. *Educational Assessment, Evaluation and Accountability, 28*(4), 347–375. http://doi.org/10.1007/s11092-015-9221-x

United Nations Educational, Scientific and Cultural Organization (UNESCO). (2021). *Guidelines to strengthen the right to education in national frameworks.* Author.

Viennet, R., & Pont, B. (2017). *Education policy implementation: A literature review and proposed framework.* OECD Education Working Paper No. 162. OECD Publishing. https://doi.org/10.1787/fc467a64-en

Ward, L., & Parr, J. M. (2011). Digitalizing our schools: Clarity and coherence in policy. *Australasian Journal of Educational Technology, 27*(2), 326–342.

Williams, M. A. (2018). *Complexity and coherence: A mixed methods study of educational leadership and the development of leadership standards in Nova Scotia.* (Unpublished doctoral dissertation). St. Francis Xavier University.

Williams, M. A., Young, D. C., & White, R. E. (2022). Educational leadership standards: From contested histories to common trends. In V. Wang (Ed.), *Handbook of research on educational leadership and research methodology* (pp. 94–115). IGI Global.

Wu, X., Ramesh, M., Howlett, M., & Fritzen, S. A. (2018). *The public policy primer: Managing the policy process* (2nd ed.). Routledge.

Chapter 8

Bridging Policy-Practice Gaps and Building Policy Capacity

By now, even the least avid of readers has come to recognize that policy analysis is not an exact science. And, by no means is it exactly art, either. Like many things, such as the practice of law, dentistry, garage mechanics and, of course, education, the development of policy, its practice and implementation are somewhere in the Lagrange point between art and science. That is to say that policy development exists as both art and science. To be sure, policy does make use of the scientific method in terms of the use of policy models and the research that is endemic in all successful policy applications. However, there is also an art to its development in terms of sensitive issues such as when, where, how and to whom the final policy will apply. Thus, policy advancement and application may, to some extent be formulaic, but it is also dependent on sense and sensitivity to the environment within which it is conceived, developed and promoted.

Should one so desire, it is possible to identify the development of the policy project as a more scientifically oriented endeavour when it is compared to the practice of policy. Similarly, the building of policy capacity is both an art and a science. To be sure, building policy capacity, when it comes to education, requires a great deal of patience, research and constructive instruction. Educational leaders realize this all too well, with some appearing to lead effortlessly, while others struggle to achieve the most mundane of policy goals.

In real life terms, there is always a theory-practice divide when it comes to implementing policy in schools and classrooms. This theory-practice divide often comes to grief when the theory, or science, if you will, of the policy supersedes the practice of that same policy. Human error is often responsible for failed policies, hence the need for capacity building to establish the most fertile ground for, not only the current policy, but for all policy matters to follow.

And at its very core, it is crucial to remember that policy development is intertwined with change. As a cautionary note, it is wise to heed the fact that change can be derailed by a myriad of factors, some of which are overt, but still others that are less visible. The analogy of an iceberg, where only part of the structure can be seen above the water rings true here. And thus, for policymakers, it is vital to realize that the '…dangers on which most change processes run aground lie hidden below the surface' (Buller, 2015, p. 155).

Policy Barriers: Where Theory Meets Practice

This chapter refers to the theory-practice divide as applies to policy analysis. In this case, policy analysis refers to the entire process of policy development, from the recognition of the need for a new policy — or the recognition that a particular policy needs to be revitalized or even dispensed with — to the point of implementation.

As an initial point, it is important to recognize at the outset that some '… are … afraid of change, especially if it comes quickly or if they feel they have little control or influence over it. People become accustomed to the status quo …' (Lunenburg & Ornstein, 2008, pp. 438–439). This is hardly startling, as human nature is to covet what we grow accustomed to and shun or resist the unknown. Harris and Cullen (2010, p. 16) provide a mundane example of how resistant we can become to something as simple as upgrading our laptop or desktop computer. While the central processing unit and storage of the new system might be vastly superior to our current system, we cling to our current unit, replete with its broken screen and stained keyboard. And why, because change brings with it a degree of unknown that is beyond control, as well as the need to learn something new. For some educators, much like the computer example, the current arrangement is satisfactory, so why fix a system that in their view is not broken. Or why simply change for the sake of change? For still others, change is met with scepticism and cynicism in that new policies signal an increased workload which will ultimately be downloaded onto teachers, who already assume several different roles within the scope of their employment. Relatedly, Friedenberg (1965) has lamented the fact that teachers tend to be conformist by their very nature. As a result, a desire to trade what is known for what is unknown is not part of the social fabric. Rather, a propensity to uphold the status quo permeates, resulting in a situation where change is the enemy. Within this subsystem, the implementation of new or revised policies is difficult, and unless a culture shift is achieved, failure seems inevitable (Hoy & Miskel, 2008; Lieberman, 1995). Ultimately, many change processes falter simply because they fail to commence by changing organizational culture as a starting point. 'Effective change leaders don't just point to a destination and say, "Let's go there!" They work on shaping culture so that it becomes an engine for producing better ideas' (Buller, 2015, p. 168).

But one should not lose hope entirely, as possibilities do exist. Essentially, what is required is an 'unfreezing' of the current reality to allow new potentialities to surface (Gazda et al., 1995; Lewin, 1951, p. 45). Without sounding too hyperbolic, this is somewhat akin to the notion of a paradigm shift, as articulated by Kuhn (1962), in which a dominant worldview is replaced with an emerging or alternative way of looking at the world. While these paradigm shifts can potentially cause upheaval and turbulence, this is the very nature of the change process. And if the policy as written is to become the policy as lived, we need to expect growing pains.

Another factor that needs to be considered is that of time (Delaney, 2017, p. 48). While some policy developments move at a glacial pace, a recent trend seems to be the development and implementation of policy at breakneck speed.

As Hanson puts it, in certain cases '... change has come so rapidly that it seems to have arrived unannounced...' (1985, p. 284). Building on this, it is not an exaggeration to state that in various scenarios, policies are literally and figuratively here today and gone tomorrow. Of course, there are situations that warrant immediate and concrete action. We have commented previously on the recent COVID-19 pandemic. Due to the unprecedented nature of this phenomenon, the rapid enactment of new polices was necessary. While the rollout might not have been smooth in all scenarios, the upheaval around how to provide students with an education necessitated a quick response. However, this is not an ideal case, and it is always preferable to choose a more deliberate and contemplative path to policy enactment. As Buller notes, 'Unless it's absolutely necessary for a decision to be implemented immediately, it's far better to spend some time learning the values and history of a program before proposing significant changes to it' (2015, p. 60). Basically, good policymakers do their homework prior to the introduction of a new policy initiative. Lunenburg and Ornstein (2008, p. 440) elaborate: 'Many people feel that if something is implemented this year, it will most likely be abandoned when another innovation appears and will thus make most of their efforts useless. There have, in fact, been enough bandwagons in education to make educators innovation-shy'. In essence, good policies cannot and should not be rushed, as time is perhaps the greatest predictor of success. As an example, in the Canadian province of Nova Scotia, bullying and cyber-bullying was a major issue in the early 2000s. Building on a high-profile case involving the suicide of a teenage student, the provincial government introduced the *Cyber-Safety Act* in 2013, which besides affording criminal sanctions, allowed victims/families of cyberbullying civil recourse for damages. In the end, while this *Act* was laudable in that it attempted to offer a response to a real and immediate problem, it might be argued that while well-intentioned, it was enacted in haste. Because of its broad definition of cyber-bullying, the courts found that it violated the federal *Charter of Rights and Freedoms* and was thus struck down. 'Often, hard cases can make for bad laws' (MacKay & Sutherland, 2020, p. 99). While the overwhelming temptation might be to barrel ahead, an incremental approach is always preferable. By adopting this approach, it provides a window for introspection, which may prevent the emergence of issues later in the policy cycle. And maybe even more importantly, incrementalism works best for teachers as they work towards implementing the policy. A period to acclimate oneself to anything new is never a bad thing and can only serve all parties well. As Darling-Hammond notes, 'policymakers who want teachers to succeed ... must understand that the process of change requires time and opportunities for teachers to reconstruct their practice through intensive study and experimentation' (1998, p. 654).

Lack of resources also affects how the policy will work in practice, as a perception that inequity in resource allocation exists tends to cause conflict to emerge (Bess & Dee, 2012). 'Targeting a change initiative, therefore, calls for thought regarding whether or not a match exists between the degree of change required and the energies and resources available to do battle' (Hanson, 1985, p. 293). This is another way that the policy may run afoul of the theory-practice gap. According to Lunenburg and Ornstein:

> People often resist change ... if no financial support or additional time is given for the effort. A project for which no monies are budgeted is rarely destined to be implemented. School districts often budget monies for materials but fail to allocate funds for the creation of the curriculum plan, its delivery within the classroom, or necessary in-service training. (2008, p. 440)

Another example from the Canadian province of Nova Scotia is helpful to illustrate how resources played a most important role in terms of inclusive education policy (see Young, 2010). In this particular case, by the early 2000s inclusion had become commonplace in schools across many jurisdictions. Nova Scotia was no exception to this norm, as most teachers openly embraced the tenets of the inclusive classroom. However, while teachers accepted the philosophy of inclusion, this is not to suggest that there were no issues with the policy of inclusion. A study conducted with Nova Scotia teachers and published in 2000 found that 75% of educators felt they lacked the adequate resources to facilitate inclusion within their classrooms.

> A distinct lack of a variety of different types of support were cited as the culprits. For example, some teachers indicated that in order for inclusion to succeed, class sizes must be reduced. Others argued that additional personnel needed to be hired in order that the varying needs of students could be adequately met. And, yet others have lamented the fact they lack the curricular materials and equipment necessary to do their job ....
> (Young, 2010, p. 60)

As such, it is clear that adequate resources — and here the reference to resources is expansive — are crucial in terms of policy. Thus, it becomes important to recognize that the policy architects are at fault in this equation by not recognizing or recommending essential resources so that the implementers of the policy and those most influenced by the policy will be able to recognize *how* the policy is intended to operate. Once again, we all need to recognize that educators do not merely educate their students. They need to also educate one another. Creating a policy that does not exist in a vacuum is likely one of the best ways to build capacity among the policy recipients.

Convoluted policy requirements can also kill an otherwise healthy and robust policy. 'There should be complete understanding of, and agreement on, the objectives to be achieved' (Delaney, 2017, p. 49). Again, the fault often lies within the policy development process, rather than within the implementation process. The 'best fit', or a streamlined policy is likely one of the best ways to prevent good policy from going off the rails. Here, the more experience one has with creating or implementing policy, the better. Book learning with respect to policy making is creditable, but so is experience when it comes to the manufacturing of successful policy. This returns us to the theory-practice divide. Wherever it exists in the formulation of the policy, it is likely to exist in the implementation of that policy, as well. Where a policy is necessarily convoluted, it may be wise to roll out the policy in stages, so that recipients become acclimatized to portions of the policy. This harkens back to the earlier notion of incrementalism in policy implementation and is not without its own risks. However, when there are few choices available, incrementalism may be the most effective way to proceed, even though this process may be somewhat redundant and may even be less than efficient.

As we have ascertained previously in this volume, the people who make the policy are seldom the people who implement it. This feature, alone, is important in that it insulates the architects from the product they have created. At the same time, it may also be viewed as the Achilles' heel of policy work, due to the simple fact that creators of policy are often removed from the battleground where the policy is to be implemented. Therefore, in many respects, and with only their art and their science to assist them, policy architects tend to work in a semi-vacuum, of sorts. This points directly at the need for capacity building.

Capacity building is an art form in its own right. It consists of fertilizing the soil and planting seeds, much in the same way that farmers cultivate their crops. The key term, here, is cultivation. To drop a policy bomb on an unsuspecting educator or, worse, on an unsuspecting classroom is tantamount to a declaration of war. Part of the policy development process requires that the people who will be most influenced by the ensuing policy need to have some awareness of what it is that is about to occur. As such, the policy architects must be in near constant communication with the eventual recipients of that policy.

This process typically begins with the recognition that there needs to be some policy investiture, whether it be a new policy, an adjustment of an existing policy or the retirement of a policy that has served its day. And while they are at it, it is always a good idea for the policy creators to ensure that their recipients are aware that there will be further policies and/or adjustment down the line. Once the recipients are aware of policy changes, and the nature of such changes, then future policy initiatives will not be met with a great degree of 'policy anxiety'. It is the reduction of such anxiety that signals that a degree of capacity building, as it pertains to policy, has been developed.

Another key understanding is the fact that policy as written is rarely the same as policy as delivered or lived. This is a dimensional problem. Once the course of a policy initiative has been decided upon and that policy has taken shape, all that remains is to implement the darned thing. This is where the three-dimensional document of policy intent — the height, length, width and content of the policy paper — meets the reality of the fourth dimension, which is time. Of course this dimension is subject to the implementation of the policy. And this is where the policy becomes interpreted by those who implement it and by those who are influenced by its very existence. Because each human being is unique, it stands to reason that the new policy is prone to being interpreted in a variety of ways, no matter how unequivocal that policy may be. For example, some classroom teachers may view the policy as an order, a fiat, or a rule to be followed, ignoring it, or misinterpreting it at one's peril. Others may see the policy as a guideline, recognizing that human circumstances vary as much as each human varies. Thus, policy becomes a tool to be used with judgment, mercy and discretion. Still others may simply ignore the policy as being irrelevant, immaterial and 'somebody else's problem'.

Given the variety in responses to policy implementation, no wonder capacity building becomes an important part of the policy project. Further to this, various other factors are in play that may thwart even the best policies. Blunt resistance to the policy as planned has seen the demise of any number of almost successful policies. The failing here is not necessarily due to the policy itself. This failure is related more to the lack of education about the need and efficacy of the policy; a failure that can be avoided by including capacity building for those who will eventually become responsible for implementing the policy. In this way, the initiators of the policy process shoulder a responsibility for the education of the policy recipients in order to create a smooth voyage for the policy-to-come. And part of this education is tied up in communication, which has an 'important contribution to make to coordination and to implementation generally' (Delaney, 2017, p. 49). Communication can serve an important role in laying the groundwork. As Rich (1974, p. 31) notes:

> The policy-maker must anticipate and evaluate a host of factors prior to deciding on the proper course of action; such factors as the complexity of the policy changes, the degree to which the policy breaks with past practices, the ability of personnel to execute the policy successfully, and the possible conflict of the policy with the vested interests are all matters that merit careful assessment in determining dissemination procedures.

And as surely as good communication can help to facilitate the policy process, poor communication can easily derail the entire endeavour. One is reminded here of the professor with an encyclopedic knowledge of the material they teach, but a general inability to communicate and disseminate the material to their students. As such, one is left with an odd and less than ideal scenario where the professor is the most brilliant person in the classroom, and through their own woes at communicating, retains the status quo! Ultimately, good communication can be a foe or a friend to the policymaker. For Clemmer, 'board, administration, staff, parents, students, and the community as a whole profit from the greater understanding and improved communication that an effective policy development process engenders' (1991, p. 33).

Of course, another bug in the system comes back to purpose. As Darling-Hammond (1995) puts it, restructuring hinges on understanding why change is being sought. If there is no clear purpose for a policy to be created, it may appear that it is simply being created for its own sake. A policy cannot be optimized under these conditions and is likely doomed to failure. Such policies that appear to have little purpose become routinely ignored and often disappear from sight. While it may look similar to a successful policy that has withstood the vicissitudes of time, policies of little purpose tend to live for a very short period of time, while more robust policies may likewise 'disappear' into the matrix of 'how

Bridging Policy-Practice Gaps and Building Policy Capacity   129

we do things around here'. Both types of policies may look similar, but they are diametrically opposed in terms of their longevity, substance and purpose.

Another factor that cannot be ignored is the very nature of the policy process itself, which has traditionally been a top-down arrangement. As Levin and Young (1998, p. 73) have noted:

> In the case of education, the policy process is often dominated by the established groups — governments and stakeholder organizations. They are already organized, and tend to have staff and money. The people know and are used to dealing with one another. They are already present in many of the decision-making forums. This fact tends to push the policy process in particular directions. Each group normally acts to protect the welfare of its own members. If the key decisions are being made by people who are already part of the system and benefiting from it, there might well be less likelihood of significant change.

Darling-Hammond (1995, p. 165) further laments the difficulties associated with a top-down approach to policy. As she writes:

> The dilemma is that this [top-down] policy strategy prevents local educators from making decisions that may be more developmentally, contextually, or individually appropriate, and locks everyone into a 'one best system' solution that invariably turns out not to work ideally in many cases, sometimes undermining its own goals. In addition, this approach does not build the capacity of local educators to deepen their knowledge, so that they can engage new practices and design new programs effectively.

Yet there is some light at the end of the tunnel, as the process of who is involved in the policy process is gradually widening. According to Owens:

> In traditional organizations [schools and school boards are prime examples], which are markedly hierarchical, the process of deciding how to make decisions is largely controlled by the administrator, not the followers. In such a case, the progress of the organization from autocratic decision making toward collaborative decision making resides largely in the extent to which the administrator sees power-sharing as a win-win proposition, a desirable state of affairs, rather than a threat to administrative hegemony. Many present-day educational organizations, though still hierarchical, have developed collaborative cultures to such an extent that reverting to the more primitive autocratic model would be difficult: the

administrator is not so much confronted with the issue of whether or not others will be involved in the decision making but, rather, how and to what extent they will be involved. (1998, p. 272)

Because there are so many ways that policy may fail, it is the wise policy architect who recognizes the need for involvement, not only from the rest of the team but also from the eventual recipients of the policy. Pal's (1997) relatively unstructured policy model is very useful in this respect because it does not presume that policy development occurs in secret, in private rooms set apart from a real-world application of the eventual policy. It is during the development stages of the policy initiative that the wise policy developer will recognize that the people who are going to implement the policy or be influenced by the policy are valuable resources that will help to guide the policy process to its eventual and successful conclusion. '...[I]f restructuring is to happen, teachers must begin to think of themselves as change agents who generate ideas, discuss plans, and implement projects...' (Bondy, 1995, p. 60). Just as it is important to reduce the theory-practice gap in the introduction of new policy, or adjustments to existing policy, recognizing the implementers and recipients of that policy as resources that are invaluable in guiding the process, policy developers will be able to better understand the anxieties, the doubts and the hopes that the eventual inheritors of that policy can make material. It is in this way that the gap between the creators of policy and the recipients of policy can be reduced. By reducing this gap, the eventual policy is bound to stand a greater chance for success, simply because it is no longer a surprise to the people most influenced by it. And, because it is no longer a surprise, and because people, other than the policy makers themselves, have been consulted or brought on board as resources to offer opinions or voice concerns, the distance between the creators of the policy and the implementers of that same policy is reduced. Each individual who has been involved in or exposed to the process allows all participants to share a common understanding of why the policy is deemed necessary, how it was developed and the way(s) in which it is to be implemented. Thus, the process is no longer a mystery, the theory-practice gap is reduced and the necessary capacity has been or is in the process of being built.

Through striving to reduce the distance between creators and recipients, educators can become empowered not only to understand the process of policy making but also to support it. In the end, we '...must find ways to build the capacity of local actors...' (Darling-Hammond, 1995, p. 160). This is not meant to imply that this is an easy task to accomplish. But good policy depends upon effective implementation. That is unequivocal. However, effective implementation depends upon teacher buy-in and the willingness to support any given policy. And buy-in can often be seen as a 'hidden construct within program implementation that can explain how individuals and organizations translate participation in program activities (such as professional development) to actual implementation in their daily work' (Grebing et al., 2023, p. 3). And in the end, motivating teachers to become more assertive in terms of their own leadership capacities may serve policy initiatives well. For Buller, '...broad-based participation in the activity of change, scenario planning, and the creation of a new organizational culture can yield impressive results...' (2015, p. 163).

Overcoming Policy Barriers: Some Useful Strategies

Thus far this chapter has chronicled many of the impediments or barriers to change, and these are real and have an impact on the policy process. However, in taking a different approach, it is also advantageous to sometimes think about how resistance to change can be seen in a positive light. Resistance might well point to a need to re-evaluate the policy to ascertain if it is well-conceived, and if in fact it will realize the goals for which it was designed. This would necessitate the need to perhaps slow down, and we have already extolled the virtues associated with time and the adoption of an incremental approach. As Weimer notes, 'The objections raised by others challenge us to keep looking at what we are doing and asking why' (2013, p. 217). And without a doubt, complacency has no place in the area of policy development, as the stakes are simply too high.

Besides resistance, Lunenburg and Ornstein (2008, pp. 441–442), in surveying the literature, offer some factors to consider so that change has a lasting and significant impact:

- *Adaptive problem solving*: For change to succeed, it must be introduced so that implementation is feasible;
- *School-level focus*: Any change plan must be focused on the school level, where teaching and learning occurs;
- *Compatibility*: Reform rests on whether teachers believe they can employ such reforms in their practice;
- *Principal's leadership*: The principal must be key for making decision around institutional arrangements and structures;
- *Teacher involvement*: Teachers must be given a voice in the policy process, and must have the time and resources required; and
- *Staff development*: School improvement hinges on supporting staff in their growth.

While this list is not exhaustive, the points advanced are worth remembering. As Delaney notes, '...there is no perfect implementation of policy. That said, policy-makers are well advised to ensure that, within reason, as many of the preconditions...be in place as possible' (2017, p. 50).

Conclusion

In this chapter, discussion has been focused on the theory-practice divide as it applies to policy analysis. It is important to remember that the policy as written is seldom the same as the policy as delivered/lived. There are many factors that can derail the change process, including but not limited to resistance, time, lack of resources, convoluted policy requirements and purpose. Ultimately, good policy depends upon effective implementation, as we saw in Chapter 7. Yet, the relationship is not independent in that effective implementation is dependent on teacher buy-in and the willingness to support any given policy. As such, motivating and empowering teachers to become more assertive in terms of their own leadership capacities may serve policy initiatives well. This is especially true given overwhelming pace and volume of educational change confronting educators today, the topic of Chapter 9.

References

Bess, J. L., & Dee, J. R. (2012). *Understanding college and university organization: Theories for effective policy and practice*. Volume II: Dynamics of the system. Stylus.

Bondy, E. (1995). Fredericks middle school and the dynamics of school reform. In A. Lieberman (Ed.), *The work of restructuring schools: Building from the ground up* (pp. 43–63). Teachers College press.

Buller, J. L. (2015). *Change leadership in higher education: A practical guide to academic transformation*. Jossey-Bass.

Clemmer, E. F. (1991). *The school policy handbook*. Allyn & Bacon.

Darling-Hammond, L. (1995). Policy for restructuring. In A. Lieberman (Ed.), *The work of restructuring schools: Building from the ground up* (pp. 157–175). Teachers College Press.

Darling-Hammond, L. (1998). Policy and change: Getting beyond bureaucracy. In A. Hargreaves, A. Lieberman, M. Fullan, & D. Hopkins (Eds.), *International handbook of educational change* (pp. 642–667). Kluwer.

Delaney, J. G. (2017). *Education policy: Bridging the divide between theory and practice* (2nd ed.). Brush.

Friedenberg, E. A. (1965). *Coming of age in America*. Random House.

Gazda, G. M., Asbury, F. R., Balzer, F. J., Childers, W. C., Phelps, R. E., & Walters, R. P. (1995). *Human relations development: A manual for educators* (5th ed.). Allyn & Bacon.

Grebing, E. M., Edmunds, J. A., & Arshavsky, N. P. (2023). The relationship between buy-in and implementation: Measuring teacher-buy-in to a high school reform effort. *Evaluation and Program Planning*, 97, 1–7.

Hanson, E. M. (1985). *Educational administration and organizational behavior* (2nd ed.). Allyn & Bacon.

Harris, M., & Cullen, R. (2010). *Leading the learner-centered campus: An administrator's framework for improving student learning outcomes*. Jossey-Bass.

Hoy, W. K., & Miskel, C. G. (2008). *Educational administration: Theory, research, and practice* (8th ed.). McGraw-Hill.

Kuhn, T. S. (1962). *The structure of scientific revolutions*. University of Chicago Press.

Levin, B., & Young, J. (1998). *Understanding Canadian schools: An introduction to educational administration*. Harcourt Brace.

Lewin, K. (1951). *Field theory in social science*. Harper & Row.

Lieberman, A. (1995). Restructuring schools: The dynamics of changing practice, structure, and culture. In A. Lieberman (Ed.), *The work of restructuring schools: Building from the ground up* (pp. 1–17). Teachers College Press.

Lunenburg, F. C., & Ornstein, A. C. (2008). *Educational administration: Concepts and practices* (5th ed.). Wadsworth.

MacKay, A. W., & Sutherland, L. (2020). *Teachers and the law: Diverse roles and new challenges* (4th ed.). Emond Montgomery.

Owens, R. G. (1998). *Organizational behavior in education*. Allyn & Bacon.

Pal, L. A. (1997). *Beyond policy analysis: Public issue management in turbulent times*. Nelson.

Rich, J. M. (1974). *New directions in educational policy*. Professional Educators.

Weimer, M. (2013). *Learner-centered teaching: Five key changes to practice* (2nd ed.). Jossey-Bass.

Young, D. C. (2010). The philosophy and policies of inclusion: An administrator's guide to action. In A. L. Edmunds & R. B. Macmillan (Eds.), *Leadership for inclusion: A practical guide* (pp. 53–63). Sense Publishers.

Chapter 9

Leadership of Change

Introduction

As described in the preceding chapters of this book, policy is closely intertwined with many other facets of education, from politics and power to contexts and change. Building upon the introduction to change presented in Chapter 8, this chapter examines the interconnections between education policy and change, including the role of educational leaders in guiding systemic change. In contemporary education systems, the amount of change and the pace of change have escalated substantially in recent years (Fullan, 2016; Robinson, 2018; Starr, 2019). In fact, 'educators at all levels stand in the midst of change today as never before' (Shirley, 2018, p. 1). Unfortunately, however, planned changes frequently fail to achieve their desired results (Fullan, 2016; Greene & McShane, 2018; Robinson, 2018). Moreover, many of the changes that have materialized have been superficial and unsustainable, especially within the volatile economic, political and social contexts of modern societies. Despite repeated policy failures, educators are under mounting pressure to transform schools and education systems and improve student outcomes (Harris et al., 2016; Harris & Jones, 2020; Robinson, 2018; Starr, 2019). As a result, education systems and schools are constantly repositioning themselves to be more receptive to change, more responsive to students and parents, and more effective in driving improvements to the delivery of education programs and services (Starr, 2019). This chapter examines the leadership of educational change, including leaders of change, barriers and supports to change, and leadership practices that build the capacity for change in schools and education systems.

Educational Change

Definition

The field of educational change is a body of knowledge and ideas that seeks to understand and enhance efforts aimed at the improvement of individual schools and entire school systems (Rincón-Gallardo, 2018a, 2018b). Within this field, 'theories of what to change and how to change abound' (Hargreaves & Shirley, 2012, p. 4). In addition, the definitions of educational change vary and different approaches are recommended for putting theories of change into practice. Fullan

(2016) states that educational change is a people-related phenomenon which requires the meaningful engagement of individuals to succeed. Accordingly, the ultimate goal of educational change is for individuals to see themselves as shareholders with a stake in the success of system-wide change initiatives. In Bell and Stevenson's (2006) view, educational change centres around challenges to the status quo in education as established assumptions, values, and practices are questioned (Bell & Stevenson, 2006). Thus, educational change is a volatile process of actions and reactions that frequently generates conflicts and power struggles. In contrast, Cobb et al. (2013) define educational change as the transformation of fundamental school and district structures, systems, and cultures to positively impact classroom relationships, enrich education systems and produce positive student outcomes. Very importantly, learning is at the heart of educational change (Fullan, 2020; Hall & Hord, 2015). In this chapter, educational change is defined as the transformation of education policies, programs, and practices by policymakers and policy actors to strengthen teaching and learning and achieve desired values, goals and outcomes.

Implementation of Educational Change

The implementation of educational change is the process of putting structures, policies, programmes and activities into practice that are new to the people implementing them (Fullan, 2016). Implementation is a socially complex, multifaceted process (Avidov-Ungar & Reingold, 2018; Fullan, 2016, 2020; Robinson, 2018). Hall and Hord (2020) describe a change process comprised of three phases: (1) *developing* (creating and testing new programs and processes); (2) *implementing* (learning how to use the new programs and processes with time and supports); and (3) *sustaining* (establishing ongoing use of new programs and processes, and adjusting supports). Generally speaking, a good deal is known about creating innovations, adopting changes and implementing changes, but relatively little is known about how to sustain educational changes over time (Hall & Hord, 2020). In addition, when education systems promote new behaviour patterns and work habits, they often end up with changes in practice that do not embrace intended values and principles (Avidov-Ungar & Reingold, 2018). Even when the need for change is widely understood, differences between the perceptions, interests and attitudes of diverse policy actors may spawn conflicts that impede the implementation process (Bell & Stevenson, 2006). Thus, the implementation of educational change is frequently derailed for a variety of reasons.

For example, implementation may be undermined by the unilateral decisions of policymakers and/or educational leaders that fail to involve educators and stakeholders (Farhadi & Winton, 2022; Harris, 2019; Starr, 2019). Educator and stakeholder involvement are crucial because their acceptance of the need for change, the conversations held among them, and their inclusion in reforms contribute to successful implementation (Avidov-Ungar & Reingold, 2018; Starr, 2019). In addition, the interconnected structures and processes for educational change, policy, reform and improvement must be aligned and coordinated to realize the goals of change.

Educational Change, Policy, Reform and Improvement

The concepts of educational change, policy, reform and improvement intersect and interact in many ways (Avidov-Ungar & Reingold, 2018; Robinson, 2018; Starr, 2019; Viennet & Pont, 2017). Cerna (2013) states that policy change entails new and innovative policies or gradual shifts in existing structures. Similarly, Gu et al. (2018, p. 386) state that 'policy enactment is, in essence, about change' because successful policy enactment is reliant upon increased capacity for change. Bell and Stevenson also argue that education policy and educational change are inextricably linked because change is a key driver of the policy process (Bell & Stevenson, 2006). Policy and change are also inextricably intertwined with educational improvement because policy reforms and structural changes are integral to the continuous improvement of schools and education systems (Pont, 2018). Given these numerous interconnections, the leaders of educational change must approach the process in a cohesive and integrated way.

Leaders of Educational Change

Harris and Jones (2020, p. 6) state that 'leadership remains the most potent lever in any change or improvement process'. Effective leaders of change systematically build the capacity of individuals and groups to make informed decisions and engage in associated actions (Fullan, 2020). They also demonstrate moral purpose, understand the change process, build positive relationships, advance knowledge creation and deep learning, and create coherence. At its core, the leadership of change is not about mobilizing others to solve problems that already have solutions; it is about helping others to confront problems that have never been successfully resolved. Moreover, the more complex the change, the more that the people directly impacted by the problem must be part of the solution (Fullan, 2020). Learning is also integral to the leadership of change because 'leading change is about helping others to focus and learn' (Fullan, 2020, p. 60). In Hargreaves and Shirley's (2012) view, the leadership of change is not so much about managing the delivery of mandated reforms, but about developing shared and sustainable ownership for innovating and changing together.

In the literature, different strategies are suggested for the leadership of change. For example, Greene and McShane (2018) recommend:

(1) focusing on creating the conditions for quality teaching and learning rather than targeting unrealistic goals;
(2) securing a strong base of political support through public dialogue, debate and consensus-building;
(3) acknowledging that research evidence informs choices but does not dictate universal courses of action; and
(4) considering the complexity of education reform, including the diverse contexts in which it occurs.

These and other leadership strategies are utilized by teachers and school, district and system leaders to advance educational change.

Teachers

Within the field of educational research, mounting evidence has confirmed the crucial role of teachers in educational change, policy reforms, and school and system improvement (Bangs & Frost, 2016; Biesta, 2016; Broekman, 2016; Evers & Kneyber, 2016; Farhadi & Winton, 2022; Harris, 2019). Teacher expertise and innovation are indispensable in all stages of the policy process, from policy design and development to review and evaluation (Farhadi & Winton, 2022; Harris & Jones, 2020). As central policy actors, teachers lead the implementation of a plethora of policies every day, including policies for curriculum, assessment, student discipline and technology integration. Throughout the policy process, teachers adapt policies to their diverse classroom and school contexts to support the learning, well-being and success of their students. Consequently, the successful development of education systems is highly dependent upon teachers as main partners in education policies and reforms (Bangs & Frost, 2016). Given teachers' pivotal roles, policymakers are well advised to involve teachers in all aspects of the policy process, listen to their advice, value their expertise, and afford them opportunities to innovate and experiment with education policy as an integral part of their work (Broekman, 2016).

School Leaders

Multiple studies have shown that school leadership impacts student outcomes, establishes the conditions for learning and advances school improvement through the enactment of specific leadership practices (Leithwood et al., 2020; Pont, 2020). As lynchpins in administrative hierarchies, school leaders serve as local leaders and partners in the implementation of educational reforms at the school level (Avidov-Ungar & Reingold, 2018). Effective school leaders build positive relationships, trust and credibility with the students, teachers, support staff, families and communities that they serve (Robinson, 2018). They also learn from and network with other school leaders and demonstrate courage in tackling difficult problems (Hargreaves & Shirley, 2012; Robinson, 2011). In addition, school leaders recognize that learning *in* leadership and leadership *as* learning are integral to the successful leadership of change (Robertson, 2018). By adopting a learning disposition, leaders position themselves to confront the complex challenges facing schools, and actively build and reinforce school capacity for change (Harris & Jones, 2020; Quinn & Fullan, 2018; Robertson, 2018; Robinson, 2018).

School leaders also act as gatekeepers of educational change who play pivotal roles in determining the outcome of internal and external innovations (Fullan, 2016). In successful schools, school leaders use education policies and reforms as opportunities for change. They support policy enactment and educational change by facilitating school and community engagement and harnessing collective ideas, experiences, relationships and knowledge to advance shared values and goals (Gu et al., 2018). School leaders also advance positive student outcomes by collaboratively developing school improvement goals, allocating essential human and financial resources for the achievement of the goals, supporting quality teaching and learning, providing professional development and creating safe and orderly learning environments (Robinson, 2011, 2018). Harris et al. (2022) contend that school leaders are, in effect, system leaders whose presence, actions and influence shape, define and maintain education systems. School leaders are well positioned to inform and guide educational change because they know children and youth and are intimately acquainted with the daily challenges and struggles that students and educators face. Therefore, the voices of school leaders must be heard for meaningful change to occur (Harris et al., 2022).

District Leaders

Whether it is a new policy, programme or practice, the initiation of educational change rarely occurs without champions and advocates, chief among them district leaders (Fullan, 2016). When district leaders are not interested in proposed changes, little may happen, but when their interest is sparked, superintendents and central office staff can furnish the requisite authority, resources and supports for educational change (Fullan, 2016). District leaders support change by concentrating school improvement efforts on a few goals and strategies aimed at enhanced student learning (Westover, 2020). They construct supportive mechanisms that advance leadership, teaching, learning and the development of communal expertise through job-embedded professional learning. As well, district leaders assist schools in overcoming problems of practice and barriers to educational change (Westover, 2020).

District leaders employ various leadership strategies to positively influence school improvement and student outcomes (DuFour & Marzano, 2011). Effective district leaders collaborate with elected school board members, district staff, and school leaders to articulate clear, non-negotiable student achievement goals for the district, individual schools, and subgroups of students. District leaders also construct supportive frameworks for realizing these goals. By clearly communicating district goals, strategies for achieving them and indicators for monitoring progress towards them, district leaders create the conditions for successful change (DuFour & Marzano, 2011).

Although they reinforce non-negotiables in school and system improvement, district leaders recognize the unique contexts of each school, and give school leaders the leeway to guide their schools towards improvement within the boundaries of district goals (DuFour & Marzano, 2011). District leaders also widely distribute information about why improvements are needed, and create guiding coalitions to champion improvement efforts. They ensure that district priorities are understood and acted upon and promote common understandings of targeted instructional practices. In addition, they concentrate on a few priorities and avoid overloading schools with multiple, uncoordinated improvement initiatives. District leaders support capacity-building by investing in job-embedded, collaborative professional learning for teachers and school leaders. They support continuous improvement through clear and consistent messages and ongoing, two-way communication with everyone involved. Very importantly, effective district leaders collaborate with educators and stakeholders and solicit and act upon their feedback as they continuously monitor and adjust improvement efforts (DuFour & Marzano, 2011; Leithwood, 2013).

System Leaders

Like their district counterparts, system leaders play major roles in creating the conditions for continuous improvement and educational change (Sharratt & Planche, 2016). System leaders build the capacity for change in a variety of ways, including the promotion of shared visions, the creation of collaborative cultures, the provision of consistent messaging and the reinforcement of accountability with appropriate supports (Quinn & Fullan, 2018). As well, they concentrate resources on key priorities, develop leaders at all levels of education who are catalysts for change and construct horizontal and vertical processes that foster clarity, innovation, sharing and the celebration of successes (Quinn & Fullan, 2018).

Although informal and formal leaders play important roles in improvement processes, system leaders occupy influential positions as lead learners and champions of school improvement processes (Sharratt & Planche, 2016). They ensure that all stakeholders have a voice and choice in new initiatives, and build positive relationships and partnerships with many different stakeholder groups. System leaders also carefully consider the current roles and responsibilities of educators and the additional work entailed in improvement activities. System leaders value all aspects of collaborative inquiry, learning and work, and recognize the importance of implementing and sustaining structural and cultural conditions that enable lasting improvements (Sharratt & Planche, 2016). Very importantly, they assist school and district educators with the identification, prevention and resolution of barriers to educational change that confound change initiatives everywhere.

Barriers to Educational Change

Unfortunately, many educational change initiatives and reforms are unsuccessful (Fullan, 2016; Greene & McShane, 2018; Robinson, 2018). Although the vast majority of education reformers act in good faith and in the best interest of students, successive education reforms continue to fall short of their intended outcomes (Greene & McShane, 2018). This is partly due to the difficult trade-offs inherent in education reform. In particular, the conflicting opinions and priorities of various education stakeholders create difficult choices for school and system leaders. Thus, education reform is difficult, uncertain and often challenging work (Greene & McShane, 2018).

Robinson (2018) contends that planned changes often fail because the leaders who plan them underestimate the complexity of implementation and fail to consider the beliefs, values, and priorities of the implementers. The most difficult aspect of educational change is not planning but implementation because the latter involves the uncertainty and complexity of integrating and aligning new practices with hundreds of established practices. Consequently, for change to succeed, leaders must concentrate on the established practices that they wish to replace, not just the new alternatives that they are recommending. This requires a major shift in leader focus from compliance with change agendas to collaborative inquiry and critical evaluation of the merits of existing and proposed practices. It also necessitates a move away from ensuring the compliance of implementers, to facilitating the authentic engagement of implementers. Thus, successful change requires strong, sustained coalitions of change leaders and implementers built on trust and shared understandings, and supportive structures, interpersonal processes, and constant leader vigilance (Robinson, 2018).

Fullan (2016) posits that educational change will always fail until essential implementation infrastructures and processes are developed that support teachers in acquiring and applying new knowledge, skills, and understandings. Key to successful implementation is the realisation that improvement plans are for the implementers, not the planners, and planning and actions must be integrated to support changes in practice. To this end, the involvement and leadership of teachers in all stages of the policy process is essential (Evers & Kneyber, 2016; Harris, 2019). As co-creators of educational change, teacher agency, leadership and collaboration are indispensable (Harris, 2019).

In recommending strategies for successful change, Wagen and Keegan (2013) highlight the importance of creating a sense of urgency, choosing a priority and sticking with it, holding high expectations for all students, and involving school and system leaders more in instructional leadership. They also advocate distributed leadership that empowers groups of educators to share their expertise and guide improvement, and the creation of administrative teams capable of simultaneously managing schools and school systems and leading school and system improvement (Wagner & Kegan, 2013).

Enacting meaningful and effective change takes considerable time, from two to three years for specific innovations, and from 5 to 10 years for large-scale renewal and system reforms (Fullan, 2016; Hall & Hord, 2015). Therefore, a gradual, phased-in approach works well in implementing improvements over time. Adequate funding and resources are also integral to the successful launch, implementation and sustainability of educational change.

Understanding why most educational changes fail requires in-depth analysis that goes beyond technical problems such as shortfalls in materials, professional development and leadership support (Fullan, 2016). Educational change fails partly because of the flawed assumptions of change planners, and partly because the substantial problems inherent in educational change defy easy solutions. Moreover, educational change often founders due to too little consideration of local contexts and cultures, and too much emphasis on planning at the expense of action (Fullan, 2016). In addition, Hall and Hord (2020) argue that many planned changes in education fail because educational change is not accomplished by simply adopting policies, rendering leadership decisions, having two-day summer workshops for teachers, or delivering new curricula and technology to schools.

Instead, change is an incremental process through which individuals and organizations gradually move as they learn new programs, practices and policies, and become skilled and competent in implementing them.

Many planned changes also fail because there is an expectation that desired outcomes will automatically materialize by virtue of being announced, which is not the case (Hall & Hord, 2020). When attention is narrowly focused on desired outcomes, and the complex realities of implementing change are overlooked, many planned changes fall short. In addition, change efforts founder when all members of schools and education systems do not receive adequate assistance and support from above, including school and district leaders (Hall & Hord, 2020). Educational change also falters due to flawed planning processes, inadequate implementation supports, and lack of teacher engagement.

Flawed Planning Processes

Although considerable research evidence has reinforced the key features of good planning, it does not typically happen in practice (Fullan, 2016). Often, change plans are too general, negative, complicated and unworkable in practice. On top of these shortcomings, fragmented plans create extra, unnecessary work for educators because they require numerous meetings and multiple edits that consume educators' time and effort. Thus, flawed planning processes can seriously undermine the successful implementation of change (Fullan, 2016).

Inadequate Implementation Supports

Educational change will not result in targeted improvements unless supportive structures and interpersonal processes are put in place (Robinson, 2018). Too often, educators are asked to make giant leaps from their established practices to new practices without adequate implementation supports (Hall & Hord, 2020). In particular, the lack of time, resources, capacity for change and professional development form formidable barriers to the implementation of change (Hall & Hord, 2020; Harris & Jones, 2020).

Lack of Teacher Engagement

The failure to engage teachers impedes change initiatives because 'educational change depends on what teachers do and think – it's as simple and as complex as that' (Fullan, 2016, p. 97). Therefore, educational change will continue to fail until supportive infrastructures and processes are developed that actively engage teachers in the acquisition and application of new knowledge and skills (Fullan, 2016).

Over the past decade, the education policy landscape has undergone major changes but the core challenges confronting teacher and leaders have remained essentially the same (Harris & Jones, 2020). Teachers are caught between increased demands for student performance, policy implementation and instructional excellence on the one hand, and the difficult life circumstances that many students face, on the other. Moreover, the collective experience, knowledge, and wisdom of teachers and leaders are often overlooked by policymakers as they introduce short-term interventions from other jurisdictions that are not workable in local contexts (Bangs & Frost, 2016; Broekman, 2016; Harris & Jones, 2020). Therefore, policymakers need to include teachers more in policy debates and decisions and listen to the professionals and support staff within their own school systems who are on the front lines of teaching and learning every day (Bangs & Frost, 2016; Broekman, 2016; Harris & Jones, 2020). By ensuring meaningful teacher engagement, strong buy-in, ownership and supports can be created for educational change.

Supports for Educational Change

While the barriers to educational change are daunting, effective strategies for overcoming them have been identified in the literature. Impactful educational change is supported by a variety of proven strategies, including a laser-like focus on teaching and learning, meaningful parent and family engagement, professional learning communities, positive school cultures, distributed leadership and ongoing professional learning centred on collaborative inquiry (Harris & Jones, 2020). In addition, specific school leadership practices have been shown to be effective in advancing equity, including setting goals and directions, managing competing priorities, coordinating and integrating improvement activities, building collaborative school cultures, and tailoring leadership to cultural norms and expectations (Harris & Jones, 2020). These practices have been identified by other scholars, including Michael Fullan, who argues that achieving meaningful change in education systems, schools and classrooms requires (a) setting priorities and focusing on a small number of ambitious goals; (b) ensuring that teaching and learning are the heart of the matter; (c) involving everyone in the school and/or education system from the start; (d) building individual and group capacity to enact the change; and (e) transparently sharing information about progress and setbacks in implementing the change and exchanging ideas for improving student outcomes (Fullan, 2016). Thus, a wide array of supports for educational change are identified in the literature, including teacher leadership; collaborative planning processes, cultures and inquiry; implementation bridges; professional learning; professional capital; and coherence.

Teacher Leadership

Teacher leadership has been a pillar of educational change and improvement for many years (Bangs & Frost, 2016; Berry et al., 2016; Broekman, 2016; Harris, 2019). In fact, teacher agency and professional influence are increasingly recognized as foundational elements in school and system improvement (Harris, 2019). Mounting evidence about teacher leadership indicates that when teachers work purposefully, collectively and collaboratively, they can significantly influence both policy and practice. As skilled professionals, teachers exercise their leadership by upholding core values, developing and pursuing visions of improved teaching practice, and identifying and rectifying problems in practice. They also influence school cultures, support their own professional learning and that of their colleagues, and contribute to policy development (Bangs & Frost, 2016).

Teacher leadership is strengthened by government-backed policies that promote teacher agency, self-efficacy, participation, voice and leadership. Bangs and Frost (2016) recommend seven strategies for creating and enabling policy environments that promote teacher leadership, including providing teachers with opportunities to lead the development and improvement of teaching practice, guaranteeing teachers the right to be heard at all levels of policymaking, supporting teachers in guiding their own professional development and recognizing teachers' vital role in building collaborative relationships with parents and the wider community.

If schools are to succeed in meeting the needs of all students, teachers' roles must change dramatically so that they can exercise leadership and utilise their ideas and expertise to advance policies and pedagogical practices (Berry et al., 2016). Nations like Finland and Singapore have built successful education systems based on teacher development and leadership. To achieve these ends, governments intentionally created policies and programs that enabled teachers to learn from one another and share their expertise. Moreover, they enacted policies that supported teaching as a career, and invested heavily in pre-service and in-service teacher education. As evidenced in these and other education systems, strengthening teacher leadership supports successful change because educators need to learn and lead together as schools confront rapid change, increased complexity, and volatile conditions (Berry et al., 2016). In the words of Harris (2019, p. 123), 'teachers as the co-constructors of educational change and key contributors to policy making is an idea that is long overdue in many education systems'.

Collaborative Planning Processes

Collaborative planning processes enable teachers and educational leaders to collegially develop plans that are grounded in good change processes that promote clarity, capacity-building and shared ownership (Fullan, 2016). In addition, plans need to be clear and readily adaptable to changing conditions. Straightforward monitoring is also essential, so that adjustments can be easily made without the need for cumbersome and time-consuming measurements. Very importantly, educational leaders must engage the people who are doing the work on the ground because they have access to essential information that policymakers don't have. If leaders do not collaborate with frontline workers, especially teachers, the planning of educational change fails every time (Fullan, 2016).

Collaborative Cultures

A significant body of research has demonstrated the importance of collaborative school and system cultures to meaningful educational change (Saphier, 2018). The creation of collaborative cultures requires changes in thinking and practice, the joint effort of everyone involved (including students, parents, teachers and leaders), and the leadership of 'lead learners' who model learning and facilitate it in others (Azorin & Fullan, 2022).

In deeply collaborative cultures, teachers and educational leaders engage in problem-solving centred on the identification of learning issues and the selection of appropriate responses from their professional repertoires (Saphier, 2018). Based on decades of research, scholars have identified seven key elements of collaborative Adult Professional Cultures (APCs):

(1) Frequent teaching in the presence of other adults (public teaching);
(2) Safety to take risks and be vulnerable in front of colleagues;
(3) Constant learning about high-expertise teaching;
(4) Deep collaboration and deliberate design for interdependent work and joint responsibility for student results;
(5) Constant, non-defensive use of data to refocus teaching;
(6) Urgency and press to reach all students and do better for our disadvantaged students; and
(7) Honest, open communication and the ability to have difficult conversations.
(Saphier, 2018, p. 96)

At the school level, leaders play pivotal roles in ensuring that schools are amenable to the creation of collaborative cultures and collegial professional networks (Azorin & Fullan, 2022). School leaders establish and sustain collaborative cultures by building trust, supporting risk-taking, enabling staff to get to know each other, and being visible in classrooms and school halls. Moreover, they provide stable and approachable, relational leadership by frequently conversing with staff, participating in all school professional development, and protecting staff from the behaviour of toxic people. In these ways, school leaders build the trust and positive relationships that are integral to collaborative cultures (Saphier, 2018).

Collaborative Inquiry

With collaborative inquiry, educators build communal expertise by joining forces to analyse evidence of student learning, identify learning challenges and try various instructional strategies to improve student learning (Westover, 2020). By focusing on the identification of teaching and leadership practices that have the greatest impact on student learning, collaborative inquiry promotes enhanced teaching practices for the benefit all learners. Collaborative inquiry is central to educational change because it enables educators to identify the necessary conditions for change at different times and in varied school and classroom contexts

(Robinson, 2018). Robust collaborative inquiry is at the heart of high-impact, job-embedded professional learning that occurs among and between teachers and school and district leaders. Moreover, feedback loops accommodate the frequent and timely sharing of evidence of student learning during collaborative inquiry, and inform improvement efforts at the district, school and classroom levels (Westover, 2020).

Implementation Bridges

Hall and Hord (2015, 2020) use the image of an Implementation Bridge to describe the importance of implementation supports to successful change. On the left is a school or school system perched on a cliff and engaged in current practices. On the right are the desired student outcomes that the school or school system is working toward, also perched on a cliff. The two are connected by an implementation bridge that spans the deep chasm between them. To cross the bridge and achieve the desired student outcomes, teachers and leaders require multiple supports to enact new policies, practices, and programs. These supports include time, professional development, resources and supportive leadership.

When educators access essential supports, they gradually move across the bridge and learn to change their practices so that desired student outcomes are realized. However, when essential supports are missing, educators may fall into the chasm as they try to take giant leaps forward without adequate reinforcement. Moreover, when several concurrent changes are implemented, multiple implementation bridges must be constructed and crossed simultaneously, which presents many challenges for teachers and educational leaders (Hall & Hord, 2015, 2020).

Professional Learning

Teachers and educational leaders require ongoing professional learning opportunities that equip them to implement educational change. In particular, practical, job-embedded professional learning helps educators to develop the knowledge, skills and competencies that they require to implement evidence-based practices and enhance key aspects of their daily work, such as data collection, analysis and utilization; lesson planning; classroom instruction; responding to diverse student learning needs; monitoring, assessing and evaluating student progress over time; and determining the impact of school improvement initiatives on teaching and learning (Bernhardt, 2018).

It is important to note that not all forms of professional learning are equally effective. In their review of several studies of teacher training in public schools, Fixsen et al. (2009) found that training that consisted of theory, discussion, and demonstration resulted in a low percentage of teachers implementing new skills in the classroom. However, training that included on-the-job coaching was associated with significant gains in teachers' knowledge and skills, and the implementation of new skills in their classrooms.

Professional Capital

Campbell (2018, p. 117) argues that the future of educational changes depends upon the recognition and prioritization of professional capital that is led by, for and with the teaching profession. Amid heightened global interest in strategies for developing teachers and teaching that support enhanced student outcomes and whole system reforms, there is a growing recognition of the centrality and importance of teachers in all aspects of school improvement. As a result, teacher professional learning and the development of professional capital have garnered increased attention. Professional capital is comprised of three, interconnected dimensions – human capital, social capital and decisional capital (Campbell, 2018).

Human capital, which centres on individual talent and the development of essential knowledge and skills, is often at the heart of education system policies for teacher development (Campbell, 2018). Policies that support the recruitment, preparation, development and retention of teachers help build human capital. In addition, professional development that is tailored to teachers' varied career stages, work contexts, and personal circumstances is key. Because there is no one-size-fits-all approach to teacher professional development, high quality, differentiated pre-service and in-service teacher education are required to meet teachers' professional learning needs at each stage of their careers (Campbell, 2018).

Robertson (2018) contends that investment in human capital to ensure that every teacher and leader develops to their full potential is central to educational change. Moreover, the development of agency in educational leaders increases their readiness and capacity to lead, act, and respond to policy directions with moral purpose. Leaders with a high level of agency have the confidence to challenge others by posing questions that query and problematize practice. They engage in the sometimes difficult conversations that are essential to change, and are supported by fellow leaders who are confronting similar challenges. As school leaders create and share new knowledge with their counterparts from other schools, leader agency is strengthened at the individual and school levels. Leaders who build agency and efficacy, two vibrant and evolving elements of leadership, step up and take responsibility for making a difference, even when it is a daunting task (Robertson, 2018).

Social capital is built through teacher collaboration with each other and with other professionals within and outside their schools (Campbell, 2018). Various kinds of professional collaboration are vital to educational change, including coaching, mentoring, peer observation, co-teaching, professional learning communities, and collegial networks. Often, these networks involve partner organizations, such as teachers' unions, professional associations, universities and community agencies. In general, teachers appreciate collaborative learning experiences that are practical and pertinent to their classroom contexts, their students' learning needs, and their own professional development goals. Educational change is advanced by collaborative learning activities when teachers observe, learn, share and connect with their school colleagues and outside professionals (Campbell, 2018).

Daly (2018) also highlights the importance of social capital in educational change, especially the interactions between teachers and school leaders and the cultures that they co-create. The quantity and quality of social ties between and among educators, and the formal and informal roles in schools and districts, are prime considerations. A whole system approach is needed to address the district and community contexts of schools, the web of social interactions in education systems, and the interdependent horizontal and vertical interfaces that occur within these complex systems. Therefore, achieving meaningful change in twenty-first-century education systems requires a heightened emphasis on relationships at all levels of the systems, ongoing investment in human and social capital, and the development of knowledge and intellectual capital among educators who reside in interconnected and interdependent social networks (Daly, 2018).

Decisional capital entails the exercise of teacher agency, responsibility, and professional judgment as trusted professionals and members of a well-regarded profession (Campbell, 2018). Through the exercise of professional judgment, teachers share their knowledge and practices and participate in networks of influence within and across schools and education systems. When making difficult decisions and choices in complex work environments, teachers rely on their competence, insights, knowledge, professional judgment, and ability to improvise. Thus, teacher choice, voice, judgement and leadership are central to educational change. System-, school- and teacher-directed professional development all play a role in building decisional capital. At the system level, policies and curricular reforms must be accompanied by adequate resources and professional development opportunities. At the school level, school improvement goals and plans impact teachers' collaborative learning priorities. At the classroom level, the learning needs of teachers and students shape teachers' voice and choice in professional development options. Thus, the exercise of decisional capital by professionals at all levels of education is critical to new forms of collaborative professionalism (Campbell, 2018).

Coherence

Coherence is a change strategy that develops the cultures of whole systems, integrates these systems horizontally and vertically around core beliefs, and enables the actions and interactions of policy actors at all levels of the systems as they navigate rapidly changing environments (Quinn & Fullan, 2018). Coherence is unwaveringly focused on whole education systems, pedagogical practices and causal pathways that support measurable student progress. Given the fluidity of education systems, coherence requires a shared, in-depth understanding among individuals and groups of educators about the nature of the work, as well as purposeful interactions that enable professional collaboration on shared agendas. In their Nonlinear Coherence Framework, Quinn and Fullan (2018) combine several supports for educational change with educational leadership to describe how successful change looks in practice.

Nonlinear Coherence Framework

After two decades of failed policy attempts at whole system change through accountability mechanisms and education standards, a new approach is required (Quinn & Fullan, 2018). Key to this approach is fostering whole system cultures of growth and innovation, catalysing ecosystems of policy actors, and building coherence as a supportive framework for change. Accordingly, the authors' Nonlinear Coherence Framework is comprised of four interdependent components: (1) focusing direction; (2) cultivating collaborative cultures; (3) deepening learning; and (4) securing accountability. All four components are connected and reinforced by leadership, which forms the hub of the framework.

Focusing Direction

To focus direction, educators must achieve clarity about their own deep moral purpose while also building clarity of common purpose, capacity and commitment to change among others (Quinn & Fullan, 2018). As more educators recognize what needs to be done and their role in achieving it, coherence is built. Key to this process is focusing on a few goals, limiting priorities, and reducing the 'initiative clutter' caused by too many competing reform efforts that distract and overwhelm educators. In addition to streamlined goals, change leadership is required that fosters common understandings and mobilizes collective action. In this way, the directional visions of education systems are operationalized through purposeful actions (Quinn & Fullan, 2018).

Cultivating Collaborative Cultures

The second component of the coherence framework, cultivating collaborative cultures, entails the construction of strong system cultures that encourage risk-taking, promote collaborative problem-solving, nurture talent, build capacity and establish mechanisms for system-wide knowledge creation, dissemination and sharing. Lead learners build collaborative cultures by modelling and promoting active learning, supporting leadership development, and developing horizontal and vertical relationships. Leaders also promote pedagogy that enhances student learning, and nurture professional teams, networks and practices that build momentum for change. Through these collegial efforts, collaborative cultures are built within and between schools and districts, and collective efficacy for change is augmented (Quinn & Fullan, 2018).

Deepening Learning

The third component, deepening learning, involves the transformation of learning through clear learning outcomes, precise pedagogies that support the outcomes, and reconceptualized learning frameworks and organizational mechanisms that move practice beyond the status quo (Quinn & Fullan, 2018). Adapting learning to turbulent global conditions necessitates the empowerment of *all* students to innovate, apply their learning to novel situations, and contribute to the advancement of humanity. It also requires the establishment of new roles and responsibilities among students, teachers, families, educational leaders, and local and global communities.

Enabling deep learning advances educational change in several ways. Deep learning makes school more relevant to students, galvanizes them into action, develops moral purpose, nurtures relationships, and prepares students for the realities of a rapidly changing world. Deep learning also enables students to acquire and apply twenty-first-century knowledge and skills in pivotal domains, such as character, citizenship, collaboration, communication, creativity and critical thinking (Fullan, 2020).

Deep student learning occurs when students become agents of change and assume more responsibility for their own learning. Deep educator learning occurs when educators engage in collaborative inquiry that is fostered by supportive cultures, resources, structures and technologies. Deep system learning occurs as school districts establish common language, practices, and mechanisms for knowledge generation and dissemination that support the implementation of change (Quinn & Fullan, 2018).

Securing Accountability

The fourth component, securing accountability, is achieved by attending to the first three components of the framework. By focusing direction on a few priorities, creating collaborative cultures and deepening learning, education systems build capacity, increase collective action and improve learning for everyone. As educators work on the first three components, they create the conditions for individual and collective responsibility and accountability for the results achieved (Quinn & Fullan, 2018).

Leadership of Coherence

Last but not least, leadership connects and integrates all four components by serving as the glue that holds the framework together (Quinn & Fullan, 2018). Educational leadership plays a pivotal role in promoting, advancing and continuing the never-ending work of coherence-making. Therefore, the coherence framework advocates new roles and skillsets for educational leaders who are committed to the advancement of whole system, deep learning cultures.

To do this, leaders must simultaneously build on existing strengths while highlighting urgently needed changes (Quinn & Fullan, 2018). They must also balance their contrasting roles as experts and apprentices who are constantly learning. Effective change leaders also experiment, learn from their failures and persevere through their reliance on the insights gained and lessons learned on change journeys. While strong leadership at all levels of education is required for successful change, Quinn and Fullan (2018) argue that district leadership from the middle is especially important. When district leadership is reinforced, capacity is increased within and across districts, districts become better partners with provincial and state governments, and district leadership becomes more effective in supporting schools and communities. As district, school and system leaders form the vanguard of educational change, they must change their practice to move schools and school systems forward. With its focus on educational leadership as the hub of educational change, Quinn and Fullan's (2018) Nonlinear Coherence Framework illustrates how change can be successfully led in a focused, collaborative and innovative way.

Conclusion

The leadership of educational change is a daunting process that is thwarted by the complexity of societal problems, exacerbated by global instability, and invigorated by the diligence, perseverance, ingenuity and dedication of educators who are determined to make a positive difference for students. The leadership of change impacts every facet of education and all educators and stakeholders around the globe. As educators confront the causes of failed changes and build supports for change, it is imperative that students remain the focus of their efforts, and student learning and well-being remain the overarching goals. By maintaining a laser-like focus on students and the changes that increase their life chances, educators can chart a path forward towards truly equitable and excellent education for the benefit of all. As we shall see in Chapter 10, however, the achievement of positive policy outcomes for students may be derailed by the unintended consequences of policies in education and in society, as a whole.

References

Avidov-Ungar, O., & Reingold, R. (2018). Israeli ministry of education district managers' and superintendents' role as educational leaders – Implementing the new policy for teachers' professional development. *International Journal of Leadership in Education*, *21*(3), 293–309. https://doi.org/10.1080/13603124.2016.1164900

Azorin, C., & Fullan, M. (2022). Leading new, deeper forms of collaborative cultures: Questions and pathways. *Journal of Educational Change*, *23*(3/4), 131–143. https://link.springer.com/article/10.1007%2Fs10833-021-09448-w

Bangs, J., & Frost, D. (2016). Non-positional teacher leadership: Distributed leadership and self-efficacy. In J. Evers & R. Kneyber (Eds.), *Flip the system: Changing education from the ground up* (pp. 91–107). Routledge.

Bell, L., & Stevenson, H. (2006). *Education policy: Process, themes and impact*. Routledge.

Bernhardt, V. L. (2018). *Data analysis for continuous school improvement* (4th ed.). Routledge.

Berry, B., Zeichner, N., & Evans, R. (2016). Teacher leadership: A reinvented teaching profession. In J. Evers & R. Kneyber (Eds.), *Flip the system: Changing education from the ground up* (pp. 209–225). Routledge.

Biesta, G. (2016). Good education and the teacher. In J. Evers & R. Kneyber (Eds.), *Flip the system: Changing education from the ground up* (pp. 79–90). Routledge.

Broekman, A. (2016). The effects of accountability: A case study from Indonesia. In J. Evers & R. Kneyber (Eds.), *Flip the system: Changing education from the ground up* (pp. 48–67). Routledge.

Campbell, C. (2018). Realizing professional capital by, for, and with the learning profession: Lessons from Canada. In H. J. Malone, S. Rincón-Gallardo, & K. Kew (Eds.), *Future directions of educational change: Social justice, professional capital, and systems change* (pp. 117–134). Routledge.

Cerna, L. (2013). *The nature of policy change and implementation: A review of different theoretical approaches*. OECD.

Cobb, C. D., Donaldson, M. L., & Mayer, A. P. (2013). Creating high leverage policies: A new framework to support policy development. *Berkeley Review of Education, 4*(2), 265–284. https://doi.org/10.5070/B84110010

Daly, A. J. (2018). Leading educational change in socially networked systems. In H. J. Malone, S. Rincón-Gallardo, & K. Kew (Eds.), *Future directions of educational change: Social justice, professional capital, and systems change* (pp. 151–161). Routledge.

DuFour, R., & Marzano, R. J. (2011). *Leaders of learning: How district, school and classroom leaders improve student achievement*. Solution Tree Press.

Evers, J., & Kneyber, R. (Eds.). (2016). *Flip the system: Changing education from the ground up*. Routledge.

Farhadi, B., & Winton, S. (2022). Ontario teachers' policy leadership during the COVID-19 pandemic. *Canadian Journal of Educational Administration and Policy, 200*, 49–62. http://doi.org/10.7202/1092707ar

Fixsen, D. L., Blase, K. A., Naoom, S. F., & Wallace, F. (2009). Core implementation components. *Research on Social Work Practice, 19*(5), 531–540. https://doi.org/10.1177/1049731509335549

Fullan, M. (2016). *The new meaning of educational change* (5th ed.). Teachers College Press.

Fullan, M. (2020). *Leading in a culture of change* (2nd ed.). Jossey-Bass.

Greene, J. P., & McShane, M. Q. (2018). Learning from failure. *Phi Delta Kappan International, 99*(8), 46–50.

Gu, Q., Sammons, P., & Chen, J. (2018). How principals of successful schools enact education policy: Perceptions and accounts from senior and middle leaders. *Leadership and Policy in Schools, 17*(3), 373–390. https://doi.org/10.1080/15700763.2018.1496344

Hall, G. E., & Hord, S. M. (2015). *Implementing change: Patterns, principles and potholes* (4th ed.). Pearson Education, Inc.

Hall, G. E., & Hord, S. M. (2020). *Implementing change: Patterns, principles and potholes* (5th ed.). Pearson Education, Inc.

Hargreaves, A., & Shirley, D. (2012). *The global fourth way: The quest for educational excellence.* Corwin.

Harris, A. (2019). Teacher leadership and educational change. *School Leadership & Management, 39*(2), 123–126. https://doi.org/10.1080/13632434.2019.1574964

Harris, A., Campbell, C., & Jones, M. (2022). A national discussion on education – So what for school leaders? *School Leadership & Management, 42*(5), 433–437. https://doi.org/10.1080/13632434.2022.2134665

Harris, A., & Jones, M. S. (2020). *System recall.* Corwin.

Harris, A., Jones, M., & Adams, D. (2016). Qualified to lead? A comparative, contextual and cultural view of educational policy borrowing. *Educational Research, 58*(2), 166–178. https://doi.org/10.1080/00131881.2016.1165412

Leithwood, K. (2013). *Strong districts and their leadership.* A Paper Commissioned by The Council of Ontario Directors of Education and the Institute for Educational Leadership.

Leithwood, K., Harris, A., & Hopkins, D. (2020). Seven strong claims about successful school leadership revisited. *School Leadership & Management, 40*(1), 5–22. http://doi.org/10.1080/13632434.2019.1596077

Pont, B. (2018). A comparative view of education system reform: Policy, politics, and people. In H. J. Malone, S. Rincón-Gallardo, & K. Kew (Eds.), *Future directions of educational change: Social justice, professional capital, and systems change* (pp. 171–187). Routledge.

Pont, B. (2020). A literature review of school leadership policy reforms. *European Journal of Education, 55*(2), 154–168. https://doi.org/10.1111/ejed.12398

Quinn, J., & Fullan, M. (2018). Coherence making: Whole system change strategy. In H. J. Malone, S. Rincón-Gallardo, & K. Kew (Eds.), *Future directions of educational change: Social justice, professional capital, and systems change* (pp. 223–237). Routledge.

Rincón-Gallardo, S. (2018a). In the pursuit of freedom and social justice: Four theses to reshape educational change. In H. J. Malone, S. Rincón-Gallardo, & K. Kew (Eds.), *Future directions of educational change: Social justice, professional capital, and systems change* (pp. 17–33). Routledge.

Rincón-Gallardo, S. (2018b). Social justice: Section introduction. In H. J. Malone, S. Rincón-Gallardo, & K. Kew (Eds.), *Future directions of educational change: Social justice, professional capital, and systems change* (pp. 11–15). Routledge.

Robertson, J. (2018). Building and sustaining capital in New Zealand education. In H. J. Malone, S. Rincón-Gallardo, & K. Kew (Eds.), *Future directions of educational change: Social justice, professional capital, and systems change* (pp. 135–150). Routledge.

Robinson, V. (2011). *Student-centered leadership.* John Wiley & Sons, Inc.

Robinson, V. (2018). *Reduce change to increase improvement.* Corwin.

Saphier, J. (2018). Strong adult professional culture: The indispensable ingredient for sustainable school improvement. In H. J. Malone, S. Rincón-Gallardo, & K. Kew (Eds.), *Future directions of educational change: Social justice, professional capital, and systems change* (pp. 93–116). Routledge.

Sharratt, L., & Planche, B. (2016). *Leading collaborative learning: Empowering excellence.* Corwin.

Shirley, D. (2018). The many future directions of educational change. In H. J. Malone, S. Rincón-Gallardo, & K. Kew (Eds.), *Future directions of educational change: Social justice, professional capital, and systems change* (pp. 1–7). Routledge.

Starr, K. (2019). *Education policy, neoliberalism, and leadership practice: A critical analysis.* Routledge.

Viennet, R., & Pont, B. (2017). *Education policy implementation: A literature review and proposed framework.* OECD Education Working Paper No. 162. OECD Publishing. https://doi.org/10.1787/fc467a64-en

Wagner, T., & Kegan, R. (2013). Bringing the outward and inward focus together. In M. Grogan (Ed.), *The Jossey-Bass reader on educational leadership* (3rd ed.) (pp. 220–254). John Wiley & Sons.

Westover, J. (2020). *Districts on the move: Leading a coherent system of continuous improvement.* Corwin Press, Inc.

Chapter 10

Navigating the Policy Process: Intended and Unintended Consequences

As the reader may have already ascertained, a policy is rarely, if ever, implemented as envisioned. This chapter explores how variations in policy development, establishment and/or implementation may function to alter the intended 'trajectory' of the policy. For example, every policy has a certain life expectancy, which may result in some policies being ignored until they are eventually abandoned. Conversely, other more effective policies may eventually become routinized until they are subsumed into the culture of the educational establishment. When this happens, they become a part of the school or organizational culture and become transformed from policy initiative into cultural artefact. When this occurs, the policy may still be effective, but it is no longer obvious as policy and simply becomes 'the way that things are done around here!' This chapter deals with some of those intended and unintended consequences of policy. In public policy, including education policy, unintended consequences are unplanned outcomes that may be positive, negative, or neutral in nature (Cheong et al., 2016). Unintended consequences permeate policymaking because of the complexity of social and political life, and because every policy enactment involves multiple stakeholders with different intentions, desires, and purposes (Karapin & Feldman, 2016). Some unintended consequences appear immediately, while others emerge over time. As we shall see in this chapter, unintended policy consequences are well documented in the literature, and have manifested themselves in education systems around the globe (Amrein-Beardsley, 2009; Cheong et al., 2016; Picton-Howell, 2022; Urbanovič et al., 2021).

A Historical Perspective

Apparently, John Locke was one of the first individuals to discuss unintended consequences of policy initiatives. In this case, he was writing to M.P. Sir John Somers regarding unintended issues relating to interest rate regulation. Currently, it may behoove parliamentarians to refresh their knowledge of Locke's argument so that interest rate regulation may no longer be used as a blunt instrument to encourage or discourage inflation and recession.

Adam Smith, of *The Wealth of Nations* fame, also discussed this concept in his work on *The Theory of Moral Sentiments*, first published in 1759 (Smith, 2005). Somewhat later, to paraphrase Friedrich Engels's (1886) cynical take on consequences, Engels believed that, although the ends of policy action may be intended, the actual results that follow may not be intended. And, when results do seem to correspond to the end intended, they ultimately have consequences *other* than those intended. There may be no escape from unintended consequences of policy action.

Of further historical note, it was Robert K. Merton who coined the term 'unintended consequences' (White & Cooper, 2022), a concept which later became popularized. While social roles were a key component of Merton's theorizing, he maintained that individuals assume a 'status set' within the existing social structure that requires a specific set of expected behaviours (Holton, 2004). Should individuals *not* assume a congruent or congenial status set, hostilities may arise or resume during the implementation of the policy. The lesson to be learned here is that, once policy has been made, it often remains up to the implementers of that policy to resolve issues created but not attended to by the developers of that policy. Thus, policy is rarely implemented as envisioned.

This recognition of the fluidity of the policy process has led to the development of the 'law of unintended consequences,' which may be one of the most cited laws within the social sciences. The law claims that every purposeful act leads to results that are unintended and unforeseen, apart from those intended. Somewhat akin to Murphy's Law that claims that if anything can go wrong, it will, the law of unintended consequences has served as a cautionary that intervention in a complex system can lead to unanticipated consequences. Remember the American politician who claimed that the best way to calm global warming was to move the Earth just slightly out of its current orbit and away from the sun? There were a few mathematicians who leapt on this but, to date, not much progress has been made – fortunately. The law of unintended consequences serves to remind humanity that arrogance may result in disaster.

The Law of Unintended Consequences

The law of unintended consequences has been associated with chaos theory, but it is unlikely that a single butterfly could cause a tsunami, as has been postulated by adherents to this theory. However, the law of unintended consequences does imply that it is impossible to recognize all of the contingencies that are dependent upon a particular action. Uncertainty always accompanies policy creation or policy change simply because of the complexity and the constantly changing conditions of the society within which we live and make policy. Because of this, not every action can be foreseen in terms of consequences, intended or not. However, there are things that can be put into place that will ensure a greater degree of success when it comes to mitigating or ameliorating some of the unintended effects of a particular policy.

One such position is to think about the possible effects of change. Thinking in terms of what the policy will look like in a matter of months or years may be a useful exercise in striving to keep the policy current over time. Also, different people have different perspectives and should be consulted. Allowing intersectionality (Crenshaw, 1991) to guide policy choices or alternatives, along with a goodly dose of creativity, never hurts, it seems. Additionally, projecting least expected outcomes or possible scenarios allows the policy developer to gain some vision into what is possible in terms of consequences, both anticipated and unintended. This may be as simple as imagining the best possible outcomes as well as the worst possible outcomes. In addition, the existential question of why this policy is being created is always an important consideration. Furthermore, purpose may not necessarily be altruistic, as personal agendas may also be in play with any given policy initiative. Once the policy is in place, however, another force seems to propel the policy, independent of the policy architects. This is the implementation process and once in place, may be difficult to adjust. For this reason, it may be essential to determine if the policy decision can be changed or even reversed, if need be, particularly if the policy proves harmful to one or more segments of society.

After all is said and done, it is evident that policy tends to work within societal boundaries and, as such, policy analysts must recognize that policy development never exists in a vacuum. It is not a closed system and, so, unforeseen issues come into play whenever people come together to develop, initiate or implement policy. Thus, it also behooves the policy makers and implementers to be guided by ethics and respect for those who will be impacted by the eventual policy, regardless of whether those impacted are humans, animals or ecosystems.

The Policy Process

As has become evident by now, the policy process strives to create policy that is directed at a specific problem or issue that requires redress. This process attempts to address the necessary point(s) without creating a worse situation than that which may already exist. As a result, the formulation of the policy, at least in theory, attempts to recognize and mitigate as many areas of potential impact as possible. Of course, this is intended to prevent unexpected or unintended consequences from devaluing the policy, its formulation and its implementation (Deleon & Steelman, 2001).

Following are several examples of policies that have somehow 'gone rogue.' These malfunctions may have been introduced along with the policy process itself, or it may be that the policy initiative itself was flawed. However, in many cases, it is the interpretation of the policy that causes issues. Consequently, it is germane to ensure that the implementation of the policy is conducted by individuals who are clear on the concept of what it is that the policy intends. A second common issue relates to the timing and life span of the policy; in many instances, once created, policies are left to their own devices and are rarely reviewed or revised. Often, such policies become ignored and, by ignoring them, they become dysfunctional.

An Example of Policy Interpretation

Ms. Bela Kosoian, a Canadian citizen, was arrested in Laval, Quebec, for not holding on to an escalator handrail. The incident occurred at the Montmorency Metro station in 2009 (CBC News, 2009). Apparently, Ms. Kosoian was looking through her purse while descending the escalator when she was arrested in plain view of a sign that proclaimed 'Caution' and 'Hold Handrail.' She refused to follow the police officer awaiting her at the bottom of the escalator, refused to identify herself and claimed that she had done nothing wrong.

As a result, Ms. Kosoian was detained, given a $100 fine for disobeying the sign and an additional $320 fine for obstruction. By 2012, she had been acquitted of the infraction. However, she turned about and sued Montreal's transit authority, the city and one police officer for $45,000 (CBC News, 2019). Eventually, the case wound up in Supreme Court, where Ms. Kosoian was awarded $20,000 in damages (Darrah, 2019). The Supreme Court said the sign in the Metro station constituted a warning, rather than a law and the officer was wrong in stopping her and searching her for breaking a non-existent law. Apparently, Ms. Kosoian was under no legal obligation to hold onto the handrail. Ms. Kosoian was pleased the judge recognized the rule of law and agreed that she had done nothing wrong.

Intended and Unintended Consequences of Policy Implementation

The example provided above is an extreme instance of 'policy malfunction.' Clearly, the police officer involved was merely trying to ensure the safety and protection of the citizenry. His overzealousness led him to misinterpret – not the policy itself but its implementation – *how* the policy should be interpreted. He was inclined to view the policy as a law – or, at least, a rule. This interpretation was, to say the least, naïve, in that he did not entertain the consequences that would logically follow from such a rule. As pointed out by the Supreme Court, the perpetrator had not broken a law because not complying with the policy was not illegal. That is, the policy was not a law and, therefore, there were no legal ramifications for non-compliance. In fact, the policy was in place to encourage greater safety, not greater compliance.

This misinterpretation created a decade-long consequence, entirely unintended, whereby Ms. Kosoian sued for damages and won. It is safe to say that, in awarding damages, the Supreme Court recognized that the perpetrator had committed no crime. By this assessment, it is clear that this body of justice recognized the policy as a guideline, not as a law. The policy that resulted in the somewhat dictatorial signs that required people to 'Hold Handrail' and to exercise 'Caution' may not have been faulty. However, its interpretation and implementation led to a great deal of justifiable consternation.

As such, it may be safe to say that intended and unintended effects of a policy frequently vary widely, depending upon the organization and context within which they have been made. The particular type of policy model may also have beneficial or adverse effects on the policy itself, depending on implementation procedures and the interpretation of that policy by those charged with enforcing or addressing it.

Policies are typically instituted in order to neutralize or bolster underperforming policies that were enacted previously. An example of such a policy, presented in the first chapter of this volume, indicated that numerous large corporations and organizations are justifiably concerned with computer security. In attempting to protect sensitive and private or professional data, as well as to minimize the potential for servers and personal computers from being 'hacked' by outside, nefarious sources, such companies frequently require employees to change their passwords, often every 90 days or during a previously identified point during the fiscal year.

While this may have a standardizing effect because employees must comply with the policy in order to protect data from being stolen, such policies may have several consequences. Firstly, an intended consequence is the protection of sensitive data. Additionally, as this policy becomes ingrained in the workplace, it seems to disappear within a huge matrix of policies that preserve the creation, development and maintenance of the culture of that organization. However, there are also frequent unintended consequences of such a common sense policy. Employees may write down their new passwords or leave them in convenient places in case they forget that password. This, alone, renders the password protection policy vulnerable. Also, not everyone commits the password to a 'safe' haven and some employees prefer to remember the password. After several cycles of 'password roulette,' memories become fuzzy and passwords are frequently forgotten. While there is a relatively convenient password recovery system available, this most commonly requires the creation of a new password. This often merely contributes to further confusion and the generating of innumerable new passwords that not only render the password creator nervous, irritable and feeling vulnerable, it may also promote 'password paralysis,' a new and aggressive epidemic of employees who develop justifiable angst whenever they turn on their computers. Such insecurity and agitation is clearly unintended by a policy that merely seeks to reassure and convince people that their data and documentation is safe.

Preservation of Antiquated Policies

As policies become one with the culture of any organization, they tend to disappear from view and simply become a part of 'that's the way we do things.' This movement into the culture of the organization may take years, however. Some policies do not survive this and may become ignored to the point that they disappear, as well. These policies may constitute 'failed' policies, although they may also be policies that have not benefitted from review. As a result, such policies may stay on the books even though they are no longer useful.

One hilarious example constitutes an urban legend, although its value as an example of an antiquated policy cannot be disputed. This legend apparently comes from the University of Toronto. Although this policy has yet to be ascertained because it has not been verified and can no longer be found, it may serve as an example, hypothetical or not, of a policy that has not become defunct, only ignored.

It has been claimed that there is a policy, which has never been recanted, that states that students attending Victoria College at the University of Toronto cannot hitch their horses at the front of the building. It is fine for them to hitch their horses at the rear of Victoria College, but not at the front. What makes this hilarious is the fact that the policy must be at least a century old, if not older, by now. It is humorous to think that, in this day and age of electric cars and all manner of technological transport, one may still hitch a horse to (the rear of) a building that is now in the heart of a large world-city.

Why is this policy a remnant of a bygone age? If this policy still exists, it has likely become a policy that was not reviewed. Not reviewing policies is a common strategy because there is a cost incurred whenever a committee meets to create, interpret, implement or even review an existing policy. Although a review phase should be included in every policy document, the fact remains that it may be less expensive to ignore the policy than to rescind it. The result is that we occasionally get rewarded with interesting but useless policy initiatives that were once important considerations but which have more recently fallen prey to the vicissitudes of time. Unfortunately, it is not just antiquated policy that this occurs with. As technology surges forward in ever more maddening 'efficiencies,' even recent policies can become quickly out dated. This suggests that the review phase for any policy initiative should not be overlooked or treated in a cavalier manner.

Such a review phase allows for the monitoring of a policy so that all people impacted by the policy, including its creators, may become aware of possible issues related to that policy. This includes intended as well as any unintended consequences of the policy. This review phase may be formalized within the policy document or it may be less formal, particularly since resources and support for the policy may decrease after it has been implemented. Needless to say, the resultant policy is much more likely to be successful when a review phase is built into the policy process.

Other Considerations

Occasionally, even the best policy analysts shoot themselves in the foot. An awareness of the 'Laffer Curve' may be a useful construct to assist in keeping policy considerations 'real.' Coming from the world of economics, the Laffer curve (Hayes, 2022) describes the relationship between tax rates and revenue generated. Simply put, the Laffer curve implies that no revenue is generated when extreme tax rates – either extremely low or exceedingly high – are instituted. However, there is a tax rate between these two poles that will generate revenue. The key is to find the optimum or maximum revenue generated. If a tax rate is reduced, this increases buying power for citizens, who will spend it and, in so doing, will create more business demand and, in turn, more business activity. In the long run, this has the potential to spur and increase employment and overall productivity (Hayes, 2022).

Because of the various stresses and priorities among members of the society in general, the exact shape of the Laffer curve may change with specific conditions being met. One implication of this construct, however, is the notion that increasing tax rates beyond the ability of the citizenry to pay those taxes becomes counterproductive. While lower taxes may increase revenue because the tax base is more accessible for more people, this curve cannot be observed directly. It can only be estimated. As a result, any policies that are built around the Laffer curve will necessarily be extremely sensitive to not only intended consequences, but to unintended consequences, as well, due to the quixotic optimal tax rate that will generate the highest revenue at the lowest cost to the tax payer.

Certainly, an unintended consequence of a poorly engineered policy may result in a policy decision to raise taxes in order to generate more revenue. However, if the tax rate is too high, the opposite may occur and tax revenue may actually be reduced as capital leaves the economy in search of better options. Another unintended consequence may be that the average citizen may decide that earning a lot of money that is taxable may be counterproductive for them. The result, then, is to either work less to earn less money, or to go underground and not declare taxable income – in short, income tax evasion. A third option, when faced with taxes that act as a disincentive to work, is to invest in the time-honoured barter system, where there is a *quid pro quo* ethic in effect that allows some goods and services to be traded for others, depending on what the citizens require.

Almost all policies tend to have some unintended consequences even when they are successful policies that are formulated and implemented properly. What follows are two examples of wildly different policies that, while dissimilar, can be compared for a commentary on societal values.

The first example features respiratory syncytial virus (RSV), also known as human respiratory syncytial virus (hRSV) or human orthopneumovirus. Despite its various sophisticated names, this virus is very common and contagious, causing infections of the respiratory tract. While urgent medical attention may be required in severe cases, there are fewer than 1,000 cases identified each year in Canada. Typically, however, this is a common infection in young children, particularly those who are pre-school age or who are in the early years of schooling. Symptoms are similar to those of the common cold and may last from several days to several weeks. RSV, like COVID-19, is transmitted through airborne exposure.

Children frequently get colds, the flu and almost any childhood infection that can be transmitted from person to person. After all, children in school often bring colds and fevers home to democratically distribute them throughout the household. And, apparently, during the winter of 2022, we experienced a surge in RSV. Dr. Earl Rubin, director of the infectious diseases division at Montreal Children's Hospital claims the surge was part of the reason his hospital struggled with long wait times and a shortage of paediatric beds, similar to what the adult hospitals were experiencing during the peak of COVID-19. The triple threat of the flu, coronavirus variants and RSV are cause for concern (Shingler, 2022) and, of course, this warranted discussion over a talk show on CBC radio, where people called in to advise on appropriate policy. The 'research' question asked if closing day care and after school facilities would help to resolve this growing contagion.

Regardless of how one feels about COVID-19, it has inserted itself in the hearts and minds of a worldwide population, for better or worse. Combining this with a perceived threat, such as RSV, the radio population roundly decided that it would be politic to close day cares and after school care.

While this may make sense on the surface, it is to the credit of policy analysts that they did not jump on this. It was all too clear that one of the unintended consequences of closing day cares and after school care would be that parents would be 'held to ransom' in their own homes. Simply put, it would prevent parents from working and, given the scope of the erstwhile decision, it would definitely have an effect on the economy, locally and possibly nationally.

This is the same line of reasoning that has defined educators as an essential service in many areas across the country. Note that the term 'educators' refers to the people educating our children rather than to the process of education itself. It is germane to realize that children need to be in school so their parents can go to work. Thus, the education project may be less about the children's education than it is about maintaining a 'vibrant' economy. This has led some to dub teachers 'glorified babysitters.' In many parts of the country, if and when teachers or support staff threaten a strike action or proceed with a strike, they are frequently mandated back to work, not because of the negative impacts on student learning, but because of the negative impacts on parents, especially disrupted childcare.

Now, for the second example. Some years ago, in 2009, inside and outside garbage workers in Toronto went on strike (Lunau et al., 2009). The strike persisted for more than three weeks. Citizens were in danger of being swallowed up by their own garbage. Rats were making their way into places that rats are never welcome. Citizens who were normally respectful of city ordinances and bylaws decided that the best option to maintain their health and sanity during this time would be to make use of public garbage containers in order to keep their garbage to a minimum level at home. This created an unintended consequence. Driving through the city of Toronto during this three-week strike, one could see armed police protecting public garbage bins from those well-meaning citizens who just wanted to get rid of their garbage. The strikers were never mandated back to work.

It appears that garbage collection is not an essential service but the education of our youngsters is. What a wonderful incongruence these two approaches to potential policy issues creates. Education workers are mandated back to work as an essential service, implying that our children's educational welfare is paramount in people's minds, but garbage collection and the prevention of disease borne by rats and whatever else may be lurking out there is not as large a concern as our children's education. These wildly differing responses to societal issues would be better received if they had been orchestrated with an eye to what the real issues are and how they can best be dealt with in a fair and equitable manner. It appears that, in both examples, the potential closure of day care and afterschool facilities, and the garbage strike that was allowed to continue unabated reveal another challenge to the policymaking process. This challenge is the notion that policymakers may accept compromise for the sake of reaching an agreement. However, problems nascent in the policy process may not surface until the policy becomes implemented or not, as the case may be. Poor policy, cast in the light of other policies, inadequate or not, call attention to their own misapplication.

Causes of Unintended Consequences

In education as in every sphere of public policy, there are many different causes of unintended consequences. First and foremost, there is the unpredictable human element for, as Karapin and Feldman (2016, p. 441) remind us, 'no agent has complete control in the messy realm of human affairs'. Diverse stakeholders react to policies differently, based on their contrasting beliefs, values, priorities, and intentions. As a result, policies may inadvertently spawn a wide range of responses, from backlash and resistance to compensatory behaviour and heightened expectations.

Other scholars have also emphasized the primacy of the human element in education policies, including the unintended consequences that they produce. For example, Prus (2003) observed that, although education policies are intended to be structures that manage people, closer examination reveals that it is people who manage policy (Prus, 2003). Therefore, it is essential that policymakers attend to the full range of human responses that policies may generate. While not every aspect of educational policy is disputed or challenged, every aspect is subject to interpretation, reflection, and response. Given this reality, the implementation of policy may engender everything from cooperation, dedication, and compromise to disregard and conflict.

Considering this wide range of potential reactions, it is important for policymakers to incorporate group input and approval into policy development by providing opportunities for input, debate, and/or questions. This is an especially important consideration, given the potential changes that policies may engender, and the impact of these changes on the hopes, dreams, fears, and anxieties of educators. To be authentic, policymaking must include a careful examination of how people actually 'do things' in school systems, how they fit policies into their daily routines, and how they experience policies in real-world educational settings (Prus, 2003).

There are a multiplicity of reasons why things do not always go as planned. Policy is but one of those areas that is susceptible to error in concept, development and/or implementation. One of the most prevalent causes may well be human error. Cognitive, emotional and other biases may also be responsible for consequences that are unintended. However, the most likely cause, in addition to those already noted, is the simple fact that policymaking, like the chaotic world that it is attempting to control or direct, is extremely complex. No one can attend to all of the factors that may or may not come into play with the making and implementing of policy.

As early as 1936, Robert Merton addressed five potential causes of unanticipated or unintended consequences of policy creation and implementation. Firstly on the list was the notion of ignorance. Since it is not possible to anticipate everything, analysis must, by necessity, be incomplete. Secondly, errors in analysing the problem, including things that may or may not have worked in the past, also may or may not apply to the current situation. Thirdly, big picture/little picture thinking may also compromise results. When immediate interests override future goals, there will be unintended consequences that may relate more to chaos theory than to policy analysis. The lesson here is to keep the eyes on the horizon, rather than what is happening immediately.

However, this may not be possible in every circumstance. It then behooves the policy analysts to move to an incremental view of policy making that may be reviewed or revised with an eye to maintaining the currency of the policy through changing or challenging circumstances. This re-envisions Lindblom's (1959) incremental approach to policy. A fourth concern is the notion that basic values may negatively influence the eventual success of any given policy. It is possible, also, that basic values may be affected by a policy that has been in place for a length of time. Mutatis mutandis – we act and are acted upon. Finally, Merton (1996) addresses the notion that the fear of a particular consequence may encourage people to find a solution prior to the inception of the policy. As a result of this, the problem does not materialize and the policy may die aborning. A final consideration has been put forth as the danger of 'groupthink' (Vyse, 2017). A horrific example that comes to mind is the development and proliferation of the Nazi movement of World War II. In this case, horrendous acts were conducted that were clearly the concerted work of many people. These horrors the world still endures, as the consequences of this benighted period of humanity still struggle to be forgotten – or forgiven. This is not an isolated incident. Among archives that one would rather not think about are US government-funded covert operations that, among other things, have helped to establish the Taliban as the ruling political class in Afghanistan (Bishara, 2021) and have helped to promote the rise (and fall) of despots such as Osama bin Laden in the Middle East.

Perverse Unintended Consequences

Some unintended consequences relating to the policy process are fascinating, as in a boomerang effect, where safety measures serve to propagate dangerous situations. The Peltzman Effect was noted in numerous instances when additional safety measures resulted in people taking greater risks because they felt safer, causing no decrease in accident statistics (Peltzman, 1975). This is considered to be akin to 'risk compensation,' where one undercompensates for the additional safety measures and actually incurs accidents as a result. For example, anti-lock brakes have allowed some motorists to become more cavalier about the distances required to stop a moving vehicle, particularly during winter driving conditions. Also, seat belts have improved crash safety but have also been found to encourage faster and less careful driving. The mandated wearing of bicycle and motorcycle helmets has also been identified as contributing to greater safety but also greater risk-taking behaviour.

In another example, car accidents involving children in the front passenger's seat of the vehicle often resulted in airbag injury to the child. Parents were informed that putting the child in the rear seat was a better choice. However, this led to parents forgetting children who were in the rear seat and, in an unattended vehicle, could lead to serious injury or death under extreme heat conditions (Worland, 2014).

Environmental and Historical Unintended Consequences

Of course, not all unintended consequences are related to government or to policy that is developed to rectify internal or external issues. History is rife with exotic flora and fauna, which has been accidentally introduced into a particular country, only to find that there are no natural enemies to curb the growth of the newly introduced species. The introduction of bamboo, zebra mussels in the Great Lakes and rabbits in Australia are just three of the examples where a newly introduced species has flourished at the expense of the local flora and fauna.

It would be fairly safe to say that virtually all of humanity's environmental issues stem from unintended consequences of policy initiatives that were intended to be positive. While the automobile and associated travel technologies have been a boon to humanity in that they have allowed for near instant relocation of individuals and goods, transportation vehicles have contributed to many societal problems, not least of which include traffic congestion and pollution which, in turn, contribute to climate change and other environmental concerns, resulting in negative and unintended consequences that may be irreversible.

Unanticipated Benefits of Unintended Consequences

Over the course of this chapter, we have engaged with unintended consequences of policy development and implementation. In most cases, the unintended consequences have proven to be more undesirable than not. However, there are also instances of unintended consequences that are of benefit to the individual in society.

The development of demilitarized zones from various wars, hot and cold, have led to large natural wildlife reserves (Connolly, 2009), including the development of artificial coral reefs (Cilli, 2009) that have occurred as a result of sinking of decommissioned ships. Also, in the field of medicine, there are many instances of drugs that have been developed for a specific purpose but have been found to be beneficial for other medical conditions. Naveed Saleh (2021) identifies five common drugs that have unintended benefits for the general populace. Among these are Proscar, used for prostate issues, which helps to regrow hair for men with male-pattern baldness; Baclofen, a skeletal muscle relaxant, also offers relief from heartburn and acid indigestion; and Levodopa, commonly prescribed for Parkinson's Disease, has also been shown to spark greater creativity. Oral contraceptive pills have been shown to improve acne, and one of the favourites of medical science is the discovery that Viagara, a phosphodiesterase type 5 (PDE5) inhibitor may be useful in treating cardiac hypertrophy and early-stage heart failure, but its real call to fame is its ability to treat erectile dysfunction (Saleh, 2021).

Details Relating to Unintended Consequences

There are many details that are associated with unintended consequences of policy development, such as the notion of collateral damage, often thought to be an unavoidable by-product of a more positive policy initiative. The society has also had experience with the 'rebound effect' that actually reverses the intent of the policy, as well as the 'boomerang effect' that tends to encourage the opposite of what was expected societal behaviour. Other possibilities include systems accidents that were not intended but had become unavoidable due to misinformation or misapplication and uncertainty as a result of lack of knowledge of a particular consequence of a policy. Self-interest and the advent of personal agendas, as noted previously, may also serve to derail or affect positive policy consequences.

Minimizing Unintended Consequences

However, things are never carved in stone. It is possible to strive to minimize unintended consequences of the policy process. What is required is some forethought and advance preparation. Here is an example that parents have become more concerned about, of late. Many parents impress upon their children that they should give strangers or people they do not know well a wide berth. This has resulted in children (and some adults) not seeking help when it is imperative that they do so (Gilbert, 2021). Although there are many, many examples of unintended consequences that could be modified, mitigated or ameliorated, almost all consequences can be minimized with a certain level of awareness and a few rational thinking techniques.

The first of these techniques is the process of inversion. In formulating good policy, we need to understand what it is that we are striving to avoid. As Tim Dahi (2022) notes, it is easier to avoid stupidity than to search for perfection. Secondly, it is always wise to seek out incongruent information. This prevents confirmation bias and groupthink by allowing 'alternate scenarios' to reveal themselves. Thirdly, bear in mind the 'Peter Principle' that suggests we rise to the level of our incompetence. Although we all have competencies, we also sport a fair number of incompetencies. The wise policymaker is able to recognize the differences between the two by understanding the limits of their own knowledge. Whenever one acts outside of their comfort zone or the 'zone of competence,' the risk of unintended consequences increases. Finally, it behooves the policy analyst to bear in mind the almost certain likelihood of unintended consequences. This lives in tandem with those consequences that have been intended and have been, hopefully, addressed by the policy initiative. However, it is unwise to believe there will be no unintended consequences.

COVID-19 and Unintended Consequences of Policy Development

The COVID-19 pandemic was a worldwide health crisis that arose in 2020 and rapidly spread to every corner of the planet. Governments everywhere had to scramble to protect the health and well-being of their citizens in the face of this ominous and volatile threat. As scientists and healthcare professionals searched for vaccines and medical interventions, unprecedented strides were made in the development, approval, and distribution of life-saving vaccines and treatments (e.g., Wyonch & Zhang, 2022).

During the COVID-19 pandemic, established public policy processes were upended. New policies enacted in response to the crisis produced a curious mixture of protections and burdens, and benefits and costs, that sparked sharply divided opinions regarding their positive and negative outcomes.

Within the realm of education, the COVID-19 pandemic seriously disrupted education around the world and negatively impacted the learning and well-being of millions of children (Fray et al., 2022; Parker & Alfaro, 2021; Picton-Howell, 2022). In particular, the prolonged school closures associated with the pandemic spawned a worldwide plethora of unintended consequences, from negative impacts on student well-being and behaviour (Caldwell et al., 2021; Fray et al., 2022) to breaches of children's physical health rights (Picton-Howell, 2022). In addition, one cannot overlook the impact of the pandemic on parents, caregivers, and teachers, all of whom were affected in various ways.

Thus, the school closure policies spawned immediate and long-term consequences, the full extent of which may not be known for years to come.

What did become immediately apparent, however, was that the longstanding interconnections between power, politics and policy were on full display throughout the course of the pandemic, as evidenced in the highly polarized public and scholarly reactions to mandatory lockdowns, travel restrictions, and vaccinations.

For example, a study conducted by researchers at the C. D. Howe Institute, a Canadian think tank, found that vaccines were very effective in reducing COVID-19 cases, hospitalizations, and deaths in Canda such that many lives were saved (Wyonch & Zhang, 2022). Based on their analysis of various economic and public health indicators, the researchers concluded that the 'vaccines were clearly economically and socially beneficial' (Wyonch & Zhang, 2022, p. 1). In addition, the mass vaccination campaign undertaken during the pandemic provided valuable insights for policymakers and healthcare leaders alike.

However, the cost-benefit analysis of Canadian COVID-19 vaccinations also revealed several complex, indirect effects which were intertwined with the impact of the pandemic itself and the public health restrictions enacted to curb its spread. Adding to this complexity were ongoing changes to public policy in response to successive mutations of the virus. One of the positive, indirect effects was that the arrival of the vaccines enabled the removal of some public health restrictions and facilitated a return to more regular economic activities (Wyonch & Zhang, 2022). In sum, the study concluded that the vaccines were highly effective, and the public policies enacted in response to the pandemic provided important insights for rapid and nimble policy responses to future medical crises.

While Wyonch and Zhang (2022) found positive conclusions about the impact of COVID-19 vaccinations and related public health measures, others reached vastly different conclusions, as illustrated by the examples cited below. This is a powerful reminder that, when evaluating unintended policy consequences, the determination of whether consequences are positive or negative is largely dependent upon *who* is making the determination. 'The issue that arises is "beneficial for whom" and "harmful for whom"' (Urbanovič et al., 2021, p. 277). This is because policy consequences are very rarely universally positive or negative for everyone involved. Instead, their impact varies widely.

As was pointed out previously, COVID-19 has been in the consciousness of the entire world since 2020. This pandemic has been likened to the Spanish Flu of 1918, more than a century ago. Even though great progress has been made since the 1920s, Bardosh et al. (2022) point out that COVID-19 is still highly problematic.

Of note is the recognition that vaccine policies have shifted rapidly with the advent of COVID-19, resulting in population wide vaccine mandates, vaccine 'passports' and differential restrictions based on vaccine status. This, in turn, has spawned numerous unintended consequences that have yet to be evaluated. In the opinion of Bardosh et al. (2022), many of these policies are not only counter-productive, they may also be harmful to the population in general. Although vaccines have significantly reduced COVID-19-related morbidity and mortality issues, mandatory vaccine policies have been questioned in some circles because they may impact access to work, education, public transportation, and social life. This can be viewed as an infringement on human rights, promotes stigma and polarization, eventually affecting overall health and wellbeing.

Bardosh et al. (2022) claim that such vaccination policies can lead to widening health and economic inequalities, distrust of government and scientific communities, and reduce the potency of future public health measures, including routine immunizations. The claim is that mandating vaccination is a powerful intervention into public health and should be used only when absolutely necessary in order to maintain trust and ethical norms.

Accordingly, the authors of that study claim that a more progressive way forward is to make better use of empowering strategies, based on public trust and consultation, along with improving healthcare infrastructure and attendant services in order to promote the health and well-being of the general public, as opposed to the prevalent attitude of fear and anger.

Some of the unintended consequences of vaccination policies have included social and political unrest. For instance, mandatory proof-of-vaccination policies, justified by governments and the scientific community and initiated across the political spectrum have spread globally. Rather than a response to a medical health issue, workplace mandates have moved the issue into the political realm where governments, instead of leading, have been by-and-large reactionary, resulting in a 'power over' rather than a 'power with' attitude towards its citizenry. Bardosh et al. (2022) list numerous restrictive policies from around the world, including limiting access to travel and to social activities, differential and segregated lockdowns for unvaccinated members of the society, vaccination metrics, inconsistent access to medical insurance and healthcare, along with taxes, fines and/or imprisonment and entry requirements, to itemize but a few of these restrictions.

Interestingly enough, also at issue are the various and inconsistent ways individual countries identify and exempt certain aspects of the society based on religious, philosophical or medical grounds, as they incorporate testing as an alternative to vaccination. Like most things written on water, changes, omissions and insertions are introduced as the policy makers strive to tinker successfully with stubborn policies that seem to menace their populations rather than delivering them.

There have been at least three significant turns in the policy initiatives, on a world scale, relating to the pandemic (Bardosh et al., 2022). The first of these was the early messaging around vaccination as a public health measure focusing on protecting the most vulnerable members of the society. This shifted to vaccination thresholds aimed at achieving 'herd' immunity (When government refers to its citizenry as a 'herd,' this is enough to make people wonder about their leaders' intentions) in order to restore normalcy. A third shift was represented by universal vaccine recommendations to reduce hospital crowding and to address unvaccinated individuals who were unwilling or unable to get vaccinated. Such a huge 'experiment' in social engineering has never before been undertaken by any society, leaving governments to 'play by ear.'

In addition to ineffective and inadequate government and medical campaigns, vaccination against COVID-19 variants appeared to be less than successful, over time, with both vaccinated and unvaccinated individuals transmitting the disease to others at similar rates (Singanayagam et al., 2021). However, despite limitations, vaccine policies became framed as 'benefits' that offer freedom and access to health, travel, work and social activities. Despite this, many people see these policies and the political 'spin' (read sociopolitical attitudes) as punitive, discriminatory and coercive. Singanayagam et al. (2021) have attempted to outline an interdisciplinary social science framework that will assist researchers, policymakers, civil society groups and public health authorities in lessening unintended social harm from governmental and corporate policies, a perspective that is not only timely but imperative in informing current and future pandemic policies.

Lack of transparency and the minimizing of potential risks and side effects have rendered policies ineffective, as governments and corporations struggle to maintain some semblance of leadership, an endangered concept in many areas of governance. In fact, these policies, according to Singanayagam et al. (2021), are more inclined to create cognitive dissonance as a result of perceived contradictory information. Non-information, misinformation and disinformation contributed to this through public messaging that implies vaccinated people could not spread the disease. Such policies often lacked clear communication, justification and transparency, not to mention a strong scientific basis. Clearly, trust must also be maintained among and within the populace.

Even though evidence was clear that infection-driven immunity offers significant protection, prior infection status has consistently been underplayed. In fact, some may have been impacted in terms of employment while others have been unable to travel or to participate in social activities even as transmission of the disease has continued among vaccinated individuals (Luster et al., 2021), reinforcing distrust in governmental, healthcare and scientific communities and institutions. Furthermore, political rhetoric descended into moralizing, scapegoating and blame, thus actively promoting stigma and discrimination as a way to attempt to improve vaccination statistics. The effect of this was to further polarize the society, physically and psychologically (Korn et al., 2020). By treating the populace as a single entity, much like the Borg on Star Trek, institutions err in presuming that all members of a society are equal or, worse, the same. Without discussing who or why some members of the populace are unwilling or unable to be vaccinated, the policymaking institutions tend to use a blanket approach that serves to create an us versus them attitude rather than creating adaptive strategies and policies (Singanayagam et al., 2021).

In addition to all of the foregoing issues relating to policy mismanagement of the pandemic, there have also been significant privacy issues relating to sharing of medical records with non-medical individuals. The danger in this is that such invasions may be expanded to include other personal data that may trigger further human rights violations and discriminatory treatment of employees and the citizenry in general, based on biological data. Political and social polarization and radicalization – anti-mandate and pro-mandate – may increase in the wake of punitive governmental, technological, healthcare and other institutional vaccine policies (Singanayagam et al., 2021).

Additionally, focusing on unvaccinated people and promoting the idea that this is the cause of the collapse of the healthcare system helps to divert attention from global equity failures and promotes a sort of vaccine colonialism that may tie vaccination metrics to international finances (Bardosh et al., 2022). Vaccine policies may also fuel existing inequity (Arguedas-Ramírez, 2021) by creating coercive and stigmatizing work and social environments, and discrimination against disadvantaged groups. Consequently, many vaccine policies may unintentionally disempower individuals. The economic effects of restricting access to work may also have indirect implications for dependents of the unvaccinated.

Commentators have also highlighted the potential impact of mandates in creating supply chain bottlenecks in certain commodities and with cross-border trade, and argued that changing vaccine rules and regulations threaten to negatively impact overall economic recovery in some sectors of the economy, including tourism (Bardosh et al., 2022). Mandates are presumed to be legally unproblematic but, when the public view these as problematic, trust in public health and scientific institutions is eroded, undermining ethical and legal criteria for policy and damaging the integrity of public health (Bardosh et al., 2022). Thus, the nature of mandates, passports and restrictions has increased public demands for scientific accountability and transparency. As a result, policymakers must now reflect on the impact of such policies in terms of the integrity of science and public health itself.

Conclusion

As can be seen, there is no policy without consequences, intended or otherwise. Unintended consequences may be beneficial or malignant. However, as this chapter has attempted to point out, unintended consequences of policy initiatives can be – to some extent – foreseen, prevented or ameliorated. While there is no perfect scenario for any given policy, it behooves policy makers and analysts to attend to some of the fallout from their policy choices so that the society can benefit to the extent possible from positive and forward thinking policy analysts. The alternatives to this are less than attractive. As we have seen from the sharply divided opinions on the policy responses to the COVID-19 pandemic presented here, policy decisions have far-reaching consequences that significantly impact lives in many ways, both good and bad. For that reason, it is essential that policy analysts consider all the facets of public policies and how people will be impacted by them. These facets are brought together in the final chapter of this book where the many different components of policymaking are addressed in our concluding remarks.

References

Amrein-Beardsley, A. (2009). The unintended, pernicious consequences of 'staying the course' on the United States' no child left behind policy. *International Journal of Education Policy & Leadership, 4*(6), 1–13.

Arguedas-Ramírez, G. (2021). Build that wall! Vaccine certificates, passes and passports, the distribution of harms and decolonial global health justice. *Journal of Global Ethics, 17*(3), 375–387.

Bardosh, K., de Figueiredo, A., Gur-Arie, R., Jamrozik, E., Doidge, J., Lemmens, T., Keshavjee, S., Graham, J. E., & Baral, S. (2022). The unintended consequences of COVID-19 vaccine policy: Why mandates, passports and restrictions may cause more harm than good. *BMJ Global Health, 7*(5), e008684. https://gh.bmj.com/content/7/5/e008684.long

Bishara, M. (2021). The US, the Taliban and the stunning defeat in Afghanistan. *Aljazeera (Opinion)*. https://www.aljazeera.com/opinions/2021/8/16/the-us-the-taliban-and-the-stunning-defeat-in

Caldwell, H. A., Hancock Friesen, C. L., & Kirk, S. F. (2021). The effects of the COVID-19 pandemic on health and well-being of children and youth in Nova Scotia: Youth and parent perspectives. *Frontiers in Pediatrics, 9*, 1–9.

CBC News. (2009). *Quebec woman gets ticket for refusing to hold handrail.* https://www.cbc.ca/news/canada/montreal/quebec-woman-gets-ticket-for-refusing-to-hold-handrail-1.822993

CBC News. (2019). *Supreme Court awards $20K to woman fined for refusing to hold escalator handrail.* https://www.cbc.ca/news/canada/montreal/bela-kosoian-supreme-court-handrail-1.5377772

Cheong, K., Hill, C., & Leong, Y. (2016). Malaysia's education policies and the law of unintended consequences. *Journal of International and Comparative Education, 5*(2), 73–85.

Cilli, L. (2009). WWII ship to become artificial reef off Key West. *Internet Archive WayBack Machine.* http://cbs4.com/local/Vandenberg.artificial.reef.2.991004.html

Connolly, K. (2009). From iron curtain to greenbelt. *The Guardian.* https://www.theguardian.com/travel/2009/jul/04/germany-green-line-iron-curtain

Crenshaw, K. (1991). Mapping the margins. *Stanford Law Review, 43,* 1241–1299.

Dahi, T. (2022, April 30). Inversion: Avoid stupidity rather than seeking excellence. *Are You Out There?* https://medium.com/are-you-out-there/inversion-avoid-stupidity-rather-than-seeking-excellence-24e7c26a5c8c

Darrah, N. (2019, December 1). Canadian woman arrested for not holding escalator handrail awarded $20G in damages. *Fox News.*

Deleon, P., & Steelman, T. A. (2001). Making public policy programs effective and relevant: The role of the policy sciences. *Journal of Policy Analysis and Management, 20*(1), 163–171.

Engels, F. (1886). *Ludwig Feuerbach and the end of classical German philosophy.* Die Neue Zeit (Translated: Progress Publishers, 1946).

Fray, L., Jaremus, F., Gore, J., & Harris, J. (2022). Schooling upheaval during COVID-19: Troubling consequences for students' return to school. *The Australian Educational Researcher,* 1–18.

Gilbert, A. C. (2021, October 26). Hiker lost in woods ignored calls from rescuers because they didn't recognize the number. *USA Today.*

Hayes, A. (2022). The Laffer curve: History and critique. *Investopedia.* https://www.investopedia.com/terms/l/laffercurve.asp

Holton, G. (2004). Robert K. Merton. *Proceedings of the American Philosophical Society, 148*(4), 505–517.

Karapin, R., & Feldman, L. (2016). Unintended consequences. *Polity, 48*(4), 441–444.

Korn, L., Böhm, R., Meier, N. W., & Betsch, C. (2020). Vaccination as a social contract. *Proceedings of the National Academy of Sciences of the United States of America, 117*(26), 14890–14899.

Lindblom, C. E. (1959). The science of muddling through. *Public Administration Review, 19,* 79–88.

Locke, J. (1824). *The works of John Locke* (Vol. 4, 12th ed.). Rivington.

Lunau, K., Brunet, J. R., Henheffer, T., & Gillis, C. (2009). Toronto's garbage strike. *The Canadian Encyclopedia.* https://www.thecanadianencyclopedia.ca/en/article/torontos-garbage-strike

Luster, T., Albin, E., Gross, A., Tabenkin, M., & Davidovitch, N. (2021). Promoting vaccination from a human rights and equity perspective: Lessons from the Israeli "Green Pass". *European Journal of Risk Regulation, 12,* 308–320.

Merton, R. K. (1996). *On social structure and science.* University of Chicago Press.

Parker, M., & Alfaro, B. (2021). *Education during the COVID-19 pandemic: Access, inclusion and psycho-social support – Leaving no Caribbean child behind.* United Nations Economic Commission for Latin America and the Caribbean (ECLAC).

Peltzman, S. (1975). The effects of automobile safety regulation. *Journal of Political Economy, 83*(4), 677–725.

Picton-Howell, Z. (2022). The unintended consequences of school closures during COVID-19 on children and young people's physical health rights – What are they and how can they be mitigated? *The International Journal of Human Rights* (ahead-of-print), 1–16.

Prus, R. (2003). Policy as a collective venture: A symbolic interactionist approach to the study of organizational directives. *International Journal of Sociology and Social Policy, 23*(6/7), 13–60.

Saleh, N. (2021). 5 weird but beneficial side effects of common drugs. *VeryWell Health.* https://www.verywellhealth.com/beneficial-side-effects-of-common-drugs-4078471

Shingler, B. (2022, October 26). What to know about RSV, a virus surging among young children in Canada. *CBC News.*

Singanayagam, A., Hakki, S., Dunning, J., Madon, K. J., Crone, M. A., Koycheva, A., Derqui-Fernandez, N., Barnett, J. L., Whitfield, M. J., Varro, R., Charlett, A., Kundu, R., Fenn, J., Cutajar, J., Quinn, V., Conibear, E., Barclay, W., Freemont, P. S., Taylor, G. P., ... ATACCC Investigators. (2021). Community transmission and viral load kinetics of the SARS-CoV-2 delta (B.1.617.2) variant in vaccinated and unvaccinated individuals in the UK: A prospective, longitudinal, cohort study. *The Lancet Infectious Diseases, 22,* 183–195.

Smith, A. (2005). In S. M. Soares (Ed.), *The theory of moral sentiments.* MetaLibri.

Urbanovič, J., de Vries, M., & Stankevič, B. (2021). Unanticipated consequences of reforms in school governance. *The NISPAcee Journal of Public Administration and Policy, 14*(2), 273–298.

Vyse, S. (2017). Can anything save us from unintended consequences? *The Skeptical Inquirer, 41*(4), 20–23.

White, R. E., & Cooper, K. (2022). *Qualitative research in the post-modern era: Critical approaches and selected methodologies.* Springer.

Worland, J. (2014, September 2). Who's to blame for hot car deaths? *Time.*

Wyonch, R., & Zhang, T. (2022). Damage averted: Estimating the effects of COVID-19 vaccines on hospitalizations, mortality and costs in Canada. Commentary 634. C.D. Howe Institute.

Chapter 11

Conclusion

And so, at last, we have arrived at the final chapter of this volume. Although this chapter is identified as a conclusion, it really serves as a summary of all that has been said throughout the pages of this volume. As such, this chapter strives to coalesce the numerous factors essential to policy analysis, its development, and its implementation.

This volume began with an introductory chapter that spoke to general parameters and conditions surrounding the policy project. Education policy is the primary subject here; however, it is also wise to note that policy looks the same in various contexts, although the models used, the policymakers and the issues and conditions surrounding the policy process may vary enormously. The chapter has hopefully served to introduce readers to basic education policy in terms of context, content and coordination. As such it forms the contextual background for the study of policy and processes associated with the development of policy. In particular, the first chapter illustrates that all facets of policy are variously conceptualized, defined and represented by different scholars. As elaborated upon throughout the rest of the book, contrasting descriptions of policy processes, actors, frameworks, consequences and models abound.

Of importance to note, first and foremost, is that any policy model is actually a decision-making model. Although all policy models may be considered decision-making models, not all decision-making models can be said to be policy models. The reason for this is simply that not all decision-making models have the various phases that all policy models require in order to produce potentially successful policies. At some point in every educator's career, (s)he will likely be tasked with some form of formal policy creation. This may occur at any level of the education project, from the classroom level to the department level to the school level and beyond, even to the board level and, possibly, even to national and international levels. Thus, education policy is merely a compilation or a series of compilations of ideas and/or plans that individuals or groups of individuals agree to follow, given a particular situation or circumstance. For almost any topic, there will be policies, which may belong to a particular group or educational community, whether they be locally administered at the school, department or classroom level, as well as more general policies that pertain to larger aspects of school and district governance. Policies may also be provincial in nature and, in Canada, given that the provinces and territories are largely responsible for the education of its citizenry, there may even be a few avenues where national policy is set. For example, policy around standardized testing may not only be a national issue, it may also extend past our country's borders and influence the entire country's subscription to international standardized testing regimens.

Policy is omnipresent in an educator's work. Policymakers vary depending on the task at hand, the complexity of the policy initiative and the people in charge of the process. Chapter 6 described the roles of educational leaders in the policy process at the school, district and system levels. As policymakers, educational leaders navigate tricky organizational shoals that separate the different levels of school systems and impede policy alignment and implementation. Common questions about education policy are examined through different policy perspectives, procedures, and processes and the diverse impacts on educators are discussed in a variety of examples, scenarios and instances.

Of importance is also the understanding of what a policy 'means', which, as we have seen throughout this volume, is variously described in the literature. Is a policy a general rule, a law or a guideline? This is an important distinction that may have significant permutations for those who are tasked with interpreting the policy, particularly in terms of its implementation. From code of conduct to method, from guideline to prescription, different levels of interpretation and, indeed, differing levels of interpreters may offer a variety of punishments or reprisals for the infringement of a particular policy. Although policy making can be viewed as 'applied problem solving' (Howlett et al., 2009, p. 4), it is always about matching goals with means, identifying issues and finding solutions for them, using policy tools and protocols.

The technical aspect of the policy process requires the identification and application of appropriate instruments for developing an optimal relationship between the espoused goals and the processes used to achieve those goals. The political aspect of the policy process seeks to recognise inherent issues and appropriate solutions to those issues. Competence, ideas, norms and principles, as well as the policymakers' composite knowledge are also considered to be requirements of any successful policy initiative and, as such, these conditions frequently create a complexity and messiness that may afford a number of consequences during policy implementation. As we saw in Chapter 10, the intended and unintended consequences of policies may, at once, be beneficial or detrimental to those impacted by the policy.

Policy is rarely made in a vacuum and is dependent on adequate, but often elusive, policy models. A common approach to policy development is a 'stage' approach, comprised of a variety of different stages. Additionally, policy frequently arrives in a concrete form or in a repository of some form that tends to include the purpose, duties and responsibilities, and the intended recipients of the policy initiative. Four types of policy include distributive and redistributive policies, and regulatory and constituent policies. Needless to say, with this level of flux, it is easy to see that policy as written may be very different from policy as lived.

Policy development is usually preceded by some form of needs assessment. Surveys are commonly used to identify a policy need. A cost/benefit or cost/effectiveness analysis may identify the parameters of the policy, prior to the formal policymaking process. As with any policy, there is always the risk of failure. Educational policies often fall victim to partisan politics, lack of information, rejection of information and any number of unhelpful influences. As new policies arrive, conflicts or discrepancies must be attended to.

With respect to the ever-present politics of education, it is necessary for policymakers at any level to understand the many and varied forces that come into play whenever a new policy need is identified. Political processes and, indeed, policy matters are fraught with issues of power. Perhaps this is because educational policy is as complex as any form of policy making simply because schools and systems of education represent microcosms of the larger society. As a result, all of the issues that may occur with developing and making policy in the larger context are also represented within the smaller context of schooling. It is roughly akin to 'large picture/small picture' thinking.

Policy, Power and Politics

Multiple forces are omnipresent in the development of policy and in its related processes. These forces may or may not be predictable; however, they invariably establish an interplay of sorts among other policy components. This interplay may create friction among competing interests within the policy process. Thus, the policy as written may not be implemented as written, due to various, unpredictable and insurmountable issues relating to the process of developing and implementing a new policy. It is within these parameters that policy becomes 'policy as lived', rather than policy as written. One important and incessant force that influences policy development is power dynamics. While this is an important force to contend with, the danger in not controlling the power dynamics that are present in every interaction is the possibility that the power dynamics may overpower the entire process of creating policy.

When political agendas try to sway the process of policy development, there can be no 'fair' policy, simply because of the partisan influence that is a function of particular political agendas. It may be easier to say that the policy process is free of influence or of controlling interests but, unhappily, this is a naïve consideration, at best. All policy is subject to the values, beliefs and attitudes that are brought to the table by the policymakers. This does not mean that all policy is corrupt, but it does mean that all policy is slanted in some particular direction. Thus, no unbiased policy exists that is completely free of power dynamics, political agendas and other possible forms of influence. This is the nature of policymaking, then. It does not exist in a vacuum but is representative of a function of the society within which it was created. At the end of the day, policy remains a contextual response to concrete initiatives, which must be responsive to personal and societal proclivities.

Policy Alignment

As has been noted, successful policy is never made in a vacuum. It is important to align upcoming policies with existing policies that connect to or which impact these nascent policies. The connection between school policies, district and system policies are essential in order for these policies to be aligned with one another for efficient and effective governance. The truth of the matter is that policies are not created uniformly and are subject to variations in time and place, timing and other conditions that require new policies to fit in with pre-existing policies. Additionally, the policy architects and the social conditions surrounding the creation of new policy rarely remain the same for very long. It is like the adage of the river – you can never put your foot in the same river twice. The water that was there before has been replaced by a new wave.

Policy initiatives may be subject to a conflict of interests at the school, district, and system levels. This is not a failing of policy process so much as a failure to understand the various contexts within which successful policy is developed. There are few guarantees that there will not be a conflict at some level. However, goodwill and intent are always available to assist in the deliverance of new policy in order to align with existing policies or with the alignment of old policies with the new. It all comes down to choice, not chance. What remains key, here, is the identification of those features that hinder or expedite the policy process. In this way, the refining of these features or the refining of the policy process to accommodate such features help to ensure that there are consistent, coherent policies functioning at each level of governance, be it in the field of education, politics, law or any other field that requires a strong policy infrastructure.

Contemporary Models of Policy Development

In order to arrive at this juncture, however, the wise policy maker will be knowledgeable about policy alternatives. Among the many policy models from which one may choose, we have visited Leslie Pal's 'all inclusive' model that seeks to address a multiplicity of external influences that necessarily impact internal policy development. Another a policy construct is represented by Yehezkel Dror's exclusive model that identifies three distinct phases of the policy development process. For the most part, however, policy models, tend to feature a combination of these two extremes.

Many policy models contain at least three levels of analysis – the pre-policy, policy and post-policy phases. The pre-policy phase identifies resources and issues relevant to the eventual determining of the policy, such as identification of adjudicators or analysts who will shepherd the process, timing and location of the process and other required resources. The purpose of the policy is also an important part of this phase. The policy phase involves researching and testing of possibilities, alternatives and the eventual selection of the 'best fit'. The post-policy phase identifies the implementers of the policy and how the policy is to be implemented. A review phase is also important to any policy initiative.

Different policy models exhibit different elements as a result of tradition and practice. Although the purpose for the policy may be consistent across models, the implementation may differ, depending on the model used. 'Standard' elements are found in all policies regardless of the field or subject matter. In addition to standard elements, there are also 'optional' elements of a more topical nature to be considered, depending on the subject and perceived needs for a new policy.

Charles Lindblom's (1959) seminal article, 'The Science of Muddling Through', identifies the complexity and limitations of policy development. His main point centres upon the fact that most policy makers are not experts in their field but are called from their career positions to make policy. In this case, incremental policy alternatives are to be considered, so that multiple successive policies can build upon one another, in order to eventually achieve a successful policy.

Unfortunately, policy analysis has not been shown to resolve numerous problems relating to a large organization, such as a school system. Emerging trends, such as the development of general descriptive and explanatory models of policy process and implementation, the effects of government, and large-scale shifts, such as globalization, have impacted policy formulation and development (Compton et al., 2019).

Unstructured and Structured Approaches

Three key elements of policy content, according to Pal (2014), include goal identification, problem definition and instrumentation. However, these three elements are influenced by a plethora of actors and related policy frameworks, all circulating within a specific loop. Not all policy models will yield similar results. Because it is not possible to isolate these elements from one another, Pal's policy model is iterative, cycling through the loop multiple times, creating or refining understanding as the process progresses. Contextual factors also serve to extend, enrich and mediate the policy initiative.

By way of contrast, Yehezkel Dror (1983) offered a controversial, systematic and structured approach for policy study that combines policy analysis, behavioural science and systems analysis. Here, policymaking is evaluated with explicit criteria and standards, based on Dror's optimal model approach, discussed earlier in this volume. The continuing problem with contemporary policymaking remains the gap between what we know about policymaking and how policy is actually made. This may be summed up by acknowledging that we have plenty of knowledge about policy and how to make it, but we lack wisdom (Maxwell, 2007) in creating policy.

Because contemporary policymaking is complex and dynamic, contemporary society relies on outmoded policymaking models (Dror, 1983) that strive to identify guidelines for action that are future-oriented. Of course, this presents a plethora of undetermined and difficult issues to be resolved. This, according to Dror (1983), requires that explicit criteria and standards replace implicit assumptions that tend to accompany most policy development initiatives. Another problem is the measurement of the final policy that regards net output as a proxy for quality in policymaking. A secondary set of criteria for determining the actual quality of policymaking is required. Both output and quality are necessary for evaluating policymaking (Dror, 1983) successfully.

Implicit assumptions regarding policy analysis include the view of human history as an unbroken series of errors and inadequacies and, conversely, the notion that regards human history as successful. Dror (1983) affirms that not only is policymaking is not as good as it could be, policymaking fails to achieve satisfactory quality. Thirdly, in the future, given these damnations, policymaking may not survive in its current form. In response to these charges, Dror (1983) offers his three-stage policy model, the components of which are interconnected by communication and feedback channels.

In addition to Pal's (2014) policy model, and Dror's (1983) model, there are a number of additional models available that combine many of the elements of both of these classic models. James Anderson (2014) identified a five-step policy model. Lasswell's (1971) stage approach offered a new approach in public policy development. According to Lasswell, the generating of knowledge, essential to the process of policymaking, supplemented by the knowledge generated, is essential to improving the process of policymaking itself (Dunn, 2018).

Of import, here, is the observation that a policy model will create an idealised view of the policy process, rather than a realistic view of how policy is created. In reality, policymaking is not so linear as policy models might suggest. In short, when it comes to selecting a policy model, some models may be linear and, therefore, rather idealistic while others attempt to capture the true complexity and messiness of policy development. That being said, policymakers may choose from an array of policy possibilities and may decide to mix chosen models in customizing an approach for the upcoming policy initiative or, they may create a policy model of their own design.

In fact, should one view policy making as an aspect of decision-making, there are models available that are not true policy models but which provide a platform for decision-making that mimics policy analysis. One such model is represented by the qualitative research methodology, known as action research. There are permutations of this form of policy analysis, also known as 'practitioner research', 'teacher research', 'participatory action research' and by a variety of other names that stress the notion of inclusivity in the policy process (White & Cooper, 2022).

The Policy Continuum

There is no 'one size fits all' policy. If we have learned nothing else, we have discovered that policies are developed for a myriad of differing purposes. It is clear that each purpose, or each need for policy, requires a specific policy initiative that is tailored to a unique set of circumstances. As a consequence of this individuality relative to policy development, it is clear that each 'incident' of policy architecture influences the way each policy is created, crafted, and implemented. The entire scope of each policy decision is also unique to its own particular set of circumstances.

One of the most important considerations in any policy process is the selection of policy 'experts' who will drive the process forward. It is for this reason alone that no two policies are ever developed alike. At best, one policy may build upon a previous policy or a previous iteration of that policy. When it comes to developing policies for and within school districts, the policy leaders will be selected 'in house' in most cases. It is relatively rare to have policy architects chosen from outside of the educational realm, even though educators, like many others who are tasked with policy creation, may not be experts in this particular field.

Depending from where the policy emanates, different parts of the educational project may be influenced by particular policies. This may or may not create harmonious policies or policies that suffer from a conflict of interests. Thus, it is of import that the policymakers examine policies that have preceded the current policy directive. School leaders may influence policy within their own areas of influence, such as a school setting. However, they may also be required to support policies in which they have neither had a hand in developing nor policies that they can support without reservation.

District leadership may also suffer from the same quandary. In such cases, dissonance may occur because, although the policy makers at the district level may have more power than their school leader counterparts, these district leaders may not have the last word on policy development, either. Increasingly, and with the onset of standardization processes around the globe, fewer and fewer policy decisions that impact the standardization process are being developed within the country where the policy will be implemented. Increasingly, policy is being made by international or transnational entities that have a vested interest in what passes for knowledge within any given school system. Member countries in this international education superstructure may opt in or out but, should they decide to opt in, are required to follow the policies set by the overseeing organization, regardless of whether the policies agree with the circumstances found within the particular school system, school district or by the specific schools found within the school district.

Although educational policy may offer some resemblance to non-educational policy, for educational leaders and policymakers, it is necessary to particularize the policy development process within educational terms. This is necessary in order to maintain relevance between the policy as created, and the policy as delivered and implemented. If this is handled adroitly, the policy will be more understandable to those teachers who are required to support that policy, simply because the policy has been developed in keeping with the educational terms that represent the vocabulary that is used by those educators who are expected to understand the policy and to be able to more deftly implement it. Key players in this process are often the school or district leaders. Each role that is envisioned and enacted by these policy creators, within the confines of the school or school district, has an enormous influence on what the eventual policy will come to look like.

Policy that is made outside of the school district may be led by policymakers whose work exists outside of the school environment. As a result, the policies developed by these policymakers may be focused more on broad societal, political, and economic issues as they relate to education than the daily operation of schools. In such cases, it may appear to be the case that the educational project is becoming subject to external values and beliefs that may point to societal agendas which intend to (ab)use the educational project for corporate or political advantage. This relates to the purpose of schooling and, for every citizen, politician or corporate executive, there may be a different purpose or purposes for each individual or group of individuals.

Policy Infrastructures and Impediments

For any policy to be successful, conditions must be optimal. This means, of course, that all phases of policy development need to be conscientiously attended to. For example, in the pre-policy phase, adequate resources, including funding, must be available. In addition, the entire policy process must be made clear. The buy-in from the educators, themselves, is essential. However, this may require revisiting and revising as the policy process moves forward.

During the policy phase, policy coherence and policy routinization must also be considered. These conditions may not be exclusive to the policy phase of the process but may continue to require attention into the post-policy phase, when implementation becomes the focus of the newly minted policy. Policy coherence refers to the ability of the new policy to mesh well with pre-existing policies. As well, the new policy needs to make sense in that it serves the purpose for which it was intended.

Frequently, a gap exists between a policy as conceived and a policy as applied. At the school level, for example, a disconnect between the policy that is handed down from school or district administrators to the classroom teachers is always subject to interpretation and, of course, misinterpretation. At a basic level, this implies that there is a distinction between theory and practice. As many educators are aware, one's theories inform one's practice and one's practice, conversely, informs one's theories. Essentially, this is a distinction between one's theoretical understandings of the educational processes as opposed to one's experiential knowledge.

Given this, it is hardly surprising that classroom teachers may struggle with policies that arrived unbidden or, at least, unanticipated. Often, there is little in-service provided when it comes to implementing policies. Consequently, teachers may feel as if they are promoting a policy in a vacuum. This allows for a huge array of variation when it comes to the enactment of a particular policy. There are definite linkages that apply, here. The policy may be delivered in a form that is different than the original written policy. For example, teachers may be informed of new policy at a staff meeting, where the information is passed on verbally, rather than in written form. Also, the classroom teachers responsible for implementing the policy may or may not be administering it consistently within or between classrooms. As well, not all teachers may agree with the policy, allowing a certain level of policy sabotage to occur. As a result, the policy as written may not correspond precisely to the policy as delivered or even as implemented.

Clearly, these factors influence the ultimate success of the policy, even if it is well written and well received. Right from the inception of the policy initiative, important factors, such as resistance to the policy intention and demanding and convoluted policy requirements and conditions, contribute to the success, the failure or the demise of any nascent policy. If the purpose of the policy remains unclear or is shrouded in ambiguities, it will struggle to be successful. Finally, a lack of resources necessary to any successful policy development process may signal an imminent policy failure. Many of these issues can be identified within the inception of the policy process and may reverberate through the entire process, rendering the eventual policy useless or, at best, inadequate.

However, the beginning phase of the policy process is not the only place where things can go sideways. The making of policy is largely an abstract process, whereas its implementation is a much more concrete undertaking. From the theory that is required in order to identify a purpose or a need for a particular policy to the crafting of the policy, itself, and, finally, to the translation of that policy into action, into words and deeds, there are many ways that those who wish to lead educational change can encounter a myriad of stumbling blocks.

However, not all policy initiatives are subject to ruination. Many policies are well conceived, developed and implemented. Because schools and school systems strive to develop effective and efficient ways of educating students, the quest for additional education, training and knowledge also applies to teachers and the administration. Thus, by creating positive, strong and resilient policies, school leaders may become powerful, impressive and compelling agents of change.

Intended and Unintended Consequences

The fluidity and complexity of the policy process may be expressed by the 'law of unintended consequences', which claims that every act leads to unintended and unforeseen results. Because uncertainty always accompanies policy creation, the law of unintended consequences suggests it is impossible to recognize all contingencies dependent upon a particular action. Although constantly changing social conditions may be at the root of this uncertainty, every political action can be foreseen in terms of consequences, intended or not. Bearing in mind how social fluidity influences policy is a useful way of not only thinking about policy but also about what that policy will look like over time.

For example, concepts such as intersectionality (Crenshaw, 1991), anticipating the least expected outcomes or other potential concerns allows policy makers some clarity as to possible consequences, anticipated or unintended. The need for the policy, in the first place, and the existence of personal agendas that may skew the effects of the eventual policy also represent and create positive and negative consequences. Within the implementation process, the policy may require some tweaking, either immediately or over time, and the review phase of the policy model is useful in identifying such needs, even to the extent that the policy may need to be discontinued or even reversed. Policy development is never created in a vacuum. As a result, policymakers and implementers may be best guided by ethical considerations and respect for those who are affected by the policy.

Policy malfunctions may be attributed to ignorance, human error, inadequate perspectives on the process, the interplay of policy and the societal values that affect and are affected by the policy, the notion that fear may trigger (over) reactions to specific policies (Merton, 1996) and, finally, groupthink (Vyse, 2017). It is also possible that some policy initiatives spawn positive unintended consequences. While these may be common, they are often overlooked, as people tend to agonize over examples of collateral damage rather than focusing on unforeseen positive outcomes.

Empowering Teachers and Educational Leaders

By now, it has become evident that a successful policy requires an efficient process, a strong policy model and effective implementation. At each juncture of the process, educator buy-in is required at every level of the organization and at every stage of the process. This will ensure that the eventual policy will be supported by the members of the educational institution. Once educators get behind all aspects of policymaking, even when they are not personally involved, the eventual policy will assist the teaching staff and administration to become more assertive in the development of their own leadership capacities. In addition, the policy initiatives that have been developed will also strengthen the belief and resolve that is necessary in order to delve into the bubbling cauldron of policy uncertainty. This process is reciprocal; policy development assists in the building of strong leadership potential, while strong leadership helps to create resilient and successful policy. Once established, the resulting spiral may inspire further successful leadership and policy initiatives and alternatives.

As we have become aware through the pages of this volume, the policy process is uneven, at best. There is no recipe for developing the perfect policy and, as a result, policy formulation remains an inexact endeavour. What we have attempted to portray is just how inexact this process can be. Policy analysis, development and implementation continue to be important components of our daily lives, however invisible the results may have become. It is incumbent upon all of society to understand the issues relating to the policy process and how to relate to those issues while attempting to resolve issues that the policy process is striving to ameliorate. It is hoped that these pages have helped to clarify some of those problems. It is also hoped that the reader will have enjoyed this book as much as the writers have enjoyed creating it.

References

Anderson, J. E. (2014). *Public policymaking* (8th ed.). Cengage Learning.
Compton, M., Luetjens, J., & Hart, P. (2019). Designing for policy success. *International Review of Public Policy*, *1*(2), 119–146.
Crenshaw, K. (1991). Mapping the margins. *Stanford Law Review*, *43*, 1241–1299.
Dror, Y. (1983). *Public policymaking: Reexamined*. Taylor & Francis.
Dunn, W. N. (2018). *Harold Lasswell and the study of public policy*. https://doi.org/10.1093/acrefore/9780190228637.013.600
Howlett, M., Ramesh, M., & Perl, A. (2009). *Studying public policy*. Oxford University Press.
Laswell, H. (1971). *A view of policy sciences*. Elsevier.
Lindblom, C. E. (1959). The science of muddling through. *Public Administration Review*, *19*, 79–88.
Maxwell, N. (2007). *From knowledge to wisdom: A revolution for science and the humanities*. Pentire Press.
Merton, R. K. (1996). *On social structure and science*. University of Chicago Press.
Pal, L. A. (2014). *Beyond policy analysis: Public issue management in turbulent times* (5th ed.). Nelson.
Vyse, S. (2017). Can anything save us from unintended consequences? *The Skeptical Inquirer*, *41*(4), 20–23.
White, R. E., & Cooper, K. (2022). *Qualitative research in the post-modern era: Critical approaches and selected methodologies*. Springer.

Index

Action research, 56–59
Adaptive problem solving, 131
Additional 'quasi-policy' models, 56–59
Additional policy models, 53–56
Administrative operability, 35–36
Adoption, 68
Adult Professional Cultures (APCs), 145
Agenda-setting, 67–68
Agricultural analogy, 32
Antiquated policies, preservation of, 159–160
Auton v. British Columbia, 35

Bell and Stevenson's policy framework, 70
Block grant, 21
Bridging, 97
British North America Act, 18–19
Brokering, 97
Budgeting, 68
Buffering, 97
Bullying, 124–125

Canadian Labour Congress, 25
Canadian province of Nova Scotia, 126
Cannabis, 11
Capacity building, 127
Categorical funding, 21
Central policy control, 21
Charter of Rights and Freedoms (1982), 22, 124–125
Coherence, 95–96, 117–118, 148–149
Collaborative cultures, 144–145
Collaborative inquiry, 145–146
Collaborative planning processes, 144

Collaborative policymaking, inadequate, 110
Communication, 39, 94–95, 128
Compatibility, 131
Conducive environments, 116–118
Constituent policies, 13
Constitution Act (*see British North America Act*)
Contemporary models of policy development, 178–179
Contemporary policy models, 43
  additional 'quasi-policy' models, 56–59
  creating policy, 43–47
  designing for policy success, 48–49
  standard and optional policy elements, 47–48
  structured approaches, 50–56
  unstructured approaches, 49–50
Cost/benefit analysis, 13–14, 35
Cost/effectiveness analysis, 13–14
COVID-19 and unintended consequences of policy development, 167–171
Crafting coherence, 96–97
Crises, 91–92
Culture, 4
Cyber-bullying, 124–125
Cyber-Safety Act, 124–125

Decision criteria, 34
Decision-driven data-making, 14
Decision-making models, 67–68, 175–176
Decisional capital, 148
Democratic governance, 33
Democratic politics, 33
Dispersed governance, implementation in, 110

Distributive policies, 13
District leaders, 87–88, 139–140
Dror's metapolicy phase, 51–52
Dror's policy phase, 52
Dror's post-policy phase, 52–53

Economic and financial possibility, 35
Education (al) policy, 1–2, 8–9, 14, 63–64, 72–73, 175
    definitions, 64–66
Education, 17, 91–92
    contextualizing layers, 22–26
    multiple layers of policy, 18–21
Education Policy Continuum, 73–74
Educational change, 135–136
    barriers to, 140–143
    flawed planning processes, 142
    implementation, 136
    inadequate implementation supports, 142
    lack of teacher engagement, 142–143
    leaders, 137–140
    policy, reform and improvement, 137
    supports for, 143–149
Educational institutions, 64
Educational leaders, 9, 83–85, 123, 184
    and policy, 85–89
Educational leadership, 83–84
    barriers to leadership of education policy, 89–92
    and management, 65
    supports for leadership of education policy, 92–97
Educational policymaking, 67, 90
Educational powerhouse, 18–19
Effective leaders of change, 137
Empowering teachers, 184
Environmental unintended consequences, 165
Equalization funding, 21
Exhortative/developmental policies, 72–73

External contexts, 107

Four-point Likert Scale, 13–14
Fox News, 25–26

Gallagher's model, 35
Goals, 50
Good governance, 64
Governance, 64

Health Act, 35
High Leverage Policy (HLP), 69–70
Historical unintended consequences, 165
Human capital, 147
Human error, 123
Human orthopneumovirus (*see* Respiratory syncytial virus (RSV))
Human respiratory syncytial virus (hRSV) (*see* Respiratory syncytial virus (RSV))

Imperative/disciplinary policies, 72–73
Implementation, 68
Implementation bridges, 146
Inclusive stakeholder engagement, 115–116
Informal agendas, 33–34
Information gathering, 45
Institutional agendas, 33–34
Instruments, 50
Insurance policy, 3
Integrated system, 20–21
Intended consequences (*see also* Unintended consequences), 183–184
    of policy implementation, 158–159
Inter-departmental boundaries, 33
Interpretation process, 9
Intersectionality, 183–184
Involvement, 116

Jewish People Policy Planning Institute, 50

Laffer Curve, 160–161
Lasswell's policy model, 55
Law of unintended consequences, 156–157
Leadership, 84
  strategies, 138
Leadership of change, 135
  educational change, 135–136
  nonlinear coherence framework, 149–151
Learning, 137
Leverage points, 70
Lobbyists, 25

Material contexts, 107
Meier's model, 55
Miscommunication, 39
Mission statements, 9–10

Neutrality, 17
Newfoundland and Labrador education system, 20–21
No Child Left Behind Policy, 22
Nonlinear coherence framework, 149–151
  cultivating collaborative cultures, 149
  deepening learning, 149–150
  focusing direction, 149
  leadership of coherence, 150–151
  securing accountability, 150
Nova Scotia, 11

OECD policy implementation framework, 114–118
  conducive environments, 116–118
  inclusive stakeholder engagement, 115–116
  smart policy design, 115
Ontario Leadership Framework, 92–93
Opportunity costs, 13–14
Optional policy elements, 47–48
Order, 3

Organisation for Economic Co-operation and Development (OECD), 71–72, 89
Overly optimistic expectations, 109–110

Pal's policy model cycles, 50
Participatory action research (*see* Action research)
Pentecostal system, 20–21
Phosphodiesterase type 5 (PDE5), 165–166
Policy, 1–3, 33, 126, 176–177
  actors, 71–72
  analysis, 8–9, 37, 123
  barriers, 124, 130–131
  blind men and elephant, 4–6
  borrowing, 89–90
  capacity, 108, 117, 123
  coherence, 96
  contexts, 66–67, 106–107
  creation and implementation, 43
  definitions, 3–4
  designing for policy success, 48–49
  development, 123, 176–177
  development and form, 12–13
  dissemination, 38
  educational leaders and, 85–89
  educational policy and policy analysis, 8–9
  enactment, 103–105
  evaluation, 67–68
  example of public policy, 7–8
  fast pace of policy change, 91
  features of quality policy document, 13–14
  formulation, 67–68
  frameworks, 69–71
  implementers, 104
  infrastructures and impediments, 182–183
  intended and unintended effects of policy deployment, 10–12
  learning, 38
  models, 43, 175–176

multiple layers of, 18–21
networks, 72
paralysis, 14
phases, 43–45
proliferation, 89
public policy, 6–7
purposes, 9–10
review, 113–114
sciences, 53–54
tools, 115
tracking, 112–113
transgression, 1–2
translation, 104–105
types of, 72–77
visions, 115
Policy alignment, 31, 117, 177–178
connecting theory and practice, 32–39
Policy Characteristics Scale, 72–73
Policy continuum, 63, 180, 182
definitions of education policy, 64–66
education policy, 63–64
policy actors, 71–72
policy contexts, 66–67
policy frameworks, 69–71
policy networks, 72
policy process, 67–69
types of policies, 72–77
Policy implementation, 67–68, 103
barriers to, 109–111
coherent and aligned legal and policy frameworks, 118
and enactment, 103–105
factors, 105–109
frameworks, 114
levels, 105
OECD policy implementation framework, 114–118
policy support programs, 112–114
supports for, 111–112
Policy interpretation, 104
example of, 158
Policy process, 31, 67, 69, 155, 157
causes of unintended consequences, 163–164

considerations, 160–163
COVID-19 and unintended consequences of policy development, 167–171
details relating to unintended consequences, 166
environmental and historical unintended consequences, 165
example of policy interpretation, 158
historical perspective, 155–156
intended and unintended consequences of policy implementation, 158–159
law of unintended consequences, 156–157
minimizing unintended consequence, 166–167
perverse unintended consequences, 164–165
preservation of antiquated policies, 159–160
unanticipated benefits of unintended consequences, 165–166
Policy support programs, 112–114
implementation support, 113
policy review, 113–114
policy tracking, 112–113
preparation, 112
Policymakers, 124–125, 176
Policymaking, 7, 51
Political agendas, 24
Political aspect of public policy, 6–7
Political viability, 35
Politics, 65–66, 106, 177
Post-policy phases, 43, 46–47
Power, 177
Practitioner research (*see* Action research)
Pre-policy phases, 43–44
Prescriptive policies, 75
Pressure groups, 25
Principal's leadership, 131
Problem definition, 50
Professional capital, 147–148

Professional contexts, 107
Professional learning, 146
Programme for International Assessment (PISA), 107
Progressive policies, 76–77
Public policy, 6–7
  example of, 7–8

Quality policy document, features of, 13–14

Redistributive policies, 13
Regulatory policies, 13
Research and policy, 90–91
Resistance, 131
Respiratory syncytial virus (RSV), 161
Return policy, 2
Roman Catholic system, 20–21

Salvation Army, 20–21
School Board of Broward County in Florida, 22
School boards, 19–20, 31
School districts, 31, 87
School leaders, 9, 83–85, 87, 138–139
School leadership, 85–86
School-level focus, 131
Schools, 21, 31
Setting direction, 93
Seventh Day Adventist system, 20–21
Situated contexts, 107
Smart policy design, 115
Social capital, 147–148
Social distancing, 23–24
Social forces, 26
Sound analysis, 37
Staff development, 131
Stakeholders, 115–116
Standard elements, 47–48
Structured approaches, 50, 56, 179–180
Successful policy, 48
Superintendents, 19–20
Supplemental Course Academy, 22
Supportive policies, 75–76
System leaders, 88–89, 140

System policy, 31
Systems approach, 95–96
Systems thinking, 95

Teacher career stages, 108
Teacher involvement, 131
Teacher leadership, 143–144
Teacher research (*see* Action research)
Teachers, 138
Teaching specialties and positions, 108–109
Technical aspect of public policy, 6–7
Technical feasibility, 34
Theory-practice divide, 123
Theory-practice gap, 130
Time and space, 109
Top-down approach, 129
Transparency, 39, 116
Trust, 94–95
Trustees, 19–20

Unintended consequences, 183–184
  causes, 163–164
  details relating to, 166
  environmental and historical unintended consequences, 165
  minimizing, 166–167
  perverse, 164–165
  of policy implementation, 156, 158–159
  unanticipated benefits of unintended consequences, 165–166
Unstructured approaches, 49–50, 179–180
Upholding values, 93–94

Vagaries of political cycle, 111
Vision statements, 9–10

World Bank, 71–72
World Health Organization (WHO), 71–72

Yehezkel Dror's Normative Optimum Model, 50–51

Printed and bound by CPI Group (UK) Ltd, Croydon, CR0 4YY
30/11/2023
08198835-0001